The Ur III Administrative Texts from Puzrish-Dagan Kept in the Harvard Museum of the Ancient Near East

Harvard Museum of the Ancient Near East Publications

Harvard Semitic Studies

VOLUME 68

The titles published in this series are listed at *brill.com/hvss*

The Ur III Administrative Texts from Puzrish-Dagan Kept in the Harvard Museum of the Ancient Near East

By

Changyu Liu

BRILL

LEIDEN | BOSTON

Library of Congress Cataloging-in-Publication Data

Names: Liu, Changyu (Assyriologist), author. | Harvard Museum of the Ancient Near East, host institution.
Title: The Ur III administrative texts from Puzrish-Dagan kept in the Harvard Museum of the Ancient Near East / by Changyu Liu.
Description: Leiden ; Boston : Brill, [2021] | Series: Harvard Semitic studies, 0147-9342 ; volume 68 | Includes index.
Identifiers: LCCN 2021007411 (print) | LCCN 2021007412 (ebook) | ISBN 9789004461369 (hardback) | ISBN 9789004461352 (ebook)
Subjects: LCSH: Sumerian language—Texts. | Cuneiform tablets—Iraq—Drehem (Extinct city) | Drehem (Extinct city)—Politics and government—Sources. | Babylonia—Politics and government—Sources.
Classification: LCC PJ4054.D8 L58 2021 (print) | LCC PJ4054.D8 (ebook) | DDC 499/.95—dc23
LC record available at https://lccn.loc.gov/2021007411
LC ebook record available at https://lccn.loc.gov/2021007412

Typeface for the Latin, Greek, and Cyrillic scripts: "Brill". See and download: brill.com/brill-typeface.

ISSN 0147-9342
ISBN 978-90-04-46135-2 (hardback)
ISBN 978-90-04-46136-9 (e-book)

This book is printed on acid-free paper and produced in a sustainable manner.

A Dedication To My Grandfather (1928–2016)

∵

Contents

1

Introduction

This volume is an edition of a collection of 689 cuneiform clay tablets kept in the Harvard Museum of the Ancient Near East (HMANE, formerly Harvard Semitic Museum), Cambridge, Massachusetts, USA.[1] These administrative documents date to the Third Dynasty of Ur (Ur III, ca. 2112-2004 BCE according to the Middle Chronology) of Mesopotamian history and are from Puzrish-Dagan (modern Drehem in southern Iraq).

Preceded by the Early Dynastic and Akkadian periods as well as the Gutian interregnum, the Ur III dynasty spans approximately one century and five kings: Ur-Namma, Shulgi, Amar-Suen, Shu-Suen and Ibbi-Suen. Since the dynasty is said in the Sumerian King List to be the third from Ur to rule over Sumer, the period has been called the Third Dynasty of Ur. Following the collapse of the Ur III dynasty, the periods of the Assyrian and Babylonian civilizations followed during the second and first millennia BCE.

The Ur III dynasty is considered one of the best-documented periods in the history of the ancient Near East. At least 120,000 cuneiform tablets have been unearthed from the southern Iraq, mainly from seven sites: Umma, Girsu, Puzrish-Dagan, Ur, Nippur, Irisagrig and Garshana.

Puzrish-Dagan, which is located about eight kilometers southeast of Nippur (modern Nuffar), was a redistribution center for animals and various products between the thirty-ninth regnal year of Shulgi and the third regnal year of Ibbi-Suen during the Ur III period. As opposed to being discovered through careful scientific excavations, all of the cuneiform tablets from Puzrish-Dagan

1 The abbreviations in this volume are listed on the Cuneiform Digital Library Initiative (CDLI) website, available at http://cdli.ox.ac.uk/wiki/abbreviations_for_assyriology. Add AS = Amar-Suen, Erm = Eremitage, GN = Geographical Name, IS = Ibbi-Suen, KM = Kelsey Museum of Archaeology, PN = Personal Name, Š = Šulgi, ŠS = Šu-Suen. Transliterations of texts with only one column of script are assigned continuous register numbering, including the obverse and reverse of a cuneiform tablet. In transliterations of multi-column texts, the registers of each column are counted separately. Indented lines within a register are preceded by "/". Empty registers are indicated by "----". When an empty register of a cuneiform tablet covers more space than the average inscribed register on that tablet, it is rendered as "====" in the transliteration. When an empty register of a cuneiform tablet is covered with seal impression(s), it is rendered as "==== (*seal*)" in the transliteration.

 | DOI:10.1163/9789004461369_002

are the result of looting and illicit excavations before 2017.[2] Since the first publication of tablets from Puzrish-Dagan in 1910 by François Thureau-Dangin,[3] there has been an ever-increasing number of tablets that have become available to scholars. According to the statistical summary of the Database of Neo-Sumerian Texts (BDTNS), there are 15,527 Neo-Sumerian documents from Puzrish-Dagan that date to the Ur III period (as of September 8, 2020). This number is still growing with more and more new textual material unearthed from Iraq and scattered texts from museums, libraries, and collections discovered and published by Assyriologists. Most of these texts are economic and administrative in nature, which help us to better understand the Ur III administration and the socioeconomic history of the period.

Cataloguing and publishing Ur III texts is fundamental and indispensable for the reconstruction of the administration and the daily life of this society, and the editing of the many tablets from HMANE is crucial in this task.

The HMANE was founded in 1889 and now houses 801 Ur III texts from Puzrish-Dagan, of which 113 texts (including No. 412 in this volume) have already been published by various scholars. Thomas Fish published the first tablet in 1955,[4] with a second appearing two years later.[5] From 1970 to 1971, David I. Owen and Gordon D. Young published twenty texts.[6] From 1976 to 1979, Piotr Michalowski published ten texts.[7] Furthermore, Owen published sixty-four texts in 1982[8] and one with Rudolf H. Mayr in 2004.[9] Tonia M. Sharlach

---

2 For the scientific excavations at Drehem undertaken in 2007, see Nawala Al-Mutawalli and Walther Sallaberger, "The Cuneiform Documents from the Iraqi Excavation at Drehem," *ZA* 107 (2017), p. 151.

3 François Thureau-Dangin, "La Trouvaille de Dréhem," *RA* 7 (1910), pp. 186-91.

4 Thomas Fish, "A Tablet from Drehem," *MCS* 5 (1955), p. 59.

5 Thomas Fish, "Some Place Names and their Contexts," *MCS* 7 (1957), p. 16.

6 David I. Owen and Gordon D. Young, "Ur III Texts in the Zion Research Library, Boston," *JCS* 23 (1970/1971), pp. 95-115.

7 Piotr Michalowski, "Royal Women of the Ur III Period, Part I: The Wife of Šulgi", *JCS* 28 (1976), pp. 169-72; Piotr Michalowski, "The Royal Correspondence of Ur," Ph.D. diss., Yale University, 1976, p. 52; Piotr Michalowski, "The Death of Šulgi," *OrNS* 46 (1977), p. 225; Piotr Michalowski, "Ur III Topographical Names," *OrAnt* 16 (1977), p. 292; Piotr Michalowski, "Dūrum and Uruk During the Ur III Period," *Mesopotamia* 12 (1977), p. 93; Piotr Michalowski, "Royal Women of the Ur III Period, Part II. Geme-Ninlila," *JCS* 31 (1979), p. 172.

8 David I. Owen, *Selected Ur III Texts from the Harvard Semitic Museum*, MVN 11, Rome: Multigraphica, 1982.

9 Rudolf H. Mayr and David I. Owen, "The Royal Gift Seal in the Ur III Period," in Hartmut Waetzoldt (ed.), *Von Sumer nach Ebla und zurück: Festschrift Giovanni Pettinato zum 27. September 1999 gewidmet von Freunden, Kollegen und Schülern*, HSAO 9, Heidelberg: Heidelberger Orientverlag, 2004, p. 171.

published one text in 2001[10] and ten in 2004.[11] Apart from those, Piotr Steinkeller published three in total,[12] and Paola Paoletti published two texts in her 2012 monograph.[13]

In the present volume, the 689 cuneiform clay tablets from six accession groups all came from the antiquities market or as gifts from private individuals who presumably purchased them from antiquities dealers. The accession groups are as follows:

The accession groups SM 1911.03 (142 texts in this volume), SM 1911.04 (eight texts in this volume) and SM 1911.10 (496 texts in this volume) were purchased from the Paris dealer I. E. Gejou on April 17, 1911.[14]

The accession group SM 1918.01 (thirty-one texts in this volume), a group of seventy-three tablets, was acquired by purchase from W. B. Clarke, a bookseller in Boston.

The accession group SM 1929.01 (three texts in this volume) was received as a gift from Mrs. Lucien Howe of Cambridge, Massachusetts, on September 26, 1929.

The accession group SM 1951.02 (three texts in this volume) was a gift of Kenneth Murdock and was received on October 29, 1951.

The accession group SM 1995.03 (three texts in this volume) was the part of the Zion Research Foundation Collection, and was received as a gift from the Zion Research Foundation, Boston (now known as the Endowment for Biblical Research) on April 29, 1983.

---

10 Tonia M. Sharlach, "Beyond Chronology: The Šakkanakkus of Mari and the Kings of Ur," in William W. Hallo and Irene J. Winter (eds.), *Proceedings of the XLVe Rencontre Assyriologique Internationale, Part II Yale University: Seals and Seal Impressions*, Bethesda, MD: CDL Press, 2001, p. 64.

11 Tonia M. Sharlach, *Provincial Taxation and the Ur III State*, CM 26, Leiden and Boston: Brill, 2004, pp. 257-65.

12 Piotr Steinkeller, "More on the Ur III Royal Wives," *ASJ* 3 (1981), p. 91 (no. 1); Piotr Steinkeller, "On Rulers, Priests and Sacred Marriage: Tracing the Evolution of Early Sumerian Kingship," in Kazuko Watanabe (ed.), *Priests and Officials in the Ancient Near East: Papers of the Second Colloquium on the Ancient Near East—The City and its Life held at the Middle Eastern Culture Center in Japan (Mitaka, Tokyo), March 22-24, 1996*, Heidelberg: Universitätsverlag, 1999, p. 119 (n. 48); Piotr Steinkeller, "Corvée Labor in Ur III Times," in Steven Garfinkle and Manuel Molina (eds.), *From the 21st Century B.C. to the 21st Century A.D.: Proceedings of the International Conference on Sumerian Studies Held in Madrid, 22-24 July 2010*, Winona Lake, IN: Eisenbrauns, 2013, p. 419 (no. 32).

13 Paola Paoletti, *Der König und sein Kreis. Das staatliche Schatzarchiv der III. Dynastie von Ur*, BPOA 10, Madrid: Consejo Superior de Investigaciones Científicas, 2012, p. 511.

14 Accession groups 1911.03, 1911.04, and 1911.10 together account for 821 tablets.

The accession group SM 1995.09 (two texts in this volume) was a part of the Harry Emerson Fosdick Collection, and was received as a gift from Elinor Fosdick Downs (his daughter) on January 5, 1995.

The accession group SM 1997.01 (one text in this volume) is from a group of eight tablets with no numbers found in the last of the tablet drawers, according to a curatorial note by Sharlach, dated May 27, 1997.

In this volume, 637 texts are records of animals, which account for approximately 92.5 percent of all texts presented herein. The other texts document various goods, such as barley, wool, textiles, silver, and so forth. The texts date between the thirty-third regnal year of Shulgi (No. 257) and the third regnal year of Ibbi-Suen (No. 393). As for the chronological distribution of the texts, 112 date to the reign of Shulgi, 355 date to the reign of Amar-Suen, 136 date to the reign of Shu-Suen, and thirty-three date to the reign of Ibbi-Suen. There are, as well, fifty-three undated or date-damaged texts. The texts in this volume are recorded primarily using four types of text formulae: the i$_3$-dab$_5$-type, the ba-zi-type, the šu ba-ti-type and the mu-DU-type. Among them, the first three types of formulae are attested in records documenting disbursement of animals or goods, whereas the last type is used in documents involving the receipt of animals or goods. A large number of official and individual names are attested in the texts, including Abba-saga, Duga, Intaea, Lu-dingira, Lugal-amarku, Nalu, Nasa, and Ur-kununa.

The editions of the 689 Ur III texts in this volume, arranged by their catalogue numbers, are significant for further study of how the Puzrish-Dagan organization functioned. The archive of Lugal-amarku is noteworthy in that it deepens our understanding of the succession of Abba-saga by Lugal-amarku. Furthermore, the archives of officials such as Turam-Dagan, Uta-misharam, Shu-Idim and Shu-Erra provide new materials for the further study of their individual administrative practices. It is particularly important that new evidence has been gleaned and new conclusions can be drawn from texts in this volume. For instance, it can now be proven that Nadi is the son of Shulgi (Na-di dumu lugal, No. 494), and the father-son relationship between Lugal-itida and Puzur-Enlil has been confirmed (PU$_3$.ŠA-^{d}En-lil$_2$ dumu Lugal-iti-da, No. 159). Also, the complete seal impression of Shabi with his father's name Basa is attested for the first time (Ša$_3$-bi dub-sar dumu Ba-sa$_6$, No. 551).

It is a great pleasure to offer special gratitude to the following people that have been helpful in preparing and writing this volume. First and foremost, I would like to thank the Harvard Museum of the Ancient Near East (formerly Harvard Semitic Museum) and Joseph A. Greene, Deputy Director & Curator of the museum, for having given me the authorization to publish these cuneiform texts. I am particularly grateful to Piotr Steinkeller for inviting me to visit the then-named Harvard Semitic Museum from March 29 to April 12 in 2018 to copy and proofread a number of tablets in this volume, and to Adam Aja, Assistant Curator of Collections of the museum, for providing me with the warmest help. I owe many debts of gratitude to Piotr Steinkeller, Tohru Ozaki, Robert K. Englund, Manuel Molina, Lorenzo Verderame, David I. Owen, Sergio Alivernini, and Marcel Sigrist, for further comments and corrections. I want to express my gratitude to Andrew Pottorf, John Nielsen and Sergio Tang, who corrected and improved my English. Thanks are due to my current institution, Zhejiang Normal University, for funding me during my stay at Harvard. My thanks also go to the publisher, Brill, and Michael D. Coogan, Director of Publications, for accepting this volume for publication in the renowned series of the Harvard Semitic Studies. Any mistakes, errors, or omissions, though, remain my sole responsibility. Finally, and most importantly, I owe the most to my family for their constant support, understanding, and love for me.

Changyu Liu
Zhejiang Normal University, Jinhua, China
September 10, 2020

Catalogue of Texts

Text	Museum No.	Date	Subject	Transaction	Bureau
1	SM 1911.03.001	-- -- --	animal	niĝ$_2$-ka$_9$	Ur-mes
2	SM 1911.03.002	-- -- --	animal	ba-zi	Shulgi-ili
3	SM 1911.03.003	AS9	animal	--	--
4	SM 1911.03.006	AS9 ii 30	animal	i$_3$-dab$_5$	Abba-saga
5	SM 1911.03.007	Š43 xii	animal	mu-DU	Nasa
6	SM 1911.03.008	ŠS9 ix 26	animal	ba-zi	Intaea
7	SM 1911.03.009	AS5 x 2	animal	mu-DU	Abba-saga
8	SM 1911.03.010	Š43 vi 5	animal	mu-DU	--
9	SM 1911.03.011	Š45 xi 17	animal	zi-ga	Nalu
10	SM 1911.03.012	Š47 iv 4	animal	ba-zi	Nasa
11	SM 1911.03.013	Š48 vii 14	animal	ba-zi	Nasa
12	SM 1911.03.014	ŠS4	animal	ba-zi	Beli-azu
13	SM 1911.03.015	Š47 viii 16	animal	ba-zi	Nasa
14	SM 1911.03.017	ŠS8 iv 28	animal	ba-zi	Puzur-Enlil
15	SM 1911.03.018	Š47 vi	animal	i$_3$-dab$_5$	Nasa
16	SM 1911.03.019	ŠS3 i	animal	i$_3$-dab$_5$	Aa-ilum
17	SM 1911.03.020	AS7	wool	šu ba-ti	En-dingirmu
18	SM 1911.03.021	AS9 x 18	animal	ba-zi	Nalu
19	SM 1911.03.022	ŠS7 vii 21	animal	mu-DU	Intaea
20	SM 1911.03.023	ŠS1 vi	animal	ba-zi	Nalu
21	SM 1911.03.027	IS2 xi 16	animal	ba-zi	Shulgi-ili
22	SM 1911.03.029	AS5 ii 3	animal	mu-DU	Abba-saga
23	SM 1911.03.032	ŠS4 iv 20	animal	ba-zi	[ ]
24	SM 1911.03.034	Š45 viii 21	animal	zi-ga	--
25	SM 1911.03.035	AS7 xi	reed	šu ba-ti	Abušuni
26	SM 1911.03.036	ŠS5 vi 2	animal	mu-DU	Intaea
27	SM 1911.03.038	ŠS2 iii	salt, flour	zi-ga	--
28	SM 1911.03.039	Š46 x 16	animal	zi-ga	Lu-dingira
29	SM 1911.03.040	AS9 iv 16	animal	ba-zi	Duga
30	SM 1911.03.043	AS5 vi 1	animal	mu-DU	Abba-saga
31	SM 1911.03.044	ŠS8 ix	animal	ba-zi	Intaea
32	SM 1911.03.046	ŠS8 viii 3	animal	ba-zi	Puzur-Enlil

 | DOI:10.1163/9789004461369_003

(*cont.*)

Text	Museum No.	Date	Subject	Transaction	Bureau
33	SM 1911.03.047	Š46 x 24	animal	zi-ga	Nalu
34	SM 1911.03.050	Š44 iv 27	animal	zi-ga	--
35	SM 1911.03.051	Š47 vii 5	animal	zi-ga	(--)
36	SM 1911.03.052	ŠS7	animal	i_3-dab_5	Nanna-maba
37	SM 1911.03.053	ŠS4 viii 21	animal	ba-zi	Intaea
38	SM 1911.03.054	Š47 vi 9	animal	ba-zi	Lu-dingira
39	SM 1911.03.055	ŠS7 xii	animal	i_3-dab_5	Sugali
40	SM 1911.03.057	Š45 xii 16	animal	zi-ga	--
41	SM 1911.03.058	ŠS5 x 13	animal	ba-zi	Ur-kununa
42	SM 1911.03.059	Š47 iii 18	animal	ba-zi	Nasa
43	SM 1911.03.060	AS5 vii 25	animal	ba-zi	Abba-saga
44	SM 1911.03.061	Š48 ix 27	animal	mu-DU	Nasa
45	SM 1911.03.063	Š46 ii 12	animal	mu-DU	--
46	SM 1911.03.065	Š47 x 29	animal	zi-ga	Lu-dingira
47	SM 1911.03.066	Š46 vi 14	animal	mu-DU	--
48	SM 1911.03.067	AS8 iv	animal	ba-zi	En-dingirmu
49	SM 1911.03.068	ŠS1 ix 11	animal	ba-zi	Intaea
50	SM 1911.03.069	ŠS7 ii 12	--	mu-DU	--
51	SM 1911.03.070	Š45 x 26	animal	mu-DU	--
52	SM 1911.03.071	AS5 ix 20	animal	mu-DU	Abba-saga
53	SM 1911.03.072	Š46 i 17	animal	zi-ga	--
54	SM 1911.03.073	AS5 xii 25	animal	ba-zi	Intaea
55	SM 1911.03.074	Š47 vii 25	animal	šu ba-ti	Lu-dingira
56	SM 1911.03.075	Š48 vi 15	animal	šu ba-ti	Lu-dingira
57	SM 1911.03.076	AS2 i 22	animal	šu ba-ti	Lu-dingira
58	SM 1911.03.077	AS5 iii 29	animal	i_3-dab_5	Abba-saga
59	SM 1911.03.078	Š48 x	animal	i_3-dab_5	Nasa
60	SM 1911.03.080	AS5 iv 30	animal	i_3-dab_5	Abba-saga
61	SM 1911.03.081	Š47 xid	animal	mu-DU	Nasa
62	SM 1911.03.082	Š47 xii 18	animal	zi-ga	Lu-dingira
63	SM 1911.03.083	ŠS4 i 22	animal	ba-zi	Ur-kununa
64	SM 1911.03.084	AS5 i 30	animal	i_3-dab_5	Abba-saga
65	SM 1911.03.085	AS5 vi 12	animal	i_3-dab_5	Abba-saga
66	SM 1911.03.086	AS5 i	animal	i_3-dab_5	Shulgi-aamu
67	SM 1911.03.087	AS5 vi 12	animal	i_3-dab_5	Abba-saga

(*cont.*)

Text	Museum No.	Date	Subject	Transaction	Bureau
68	SM 1911.03.089	AS8 iv/v 19	animal	ba-zi	Igi-Enlilshe
69	SM 1911.03.094	Š47 xi 2	animal	šu ba-ti	Lu-dingira
70	SM 1911.03.095	Š47 ii 27	animal	zi-ga	Lu-dingira
71	SM 1911.03.096	Š47 iv 18	animal	mu-DU	Nasa
72	SM 1911.03.100	Š47 viii 20	animal	šu ba-ti	Lu-dingira
73	SM 1911.03.101	AS1 x 10	animal	i_3-dab_5	Nalu
74	SM 1911.03.103	Š46 iv 18	animal	šu ba-ti	Lu-dingira
75	SM 1911.03.104	ŠS3 xii 9	animal	ba-zi	Duga
76	SM 1911.03.105	Š45 xii 17	animal	zi-ga	Nalu
77	SM 1911.03.106	Š46 ii 12	animal	i_3-dab_5	Ahuni
78	SM 1911.03.107	-- -- 3	animal	[ ]	[ ]
79	SM 1911.03.109	Š48 i 5	animal	ba-zi	Nalu
80	SM 1911.03.110	ŠS3 ii 5	animal	ba-zi	Intaea
81	SM 1911.03.112	AS1 v 20	animal	šu ba-ti	Lu-dingira
82	SM 1911.03.113	Š47 v 19	animal	ba-zi	Nasa
83	SM 1911.03.114	AS5 iv 25	animal	i_3-dab_5	Abba-saga
84	SM 1911.03.115	-- viii 27	animal	zi-ga	[ ]
85	SM 1911.03.116	Š46 viii 9	animal	mu-DU	Nasa
86	SM 1911.03.117	AS5 xii 28	animal	ba-zi	Abba-saga
87	SM 1911.03.118	AS8 xi	animal	i_3-dab_5	Abba-saga
88	SM 1911.03.120	Š47 ii	animal	i_3-dab_5	Nasa
89	SM 1911.03.121	AS1 xii 2	animal	ba-zi	Nalu
90	SM 1911.03.122	Š44 vi 16	animal	zi-ga	Nalu
91	SM 1911.03.124	AS5 viii 13	animal	i_3-dab_5	Abba-saga
92	SM 1911.03.125	Š47 viii 17	animal	šu ba-ti	Lu-dingira
93	SM 1911.03.126	AS7 ii 1	animal	i_3-dab_5	Intaea
94	SM 1911.03.127	AS7 xii 3	animal	i_3-dab_5	Abba-saga
95	SM 1911.03.128	AS8 ix 3	animal	ba-zi	Zubaga
96	SM 1911.03.129	AS5 vi 17	animal	i_3-dab_5	Abba-saga
97	SM 1911.03.130	AS2 ii 4	animal	i_3-dab_5	Abba-saga
98	SM 1911.03.131	AS8 iv 20+	animal	ba-zi	En-dingirmu
99	SM 1911.03.132	AS6 v 13	animal	i_3-dab_5	Abba-saga
100	SM 1911.03.133	Š47 ii 14	animal	šu ba-ti	Lu-dingira
101	SM 1911.03.134	Š46 vii 21	animal	zi-ga	Ur-Lugal-edin
102	SM 1911.03.135	AS8 ix 1	animal	i_3-dab_5	Abba-saga

(cont.)

Text	Museum No.	Date	Subject	Transaction	Bureau
103	SM 1911.03.136	AS3 xi 26	animal	ba-zi	Intaea
104	SM 1911.03.137	AS4 x	textile	mu-DU	Nur-Suen
105	SM 1911.03.138	AS4 xi 20	animal	i_3-dab$_5$	Abba-saga
106	SM 1911.03.139	AS4 xi 3	animal	šu ba-ti	Lu-dingira
107	SM 1911.03.140	AS1 vi 30	animal	i_3-dab$_5$	Nalu
108	SM 1911.03.141	AS4 vi 6	animal	šu ba-ti	Zubaga
109	SM 1911.03.142	Š46 vii 1	animal	šu ba-ti	Nalu
110	SM 1911.03.143	ŠS3 ii 5	animal	šu ba-ti	Ahu-Wer
111	SM 1911.03.144	Š44 v 21	animal	šu ba-ti	Nalu
112	SM 1911.03.145	AS7 iv --	animal	šu ba-ti	Ahu-Wer
113	SM 1911.03.146	-- xii 18	animal	šu ba-ti	Lu-dingira
114	SM 1911.03.147	AS5 viii 11	animal	i_3-dab$_5$	Abba-saga
115	SM 1911.03.148	Š45 xii 7	animal	šu ba-ti	Nalu
116	SM 1911.03.149	AS2 vii 26	animal	šu ba-ti	Shu-Idim
117	SM 1911.03.150	AS1 xii 17	animal	šu ba-ti	Nalu
118	SM 1911.03.151	AS2 xii 27	animal	šu ba-ti	Shu-Erra
119	SM 1911.03.152	Š43 iii 9	animal	mu-DU	--
120	SM 1911.03.153	Š48 vii 13	animal	šu ba-ti	Nalu
121	SM 1911.03.154	Š--v	animal	šu ba-ti	Shukubum
122	SM 1911.03.155	ŠS3 xi 8	animal	šu ba-ti	Ur-Nanna
123	SM 1911.03.156	AS2 viii 18	animal	šu ba-ti	Lu-dingira
124	SM 1911.03.157	AS6 vii 26	animal	šu ba-ti	Nalu
125	SM 1911.03.158	Š46 i 17	animal	šu ba-ti	Nalu
126	SM 1911.03.160	AS3 vi 17	animal	šu ba-ti	Lu-dingira
127	SM 1911.03.161	AS5 xi 25	animal	i_3-dab$_5$	Abba-saga
128	SM 1911.03.162	AS6 vi 1	animal	šu ba-ti	Nalu
129	SM 1911.03.163	AS5 i 22	animal	i_3-dab$_5$	Abba-saga
130	SM 1911.03.164	AS1 viii 7	animal	šu ba-ti	Nalu
131	SM 1911.03.165	Š47 vii 25	animal	šu ba-ti	Nalu
132	SM 1911.03.166	AS7 ii 25	animal	šu ba-ti	Ahu-Wer
133	SM 1911.03.167	Š48 i 11	animal	šu ba-ti	En-dingirmu
134	SM 1911.03.168	AS1 x 19	animal	šu ba-ti	Nalu
135	SM 1911.03.169	AS1 xi 7	animal	i_3-dab$_5$	Abba-saga
136	SM 1911.03.170	ŠS4 xi 9	animal	šu ba-ti	Beli-ili
137	SM 1911.03.171	AS5 x 24	animal	šu ba-ti	Turam-Dagan

(*cont.*)

Text	Museum No.	Date	Subject	Transaction	Bureau
138	SM 1911.03.172	AS5 i 8	animal	i_3-dab_5	Abba-saga
139	SM 1911.03.173	Š46 v 1	animal	šu ba-ti	Nalu
140	SM 1911.03.174	AS6 x 25	animal	šu ba-ti	Lu-dingira
141	SM 1911.03.175	Š46 ii 15	animal	šu ba-ti	Nalu
142	SM 1911.03.176	-- v 1	animal	šu ba-ti	En-dingirmu
143	SM 1911.04.001	-- iv	animal	i_3-dab_5	Ibni-ilum
144	SM 1911.04.002	ŠS1 xiid 9	animal	ba-zi	Duga
145	SM 1911.04.004	ŠS9 v 4+	animal	ba-zi	Ur-kununa
146	SM 1911.04.005	AS1 xii 27	animal	šu ba-ti	Lu-dingira
147	SM 1911.04.006	AS9 xii 1	animal	ba-zi	Duga
148	SM 1911.04.012	ŠS2 ii	animal	i_3-dab_5	Tahsh-atal
149	SM 1911.04.014	AS9 xii 29	animal	ba-zi	Intaea
150	SM 1911.04.015	-- -- --	animal	zi-ga-am_3	--
151	SM 1911.10.002	IS1 vii 2	animal	ba-zi	Intaea
152	SM 1911.10.003	ŠS2 i	animal	i_3-dab_5	Ahu-Wer
153	SM 1911.10.004	ŠS1 vii 19	animal	ba-zi	Tahsh-atal
154	SM 1911.10.006	Š46 ii	animal	i_3-dab_5	Naram-ili
155	SM 1911.10.007	AS6 xi	animal	i_3-dab_5	Abba-saga
156	SM 1911.10.008	-- -- --	animal	i_3-dab_5	Ibni-ilum
157	SM 1911.10.009	AS2 xi	animal	šu ba-ti	Abba-saga
158	SM 1911.10.011	AS9 iv	animal	i_3-dab_5	Abba-saga
159	SM 1911.10.012	IS2 vii	animal	--	Intaea
160	SM 1911.10.015	AS9 iv 16	animal	ba-zi	Abba-saga
161	SM 1911.10.016	AS2 ix 21	animal	i_3-dab_5	Abba-saga
162	SM 1911.10.017	AS7 i	animal	i_3-dab_5	Abba-saga
163	SM 1911.10.018	Š46 i	animal	i_3-dab_5	Nalu
164	SM 1911.10.019	AS7 x 18	animal	i_3-dab_5	Abba-saga
165	SM 1911.10.020	AS9 iii 28	animal	i_3-dab_5	Abba-saga
166	SM 1911.10.021	AS6 xi 24	animal	ba-zi	Abba-saga
167	SM 1911.10.022	AS7 ix	animal	i_3-dab_5	Abba-saga
168	SM 1911.10.023	IS2 v 8	animal	ba-zi	[ ]
169	SM 1911.10.024	AS1 x --	animal	zi-ga	Enlila
170	SM 1911.10.025	Š46 x	animal	i_3-dab_5	Nalu
171	SM 1911.10.026	AS4 viii 1	animal	i_3-dab_5	Abba-saga
172	SM 1911.10.027	AS8 x 24	animal	i_3-dab_5	Abba-saga

(*cont.*)

Text	Museum No.	Date	Subject	Transaction	Bureau
173	SM 1911.10.028	AS2 iv 16	animal	i_3-dab_5	Abba-saga
174	SM 1911.10.029	AS6 ix 1	animal	i_3-dab_5	Abba-saga
175	SM 1911.10.030	AS1 vii --	animal	zi-ga	Enlila
176	SM 1911.10.031	AS6 vi 30	animal	i_3-dab_5	Abba-saga
177	SM 1911.10.032	AS6 xii 25	animal	ba-zi	Abba-saga
178	SM 1911.10.033	AS1 x 9	animal	i_3-dab_5	Abba-saga
179	SM 1911.10.034	AS6 viii 14	animal	i_3-dab_5	Abba-saga
180	SM 1911.10.035	AS7 viii 5	animal	i_3-dab_5	Abba-saga
181	SM 1911.10.036	AS3 x 11	animal	i_3-dab_5	Abba-saga
182	SM 1911.10.037	AS3 x 16	animal	i_3-dab_5	Abba-saga
183	SM 1911.10.038	Š46 iv	animal	mu-DU	Ur-kununa
184	SM 1911.10.039	-- -- 18	animal	[ ]	[ ]
185	SM 1911.10.040	AS6 iv 28	animal	i_3-dab_5	Abba-saga
186	SM 1911.10.041	AS1 ix 16	animal	i_3-dab_5	Abba-saga
187	SM 1911.10.042	AS7 iii 25	animal	i_3-dab_5	Abba-saga
188	SM 1911.10.043	AS1 iii 16	animal	i_3-dab_5	Nasa
189	SM 1911.10.044	AS2 vi 14	animal	i_3-dab_5	Abba-saga
190	SM 1911.10.045	AS8 ii 13	animal	i_3-dab_5	Lugal-amarku
191	SM 1911.10.046	AS7 x 12	animal	i_3-dab_5	Abba-saga
192	SM 1911.10.047	Š46 v	animal	mu-DU	Enlila
193	SM 1911.10.048	AS7 ix 8	animal	i_3-dab_5	Abba-saga
194	SM 1911.10.049	AS7 xii 18	animal	i_3-dab_5	Abba-saga
195	SM 1911.10.050	AS6 v 19	animal	i_3-dab_5	Abba-saga
196	SM 1911.10.051	AS3 x 11	animal	i_3-dab_5	Abba-saga
197	SM 1911.10.052	AS2 ix 25	animal	i_3-dab_5	Abba-saga
198	SM 1911.10.053	AS3 x 4	animal	i_3-dab_5	Abba-saga
199	SM 1911.10.054	AS2 v 10	animal	ba-zi	Abba-saga
200	SM 1911.10.057	AS3 vi 10	animal	ba-zi	Abba-saga
201	SM 1911.10.058	Š47 xi	animal	i_3-dab_5	Ipqusha
202	SM 1911.10.059	AS7 ix 7	animal	i_3-dab_5	Abba-saga
203	SM 1911.10.060	AS6 viii 30	animal	i_3-dab_5	Abba-saga
204	SM 1911.10.061	AS6 vi 13	animal	i_3-dab_5	Abba-saga
205	SM 1911.10.062	AS7 v 13	animal	i_3-dab_5	Abba-saga
206	SM 1911.10.063	AS3 v	animal	i_3-dab_5	Abba-saga
207	SM 1911.10.064	AS4 viii 3	animal	i_3-dab_5	Abba-saga

(*cont.*)

Text	Museum No.	Date	Subject	Transaction	Bureau
208	SM 1911.10.065	AS2 ii 6	animal	i_3-dab_5	Abba-saga
209	SM 1911.10.066	Š46 ii 24	animal	zi-ga	Ur-kununa
210	SM 1911.10.067	AS2 vi 29	animal	i_3-dab_5	Abba-saga
211	SM 1911.10.068	AS2 v 5	animal	ba-zi	Abba-saga
212	SM 1911.10.069	AS6 viii 21	animal	i_3-dab_5	Abba-saga
213	SM 1911.10.070	AS3 x 8	animal	i_3-dab_5	Abba-saga
214	SM 1911.10.071	AS2 ii 22	animal	i_3-dab_5	Abba-saga
215	SM 1911.10.072	AS4 i 1	animal	i_3-dab_5	Abba-saga
216	SM 1911.10.073	AS3 xii 11	animal	i_3-dab_5	Abba-saga
217	SM 1911.10.074	AS6 xii 13	animal	i_3-dab_5	Abba-saga
218	SM 1911.10.075	AS7 viii 1	animal	i_3-dab_5	Abba-saga
219	SM 1911.10.076	AS8 ii 25	animal	i_3-dab_5	Lugal-amarku
220	SM 1911.10.078	AS6 ii 2	animal	i_3-dab_5	Abba-saga
221	SM 1911.10.079	AS2 i 7	animal	ba-zi	Abba-saga
222	SM 1911.10.080	-- -- --	animal	zi-ga	Nasa
223	SM 1911.10.081	AS4 x 13	animal	i_3-dab_5	Abba-saga
224	SM 1911.10.082	AS3 i 23	animal	i_3-dab_5	Abba-saga
225	SM 1911.10.083	AS1 ix 25	animal	i_3-dab_5	Abba-saga
226	SM 1911.10.084	AS2 viii 24	animal	i_3-dab_5	Abba-saga
227	SM 1911.10.085	AS2 x 1	animal	i_3-dab_5	Abba-saga
228	SM 1911.10.086	AS8 v 2	animal	i_3-dab_5	Abba-saga
229	SM 1911.10.087	AS6 x 23	animal	i_3-dab_5	Abba-saga
230	SM 1911.10.088	AS2 v 18	animal	i_3-dab_5	Abba-saga
231	SM 1911.10.089	AS1 ix 26	animal	i_3-dab_5	Abba-saga
232	SM 1911.10.090	AS4 viii 14	animal	i_3-dab_5	Abba-saga
233	SM 1911.10.091	AS2 x	animal	i_3-dab_5	Abba-saga
234	SM 1911.10.092	AS4 iv 24	animal	i_3-dab_5	Abba-saga
235	SM 1911.10.093	AS1 xi 10	animal	i_3-dab_5	Abba-saga
236	SM 1911.10.094	AS7 vii 21	animal	i_3-dab_5	Abba-saga
237	SM 1911.10.095	AS4 viii 8	animal	i_3-dab_5	Abba-saga
238	SM 1911.10.096	AS4 iv 7	animal	i_3-dab_5	Abba-saga
239	SM 1911.10.097	Š47 viii 12	animal	mu-DU	Enlila
240	SM 1911.10.098	AS1 vii 22	animal	ba-zi	Nasa
241	SM 1911.10.099	AS2 v 7	animal	i_3-dab_5	Abba-saga
242	SM 1911.10.101	Š47 viii 17	animal	zi-ga	Ur-kununa

(*cont.*)

Text	Museum No.	Date	Subject	Transaction	Bureau
243	SM 1911.10.102	AS6 vi 14	animal	i_3-dab_5	Abba-saga
244	SM 1911.10.103	Š47 vi 16	animal	mu-DU	Enlila
245	SM 1911.10.104	Š47 viii 9	animal	zi-ga	Enlila
246	SM 1911.10.105	-- vii 4	animal	zi-ga	Ur-kununa
247	SM 1911.10.106	Š47 ix 7	animal	zi-ga	Ur-kununa
248	SM 1911.10.107	AS4 xii 10	animal	i_3-dab_5	Abba-saga
249	SM 1911.10.108	Š47 ix 11	animal	zi-ga	Ur-kununa
250	SM 1911.10.109	AS2 vi	animal	niĝ$_2$-ka$_9$-ak	ĝiri$_3$ Intaea
251	SM 1911.10.110	AS2 vii	animal	niĝ$_2$-ka$_9$-ak	ĝiri$_3$ Intaea
252	SM 1911.10.114	-- -- 19	animal	--	--
253	SM 1911.10.115	-- -- --	animal	--	--
254	SM 1911.10.117	-- -- --	animal	[ ]	[ ]
255	SM 1911.10.118	AS5 xii	animal	ki-be$_2$ gi$_4$-a	Ur-kununa
256	SM 1911.10.119	-- -- --	animal	[ ]	[ ]
257	SM 1911.10.120	Š33 ii	animal	--	Shukubum
258	SM 1911.10.123	AS3 ii 28	animal	zi-ga	Ur-kununa
259	SM 1911.10.124	-- -- --	animal	[ ]	[ ]
260	SM 1911.10.125	-- -- --	animal	[ ]	[ ]
261	SM 1911.10.126	-- -- --	animal	[ ]	[ ]
262	SM 1911.10.128	Š42 xii	animal	zi-ga	Ur-kununa
263	SM 1911.10.133	Š46 iii	animal	--	--
264	SM 1911.10.135	ŠS1 xii 28	animal	i_3-dab_5	Nalu
265	SM 1911.10.137	-- -- --	animal	--	--
266	SM 1911.10.138	-- xii	goods	--	--
267	SM 1911.10.139	AS3 xii	animal	--	--
268	SM 1911.10.140	-- -- --	animal	[ ]	[ ]
269	SM 1911.10.141	Š47 iv	animal	i_3-dab_5	Beli-azu
270	SM 1911.10.143	IS2 x 4	animal	šu ba-ti	Ur-kununa
271	SM 1911.10.144	AS2 iii 27	animal	i_3-dab_5	Abba-saga
272	SM 1911.10.146	ŠS6 viii 28	animal	mu-DU	Intaea
273	SM 1911.10.148	IS1 iii 29	animal	ba-zi	Shulgi-ili
274	SM 1911.10.149	Š46 xi 9	animal	i_3-dab_5	Nalu
275	SM 1911.10.150	AS9 i 8	animal	ba-zi	Abba-saga
276	SM 1911.10.151	Š48 xi	animal	i_3 dab_5	Nasa
277	SM 1911.10.152	AS1 viii 10	animal	i_3-dab_5	Nasa

(*cont.*)

Text	Museum No.	Date	Subject	Transaction	Bureau
278	SM 1911.10.153	AS4 xi 8	animal	i_3-dab_5	Abba-saga
279	SM 1911.10.154	Š46 ii	animal	--	--
280	SM 1911.10.155	AS4	--	--	--
281	SM 1911.10.156	AS6 iv	--	ba-zi	Abba-saga
282	SM 1911.10.161	-- -- --	animal	[ ]	[ ]
283	SM 1911.10.164	-- viii	animal	ba-zi	Shu-Suen-bani
284	SM 1911.10.165	ŠS8 ix	animal	i_3-dab_5	Nur-ili
285	SM 1911.10.167	ŠS7 viii 24	animal	mu-DU	Intaea
286	SM 1911.10.169	ŠS6 iv --	animal	mu-DU	Intaea
287	SM 1911.10.170	Š48 xii	animal	i_3-dab_5	Nasa
288	SM 1911.10.173	AS9 xii 29	animal	ba-zi	Lu-saga
289	SM 1911.10.174	-- ix	animal	[ ]	[ ]
290	SM 1911.10.177	AS1 xi 18	animal	mu-DU	Abba-saga
291	SM 1911.10.178	ŠS3 xid 16	animal	mu-DU	Intaea
292	SM 1911.10.179	-- v	animal	i_3-dab_5	Nasa
293	SM 1911.10.180	ŠS4 i	animal	i_3-dab_5	Lugal-amarku
294	SM 1911.10.181	-- vi 24	animal	ba-zi	Ibni-Suen
295	SM 1911.10.183	IS1 x	animal	ba-zi	Allamu
296	SM 1911.10.184	AS8 i	barley	šu ba-ti	Shu-Eshtar
297	SM 1911.10.186	IS1 xii	animal	i_3-dab_5	Intaea
298	SM 1911.10.187	AS6 iv 4	animal	i_3-dab_5	Abba-saga
299	SM 1911.10.190	Š48 xi 22	animal	ba-zi	Nasa
300	SM 1911.10.192	AS3 viii	animal	[ ]	Abba-saga
301	SM 1911.10.194	AS1 viii 7	animal	ba-zi	Nasa
302	SM 1911.10.197	ŠS9 ix 25	animal	ba-zi	Ur-kununa
303	SM 1911.10.199	Š48 xi 27	animal	ba-zi	Nasa
304	SM 1911.10.200	Š45 ix	animal	mu-DU	Nanshekam
305	SM 1911.10.202	-- -- 10	animal	ba-zi	Abba-saga
306	SM 1911.10.207	AS7 xii 1+	animal	ba-zi	Abba-saga
307	SM 1911.10.208	IS1 xii 3	animal	ba-zi	Intaea
308	SM 1911.10.209	AS4 ix	barley	šu ba-ti	Shu-Ishhara
309	SM 1911.10.211	Š39 ii	wool	ba-zi	Lugal-dubla
310	SM 1911.10.212	AS4 xii 5	animal	i_3-dab_5	Abba-saga
311	SM 1911.10.213	ŠS1 iv 2	animal	ba-zi	Nalu
312	SM 1911.10.215	AS6 iv 4	animal	i_3-dab_5	Ur-kununa

(*cont.*)

Text	Museum No.	Date	Subject	Transaction	Bureau
313	SM 1911.10.217	AS8 i 16	animal	ba-zi	Lu-dingira
314	SM 1911.10.218	AS9 iii	animal	i_3-dab_5	Abba-saga
315	SM 1911.10.219	IS1 viii 4	animal	ba-zi	Ur-kununa
316	SM 1911.10.220	-- xi	animal	[ ]	[ ]
317	SM 1911.10.221	AS1 i	animal	i_3-dab_5	Nasa
318	SM 1911.10.222	IS1 vi	animal	--	--
319	SM 1911.10.223	AS2 vii 20	animal	i_3-dab_5	Abba-saga
320	SM 1911.10.224	AS8 viii 13	animal	i_3-dab_5	Abba-saga
321	SM 1911.10.227	AS7 vii 15	animal	ba-zi	Abba-saga
322	SM 1911.10.228	Š48 viii	animal	i_3-dab_5	Naram-ili
323	SM 1911.10.230	AS2 v	barley	šu ba-ti	Shu-Ishhara
324	SM 1911.10.231	Š47 ii	animal	zi-ga	Beli-azu
325	SM 1911.10.232	AS6 ix 17	animal	i_3-dab_5	Abba-saga
326	SM 1911.10.233	AS9 iii 2	animal	i_3-dab_5	Nalu
327	SM 1911.10.235	Š43 i	barley	šu ba-ti	Ur-Baba
328	SM 1911.10.236	AS4 ix	barley	šu ba-ti	Lu-shalim
329	SM 1911.10.237	AS2 ix 19	animal	ba-zi	Abba-saga
330	SM 1911.10.238	-- -- 24	animal	--	--
331	SM 1911.10.239	ŠS1 xi	[ ]	--	--
332	SM 1911.10.240	AS4 viii 16	animal	mu-DU	Abba-saga
333	SM 1911.10.241	AS7 viii 17	animal	i_3-dab_5	Abba-saga
334	SM 1911.10.242	AS9 ii 27	animal	i_3-dab_5	Abba-saga
335	SM 1911.10.243	AS6 vi 9	animal	i_3-dab_5	Abba-saga
336	SM 1911.10.244	AS9 i	[ ]	[ ]	[ ]
337	SM 1911.10.245	AS8 ii 2	animal	ba-zi	Lugal-amarku
338	SM 1911.10.247	Š45 xii	wool	--	--
339	SM 1911.10.248	AS8 i 13	animal	i_3-dab_5	Abba-saga
340	SM 1911.10.249	-- i 22	animal	--	--
341	SM 1911.10.250	AS4 i 18	animal	mu-DU	Abba-saga
342	SM 1911.10.251	AS7 iii 25	animal	i_3-dab_5	Abba-saga
343	SM 1911.10.253	Š46 ii	animal	--	--
344	SM 1911.10.254	AS1 iii	animal	i_3-dab_5	Kuli
345	SM 1911.10.255	AS4 iii 28	animal	i_3-dab_5	Abba-saga
346	SM 1911.10.256	AS4 vii 20	animal	i_3-dab_5	Abba-saga
347	SM 1911.10.257	Š47 ix	animal	šu ba-ti	Naram-ili

(*cont.*)

Text	Museum No.	Date	Subject	Transaction	Bureau
348	SM 1911.10.258	AS8 i 8	animal	i_3-dab_5	Abba-saga
349	SM 1911.10.260	AS6 x 9	animal	i_3-dab_5	Abba-saga
350	SM 1911.10.261	IS1 viii	animal	i_3-dab_5	Intaea
351	SM 1911.10.262	AS6 vii 22	animal	i_3-dab_5	Abba-saga
352	SM 1911.10.263	AS2 x 25	animal	šu ba-ti	Lu-dingira
353	SM 1911.10.265	AS3 xii 27	animal	šu ba-ti	Ahu-Wer
354	SM 1911.10.266	AS8 xi 14	animal	i_3-dab_5	Abba-saga
355	SM 1911.10.267	AS3 i	animal	ba-zi	Enlila
356	SM 1911.10.268	AS8 i 12	animal	ba-zi	Abba-saga
357	SM 1911.10.269	Š37 viii	textiles	mu-DU	Idin-Erra
358	SM 1911.10.270	AS8 i 2	animal	i_3-dab_5	Abba-saga
359	SM 1911.10.271	AS1 x 28	animal	i_3-dab_5	Abba-saga
360	SM 1911.10.272	AS7 vii 17	animal	i_3-dab_5	Abba-saga
361	SM 1911.10.273	AS4 iv 13	animal	i_3-dab_5	Abba-saga
362	SM 1911.10.274	AS9 ix 29	animal	šu ba-ti	Igi-Enlilshe
363	SM 1911.10.275	AS5 i 11	animal	šu ba-ti	Nalu
364	SM 1911.10.276	AS1 xii 17	animal	i_3-dab_5	Abba-saga
365	SM 1911.10.277	AS3 vii 28	animal	--	--
366	SM 1911.10.279	AS4 i	barley	šu ba-ti	Nanna-kiag
367	SM 1911.10.280	ŠS8 x	goods	šu ba-ti	Ur-nigar
368	SM 1911.10.282	-- -- --	animal	i_3-dab_5	Ahu-Wer
369	SM 1911.10.283	-- ix 6	labor	--	--
370	SM 1911.10.286	AS9 xiid 17	animal	ba-zi	En-dingirmu
371	SM 1911.10.287	-- -- --	animal	--	--
372	SM 1911.10.288	ŠS1 v 4	animal	ba-zi	Duga
373	SM 1911.10.289	ŠS9 xi 21	animal	ba-zi	Ur-kununa
374	SM 1911.10.291	IS1 v/vi --	animal	mu-DU	Intaea
375	SM 1911.10.292	IS1 xii	animal	šu ba-ti	Lu-Suen
376	SM 1911.10.295	ŠS5 ix 15	animal	mu-DU	Intaea
377	SM 1911.10.296	ŠS4 vi	dates	--	--
378	SM 1911.10.298	ŠS8 v	animal	i_3-dab_5	Aba-Enlilgin
379	SM 1911.10.301	AS9 v	flour	šu ba-ti	Shu-Eshtar
380	SM 1911.10.306	ŠS3 i 6	animal	i_3-dab_5	Intaea
381	SM 1911.10.307	ŠS--i	vegetables	--	--
382	SM 1911.10.309	AS2 xii	animal	i_3-dab_5	Naram-ili

(*cont.*)

Text	Museum No.	Date	Subject	Transaction	Bureau
383	SM 1911.10.311	AS8 --	textiles	šu ba-ti	Amur-ili
384	SM 1911.10.315	ŠS2 x 11	animal	ba-zi	Intaea
385	SM 1911.10.316	ŠS1 xiid 17	animal	ba-zi	Duga
386	SM 1911.10.317	ŠS2 iv	textiles	šu ba-ti	Amur-ili
387	SM 1911.10.318	IS2 vi	straw	--	--
388	SM 1911.10.319	ŠS3 vi 20	animal	ba-zi	Ur-Nanna
389	SM 1911.10.320	Š44 x	animal	i_3-dab_5	Naram-ili
390	SM 1911.10.321	ŠS1 xii 19	animal	ba-zi	Duga
391	SM 1911.10.323	ŠS2 ix	animal	i_3-dab_5	Intaea
392	SM 1911.10.324	ŠS2 xii	animal	i_3-dab_5	Tahish-atal
393	SM 1911.10.325	IS3 iii	barley	šu ba-ti	Siru
394	SM 1911.10.326	ŠS7 vii 19	animal	ba-zi	Ur-kununa
395	SM 1911.10.327	-- -- --	animal	[ ]	[ ]
396	SM 1911.10.328	AS8 i 7	animal	i_3-dab_5	Ur-Baba
397	SM 1911.10.329	IS2 vi 23	animal	ba-zi	Ur-kununa
398	SM 1911.10.330	ŠS9	wool	šu ba-ti	Ur-Enlila
399	SM 1911.10.333	IS2 xi 6	[ ]	[ ]	[ ]
400	SM 1911.10.336	AS8 iii 27	animal	ba-zi	Shu-Mama
401	SM 1911.10.338	IS2 xi 17	animal	ba-zi	Intaea
402	SM 1911.10.340	AS4 vi 11	animal	mu-DU	Abba-saga
403	SM 1911.10.342	Š47 iii	oil	šu ba-ti	Ur-Lamma
404	SM 1911.10.343	-- -- --	animal	--	--
405	SM 1911.10.345	AS9 iv 16	animal	i_3-dab_5	Abba-saga
406	SM 1911.10.346	ŠS1 iii	$imgaga_3$	šu ba-ti	Lu-shalim
407	SM 1911.10.347 = SM 1911.10.635	-- -- --	animal	--	--
408	SM 1911.10.349	ŠS7 i 20	animal	ba-zi	Ur-kununa
409	SM 1911.10.351	-- x	animal	i_3-dab_5	Ahuni
410	SM 1911.10.352	AS7 viii	barley	šu ba-ti	Diku-ili
411	SM 1911.10.353	Š41 viii	[ ]	ba-zi	Ea-ilum
412	SM 1911.10.354	AS2 vi	silver	[ ]	[ ]
413	SM 1911.10.355	AS7 vi 5	animal	mu-DU	Abba-saga
414	SM 1911.10.356	AS4 xi	cooper	[ ]	[ ]
415	SM 1911.10.357	AS9 xii 12	animal	ba-zi	Nalu
416	SM 1911.10.358	ŠS4 vi	animal	ba-zi	Nalu

(*cont.*)

Text	Museum No.	Date	Subject	Transaction	Bureau
417	SM 1911.10.359	ŠS2 xi	wheat	[ ]	[ ]
418	SM 1911.10.361	AS6 v	oil	šu ba-ti	Lu-Ninshubur
419	SM 1911.10.362	-- -- --	animal	ba-zi	Allamu
420	SM 1911.10.363	ŠS9 i	animal	--	--
421	SM 1911.10.365	ŠS3 vi	wool	mu-DU	Nur-Suen
422	SM 1911.10.366	AS6 iii 4	animal	--	--
423	SM 1911.10.367	ŠS1 iv 19	animal	ba-zi	Nalu
424	SM 1911.10.368	-- -- --	animal	mu-DU	Abba-saga
425	SM 1911.10.370	AS2 iii	silver	ba-zi	Puzur-Erra
426	SM 1911.10.372	AS8 viii 25	animal	i_3-dab_5	Abba-saga
427	SM 1911.10.373	Š40 vii	animal	--	--
428	SM 1911.10.374	Š38 vii	barley	šu ba-ti	Kikulu
429	SM 1911.10.375	AS8 x 4	animal	i_3-dab_5	Abba-saga
430	SM 1911.10.376	ŠS4 vii 19	animal	ba-zi	Ur-kununa
431	SM 1911.10.377	AS--ix 18	animal	i_3-dab_5	Abba-saga
432	SM 1911.10.378	ŠS1 ix	animal	--	--
433	SM 1911.10.379	AS8 viii 10+	animal	i_3-dab_5	Abba-saga
434	SM 1911.10.381	Š36 v	animal	i_3-dab_5	Abba-saga
435	SM 1911.10.382	IS1 iv	animal	--	--
436	SM 1911.10.383	AS7 i 10	animal	mu-DU	Abba-saga
437	SM 1911.10.384	ŠS7 vii 6	animal	šu ba-ti	Ur-kununa
438	SM 1911.10.385	AS6 v 7	animal	i_3-dab_5	Abba-saga
439	SM 1911.10.386	AS5 i 30	animal	zi-ga	Shulgi-Lammamu
440	SM 1911.10.387	-- vi	animal	i_3-dab_5	Tab-ili
441	SM 1911.10.388	AS5 x	barley	šu ba-ti	Ur-shugalama
442	SM 1911.10.389	Š45 iii	animal	--	--
443	SM 1911.10.390	Š45 i 3	animal	šu ba-ti	Ahuni
444	SM 1911.10.391	ŠS1 xii 23	animal	šu ba-ti	Ur-Igalim
445	SM 1911.10.392	ŠS1 v 13	animal	šu ba-ti	Beli-ili
446	SM 1911.10.393	AS2 vii 16	animal	i_3-dab_5	Abba-saga
447	SM 1911.10.394	AS4 x 6	animal	i_3-dab_5	Abba-saga
448	SM 1911.10.395	ŠS8 v 18	animal	ba-zi	Puzur-Enlil
449	SM 1911.10.398	ŠS1 i 8	animal	ba-zi	Nalu
450	SM 1911.10.399	ŠS3 xi 5	animal	ba-zi	Enlil-zishagal
451	SM 1911.10.402	Š42 xi	barley	zi-ga	--

(*cont.*)

Text	Museum No.	Date	Subject	Transaction	Bureau
452	SM 1911.10.404	AS9 vii 27	animal	ba-zi	Igi-Enlilshe
453	SM 1911.10.409	Š35 xi	animal	[ ]	Naram-ili
454	SM 1911.10.411	Š35	animal	--	--
455	SM 1911.10.412	AS7 xi	animal	i_3-dab_5	Intaea
456	SM 1911.10.413	AS6 xi	animal	i_3-dab_5	Shulgi-ayamu
457	SM 1911.10.414	-- -- --	animal	--	--
458	SM 1911.10.415	ŠS4 viii 6	animal	mu-DU	Intaea
459	SM 1911.10.416	ŠS9 x 16	animal	ba-zi	Puzur-Enlil
460	SM 1911.10.417	ŠS4 vii 2	animal	ba-zi	Ur-kununa
461	SM 1911.10.418	AS9 v	animal	i_3-dab_5	Lugal-itida
462	SM 1911.10.420	Š33 ix	animal	šu ba-ti	Shukubum
463	SM 1911.10.421	-- -- --	animal	--	--
464	SM 1911.10.422	ŠS7 vii	barley	--	--
465	SM 1911.10.423	IS1 iv	animal	ba-zi	Ur-kununa
466	SM 1911.10.425	ŠS6 iii 6	animal	mu-DU	Intaea
467	SM 1911.10.426	ŠS3 i 29	animal	ba-zi	Intaea
468	SM 1911.10.427	-- iii 24	animal	ba-zi	Nalu
469	SM 1911.10.428	ŠS9 iv	wool	--	--
470	SM 1911.10.429	AS - ii	wood	[ ]	[ ]
471	SM 1911.10.430	ŠS5 xi 28	animal	ba-zi	Ur-kununa
472	SM 1911.10.431	IS2 x 1	animal	ba-zi	Intaea
473	SM 1911.10.433	ŠS1 xi 23	animal	ba-zi	Duga
474	SM 1911.10.435	ŠS4 ix 12	animal	ba-zi	Enlil-zishagal
475	SM 1911.10.436	AS9 iv	barley	--	--
476	SM 1911.10.437	ŠS4 ix	animal	i_3-dab_5	Ahu-Wer
477	SM 1911.10.438	Š41 xiid	animal	--	--
478	SM 1911.10.439	AS9 xi	barley	šu ba-ti	Nisaba-andul
479	SM 1911.10.440	AS3 ix 25	animal	ba-zi	Nalu
480	SM 1911.10.441	ŠS1 i 15	animal	ba-zi	Beli-ili
481	SM 1911.10.444	ŠS4 vii 22	animal	ba-zi	Ibni-Suen
482	SM 1911.10.445	ŠS8 ix 1	animal	ba-zi	Ur-kununa
483	SM 1911.10.446	ŠS9 xii 13	animal	ba-zi	Intaea
484	SM 1911.10.449	IS2 ii	animal	ba-zi	[ ]
485	SM 1911.10.450	AS9 xii 22	animal	ba-zi	Tahish-atal
486	SM 1911.10.451	AS6 x 4	animal	mu-DU	Abba-saga

(*cont.*)

Text	Museum No.	Date	Subject	Transaction	Bureau
487	SM 1911.10.452	ŠS2 ii 24	animal	ba-zi	Duga
488	SM 1911.10.453	ŠS3 i 8	animal	ba-zi	Intaea
489	SM 1911.10.454	-- iii	wool	--	--
490	SM 1911.10.455	AS8 iii 6	animal	ba-zi	Duga
491	SM 1911.10.456	IS2 vi 12	animal	ba-zi	Intaea
492	SM 1911.10.458	AS2 i 9	animal	ba-zi	Abba-saga
493	SM 1911.10.461	ŠS5 ii 12	animal	ki-be$_2$ gi$_4$-a	Intaea
494	SM 1911.10.463	Š43 iii	animal	šu ba-ti	Nasa
495	SM 1911.10.465	ŠS8 ix 22	animal	niĝ$_2$-ka$_9$-ak	Zazi
496	SM 1911.10.466	-- -- --	animal	--	--
497	SM 1911.10.467	Š45 iv	animal	niĝ$_2$-ka$_9$-ak	--
498	SM 1911.10.468	AS8 iv	animal	niĝ$_2$-ka$_9$-ak	Huru[x]
499	SM 1911.10.469	AS3 viii	animal	i$_3$-dab$_5$	Abba-saga
500	SM 1911.10.470	Š41 ix --	animal	zi-ga	--
501	SM 1911.10.471	ŠS8 x 26	animal	niĝ$_2$-ka$_9$-ak	Lugal-ezem
502	SM 1911.10.472	AS8 iv	animal	i$_3$-dab$_5$	Abba-saga
503	SM 1911.10.473	AS2 viii 14	animal	i$_3$-dab$_5$	Abba-saga
504	SM 1911.10.474	AS4 ix 1	animal	ba-zi	Abba-saga
505	SM 1911.10.475	ŠS2 xi 27	animal	ba-zi	Enlila
506	SM 1911.10.476	AS4 viii 8	animal	ba-zi	Abba-saga
507	SM 1911.10.477	-- xi --	animal	[ ]	[ ]
508	SM 1911.10.479	AS6 vii	animal	i$_3$-dab$_5$	Ur-kununa
509	SM 1911.10.480	AS5 x	animal	i$_3$-dab$_5$	Intaea
510	SM 1911.10.481	-- -- --	animal	--	--
511	SM 1911.10.482	Š41 viii 30	animal	mu-DU	--
512	SM 1911.10.484	AS2 xi 20	animal	ba-zi	Abba-saga
513	SM 1911.10.486	Š42 vi	animal	--	--
514	SM 1911.10.487	AS8 ii 26	animal	ba-zi	Lugal-amarku
515	SM 1911.10.488	AS8 ix 20	animal	ba-zi	Abba-saga
516	SM 1911.10.489	AS7 iii	animal	niĝ$_2$-ka$_9$-ak	Alid
517	SM 1911.10.490	AS8 vi 12	animal	ba-zi	Abba-saga
518	SM 1911.10.492	AS3 ix	animal	ba-zi	Abba-saga
519	SM 1911.10.493	ŠS2 x --	animal	i$_3$-dab$_5$	Intaea
520	SM 1911.10.495	Š46 iv	animal	mu-DU	--
521	SM 1911.10.496	AS2 ix	animal	ba-zi	Abba-saga

(*cont.*)

Text	Museum No.	Date	Subject	Transaction	Bureau
522	SM 1911.10.497	AS7 xii 23	animal	ba-zi	Abba-saga
523	SM 1911.10.499	AS8 vii	animal	i_3-dab_5	Abba-saga
524	SM 1911.10.500	AS8 vi	animal	i_3-dab_5	Abba-saga
525	SM 1911.10.501	AS4 x 21	animal	ba-zi	Intaea
526	SM 1911.10.502	ŠS3 viii	animal	ba-zi	Ahannishu
527	SM 1911.10.503	AS4 viii 24	animal	i_3-dab_5	Abba-saga
528	SM 1911.10.504	AS4 iii 26	animal	ba-zi	Abba-saga
529	SM 1911.10.505	-- -- 7	animal	ba-zi	Ur-kununa
530	SM 1911.10.506	AS8 ix 19	animal	i_3-dab_5	Abba-saga
531	SM 1911.10.507	ŠS3 iii	animal	i_3-dab_5	Duga
532	SM 1911.10.509	ŠS9 i	animal	i_3-dab_5	Aba-Enlilgin
533	SM 1911.10.510	ŠS9 x 13	animal	i_3-dab_5	Intaea
534	SM 1911.10.511	ŠS9 x 13	animal	i_3-dab_5	Intaea
535	SM 1911.10.512	ŠS2 i	animal	i_3-dab_5	Ahu-Wer
536	SM 1911.10.513	ŠS9 viii 14	animal	i_3-dab_5	Intaea
537	SM 1911.10.514	ŠS9 vii 13	animal	i_3-dab_5	Aya-dingir
538	SM 1911.10.515	ŠS8 iii 20	animal	i_3-dab_5	Puzur-Enlil
539	SM 1911.10.516	ŠS9	animal	i_3-dab_5	Lu-Suen
540	SM 1911.10.517	ŠS9 iv 15	animal	i_3-dab_5	Intaea
541	SM 1911.10.518	ŠS9 vii	animal	ba-zi	Duga
542	SM 1911.10.519	ŠS9 i 11	animal	--	--
543	SM 1911.10.520	ŠS3 i 24	animal	i_3-dab_5	Intaea
544	SM 1911.10.521	ŠS8 x	animal	ba-zi	Allamu
545	SM 1911.10.522	IS1 xiid	animal	i_3-dab_5	Ur-kununa
546	SM 1911.10.523	ŠS3 viii 25	animal	i_3-dab_5	Intaea
547	SM 1911.10.524	IS1	animal	i_3-dab_5	Shulgi-irimu
548	SM 1911.10.525	ŠS1 xiid	animal	ba-zi	Ur-ezem
549	SM 1911.10.526	AS8 xii	animal	i_3-dab_5	Duga
550	SM 1911.10.527	IS1 xiid	animal	ba-zi	Ishme-ilum
551	SM 1911.10.528	ŠS7 vii	animal	i_3-dab_5	Intaea
552	SM 1911.10.529	ŠS3 viii 18	animal	i_3-dab_5	Intaea
553	SM 1911.10.530	ŠS2 iii	animal	i_3-dab_5	Nalu
554	SM 1911.10.531	ŠS2 viii	animal	i_3-dab_5	Ur-Nanshe
555	SM 1911.10.533	ŠS9 vii	ghee	šu ba-ti	Lu-kala
556	SM 1911.10.534	ŠS3 vii 1	animal	i_3-dab_5	Intaea

(*cont.*)

Text	Museum No.	Date	Subject	Transaction	Bureau
557	SM 1911.10.535	ŠS1 xiid 16	animal	i_3-dab_5	Kurbilak
558	SM 1911.10.536	ŠS9 viii	animal	i_3-dab_5	Puzur-Enlil
559	SM 1911.10.537	IS1 xi	animal	ba-zi	Aya-dingir
560	SM 1911.10.539	AS1-29	animal	i_3-dab_5	Nasa
561	SM 1911.10.540	ŠS2 x 24	animal	i_3-dab_5	Beli-ili
562	SM 1911.10.541	IS1 xiid	animal	i_3-dab_5	Aba-Enlilgin
563	SM 1911.10.542	IS1 ii	animal	i_3-dab_5	Intaea
564	SM 1911.10.543	ŠS9	animal	--	--
565	SM 1911.10.544	ŠS3 viii 17	animal	i_3-dab_5	Intaea
566	SM 1911.10.545	ŠS9 vii	animal	i_3-dab_5	Shulgi-ili
567	SM 1911.10.546	ŠS1 vi	animal	i_3-dab_5	Puzur-Enlil
568	SM 1911.10.547	AS5 x	animal	i_3-dab_5	Ur-Baba
569	SM 1911.10.548	IS1	silver	šu ba-ti	Igisasa
570	SM 1911.10.549	ŠS9 viii	animal	i_3-dab_5	Intaea
571	SM 1911.10.550	ŠS3 i 1	animal	i_3-dab_5	Intaea
572	SM 1911.10.551	AS9 iv	animal	i_3-dab_5	Abba-saga
573	SM 1911.10.552	ŠS3 xi 21	animal	mu-DU	Intaea
574	SM 1911.10.553	ŠS2 iii	animal	i_3-dab_5	Kurbilak
575	SM 1911.10.554	ŠS1 xiid	animal	ba-zi	Ur-mes
576	SM 1911.10.555	AS7 x	animal	i_3-dab_5	Abba-saga
577	SM 1911.10.556	ŠS3 ix	animal	i_3-dab_5	Nalu
578	SM 1911.10.557	ŠS8 xi	--	šu ba-ti	Duga
579	SM 1911.10.558	ŠS9 i	animal	ba-zi	Alamu
580	SM 1911.10.559	ŠS2 iv	animal	i_3-dab_5	Nalu
581	SM 1911.10.560	IS2 x	animal	i_3-dab_5	Ur-kununa
582	SM 1911.10.561	AS4 x 7	animal	ba-zi	Abba-saga
583	SM 1911.10.562	AS1 vi	animal	i_3-dab_5	Nasa
584	SM 1911.10.563	ŠS4 xi	animal	i_3-dab_5	Ur-mes
585	SM 1911.10.564	-- -- --	animal	i_3-dab_5	Ur-Nanshe
586	SM 1911.10.565	AS6 v 26	animal	i_3-dab_5	Abba-saga
587	SM 1911.10.567	ŠS1 xii 29	animal	i_3-dab_5	Intaea
588	SM 1911.10.568	AS8 ix 8	animal	i_3-dab_5	Abba-saga
589	SM 1911.10.569	AS4 i 11	animal	i_3-dab_5	Abba-saga
590	SM 1911.10.570	ŠS2 x 25	animal	i_3-dab_5	Kurbilak
591	SM 1911.10.571	AS2 ii 8	animal	i_3-dab_5	Abba-saga

(*cont.*)

Text	Museum No.	Date	Subject	Transaction	Bureau
592	SM 1911.10.572	AS8 xi 23	animal	ba-zi	Abba-saga
593	SM 1911.10.576	AS4 vi 23	animal	i_3-dab_5	Abba-saga
594	SM 1911.10.578	AS8 iv 14	animal	i_3-dab_5	Lugal-amarku
595	SM 1911.10.579	AS8 ii 25	animal	i_3-dab_5	Lugal-amarku
596	SM 1911.10.580	AS8 i 19	animal	i_3-dab_5	Lugal-amarku
597	SM 1911.10.581	AS8 ii 30	animal	i_3-dab_5	Lugal-amarku
598	SM 1911.10.582	AS6 iii 27	animal	i_3-dab_5	Abba-saga
599	SM 1911.10.583	AS6 iii 6	animal	i_3-dab_5	Abba-saga
600	SM 1911.10.584	AS4 viii 1	animal	i_3-dab_5	Abba-saga
601	SM 1911.10.585	AS8 vii	animal	i_3-dab_5	Tahish-atal
602	SM 1911.10.586	AS8 i 20	animal	i_3-dab_5	Lugal-amarku
603	SM 1911.10.587	AS6 ix 9	animal	ba-zi	Abba-saga
604	SM 1911.10.588	AS8 i 21	animal	i_3-dab_5	Lugal-amarku
605	SM 1911.10.589	AS6 xi 13	animal	i_3-dab_5	Abba-saga
606	SM 1911.10.590	AS6 iii 8	animal	i_3-dab_5	Abba-saga
607	SM 1911.10.591	AS8 xii 29	animal	i_3-dab_5	Abba-saga
608	SM 1911.10.592	AS8 i 16	animal	i_3-dab_5	Lugal-amarku
609	SM 1911.10.593	AS8 vii 12	animal	i_3-dab_5	Abba-saga
610	SM 1911.10.594	AS8 v 24	animal	ba-zi	Abba-saga
611	SM 1911.10.595	AS8 vi 4	animal	i_3-dab_5	Abba-saga
612	SM 1911.10.596	ŠS1 xii 1	animal	i_3-dab_5	Intaea
613	SM 1911.10.597	AS8 iii 18	animal	ba-zi	Lugal-amarku
614	SM 1911.10.598	AS8 vi 15	animal	i_3-dab_5	Abba-saga
615	SM 1911.10.600	AS8 iv 9	animal	i_3-dab_5	Lugal-amarku
616	SM 1911.10.601	AS8 iv 17	animal	i_3-dab_5	Lugal-amarku
617	SM 1911.10.602	AS8 ii 3	animal	i_3-dab_5	Lugal-amarku
618	SM 1911.10.603	AS6 iv 26	animal	i_3-dab_5	Abba-saga
619	SM 1911.10.604	AS1 v 21	animal	i_3-dab_5	Nasa
620	SM 1911.10.605	AS2 i 9	animal	zi-ga	Enlila
621	SM 1911.10.606	AS4 vi 20	animal	i_3-dab_5	Abba-saga
622	SM 1911.10.607	AS8 ix 11	animal	i_3-dab_5	Abba-saga
623	SM 1911.10.608	AS3 v 27	animal	ba-zi	Abba-saga
624	SM 1911.10.609	AS8 vii 25	animal	i_3-dab_5	Abba-saga
625	SM 1911.10.610	AS7 ix 26	animal	i_3-dab_5	Abba-saga
626	SM 1911.10.611	AS4 x 10	animal	i_3-dab_5	Abba-saga

(*cont.*)

Text	Museum No.	Date	Subject	Transaction	Bureau
627	SM 1911.10.612	-- xi	animal	--	--
628	SM 1911.10.613	AS8 iii 16	animal	i_3-dab_5	Lugal-amarku
629	SM 1911.10.614	AS8 xi 14	animal	i_3-dab_5	Abba-saga
630	SM 1911.10.615	AS8 ii 23	animal	i_3-dab_5	Lugal-amarku
631	SM 1911.10.616	AS8 iii 19	animal	i_3-dab_5	Lugal-amarku
632	SM 1911.10.617	AS4 vi 23	animal	i_3-dab_5	Abba-saga
633	SM 1911.10.618	AS4 vi 21	animal	i_3-dab_5	Abba-saga
634	SM 1911.10.619	AS8 xi 6	animal	i_3-dab_5	Abba-saga
635	SM 1911.10.620	Š45 iv	animal	mu-DU	--
636	SM 1911.10.621	AS4 vi 18	animal	i_3-dab_5	Abba-saga
637	SM 1911.10.622	AS8 viii 18	animal	ba-zi	Abba-saga
638	SM 1911.10.623	AS4 ix 10	animal	ba-zi	Abba-saga
639	SM 1911.10.624	AS4 vii 8	animal	i_3-dab_5	Abba-saga
640	SM 1911.10.625	AS2 iv 27	animal	i_3-dab_5	Abba-saga
641	SM 1911.10.626	AS2 v 9	animal	i_3-dab_5	Abba-saga
642	SM 1911.10.627	AS6 i 13	animal	i_3-dab_5	Abba-saga
643	SM 1911.10.628	Š47 viii 6	animal	zi-ga	Enlila
644	SM 1911.10.629	Š47 vi 2	animal	zi-ga	Ur-kununa
645	SM 1911.10.630	Š47 vii 19	animal	zi-ga	Ur-kununa
646	SM 1911.10.632	-- -- 12	animal	i_3-dab_5	Nasa
647	SM 1918.01.007	AS4 iv 29	animal	i_3-dab_5	Abba-saga
648	SM 1918.01.008	AS7 vii 14	animal	i_3-dab_5	Abba-saga
649	SM 1918.01.009	Š47 ix	animal	i_3-dab_5	Lu-Ninshubur
650	SM 1918.01.010	AS7 xi 8	animal	i_3-dab_5	Abba-saga
651	SM 1918.01.011	AS7 xi 9	animal	i_3-dab_5	Abba-saga
652	SM 1918.01.012	AS7 i 29	animal	i_3-dab_5	Abba-saga
653	SM 1918.01.013	AS7 ii 3	animal	i_3-dab_5	Abba-saga
654	SM 1918.01.016	Š46 viii	animal	zi-ga	Ur-kununa
655	SM 1918.01.017	AS3 x 28	animal	i_3-dab_5	Abba-saga
656	SM 1918.01.018	AS4 x 29	animal	i_3-dab_5	Abba-saga
657	SM 1918.01.019	AS6 vii 27	animal	i_3-dab_5	Abba-saga
658	SM 1918.01.020	AS7 vii 13	animal	i_3-dab_5	Abba-saga
659	SM 1918.01.021	AS6 ix 1	animal	i_3-dab_5	Abba-saga
660	SM 1918.01.022	AS7 i 28	animal	i_3-dab_5	Abba-saga
661	SM 1918.01.023	-- -- --	animal	i_3-dab_5	Intaea

(*cont.*)

Text	Museum No.	Date	Subject	Transaction	Bureau
662	SM 1918.01.024	AS3 x 22	animal	i_3-dab$_5$	Abba-saga
663	SM 1918.01.025	AS7 ii 21	animal	i_3-dab$_5$	Abba-saga
664	SM 1918.01.026	AS4 viii 30	animal	i_3-dab$_5$	Abba-saga
665	SM 1918.01.027	AS6 iv 18	animal	i_3-dab$_5$	Abba-saga
666	SM 1918.01.028	AS2 v 9	animal	i_3-dab$_5$	Abba-saga
667	SM 1918.01.029	AS4 vii 4	animal	i_3-dab$_5$	Abba-saga
668	SM 1918.01.030	AS4 ii 25	animal	i_3-dab$_5$	Abba-saga
669	SM 1918.01.031	AS7 vii 29	animal	i_3-dab$_5$	Abba-saga
670	SM 1918.01.032	AS2 iii 12	animal	i_3-dab$_5$	Abba-saga
671	SM 1918.01.033	AS6 xi 26	animal	i_3-dab$_5$	Abba-saga
672	SM 1918.01.034	AS2 xi 17	animal	i_3-dab$_5$	Abba-saga
673	SM 1918.01.035	AS2 v 30	animal	i_3-dab$_5$	Abba-saga
674	SM 1918.01.036	AS7 iv 3	animal	i_3-dab$_5$	Abba-saga
675	SM 1918.01.037	AS6 iii 12	animal	i_3-dab$_5$	Abba-saga
676	SM 1918.01.038	Š45 x 10	animal	šu ba-ti	En-dingirmu
677	SM 1918.01.039	AS4 vii 24	animal	i_3-dab$_5$	Abba-saga
678	SM 1929.01.003	AS8 viii 20	animal	šu ba-ti	Lu-dingira
679	SM 1929.01.009	AS1 xii 24	animal	šu ba-ti	Nalu
680	SM 1929.01.010	AS2 v 23	animal	i_3-dab$_5$	Shulgi-ayamu
681	SM 1951.02.001	AS6 viii 28	animal	ba-zi	Abba-saga
682	SM 1951.02.002	AS8 v 12	animal	i_3-dab$_5$	Abba-saga
683	SM 1951.02.003	IS1 v 6	wool	šu ba-ti	--
684	SM 1995.03.092	AS2 viii --	animal	šu ba-ti	Lu-dingira
685	SM 1995.03.093	AS2 viii 10	animal	i_3-dab$_5$	Shulgi-ayamu
686	SM 1995.03.095	ŠS2 iii 24	animal	šu ba-ti	Nalu
687	SM 1995.09.004	ŠS2 i 5	animal	zi-ga	Ur-Igalim
688	SM 1995.09.006	AS2 viii 28	animal	šu ba-ti	En-dingirmu
689	SM 1997.01.005	Š38 ix	animal	i_3-dab$_5$	En-dingirmu

Chronological List

Date	No.
Š33 ii	257
Š33 ix	462
Š35	454
Š35 xi	453
Š36 v	434
Š37 viii	357
Š38 vii	428
Š38 ix	689
Š39 ii	309
Š40 vii	427
Š41 viii	411
Š41 viii 30	511
Š41 ix --	500
Š41 xiid	477
Š42 vi	513
Š42 xi	451
Š42 xii	262
Š43 i	327
Š43 iii	494
Š43 iii 9	119
Š43 vi 5	8
Š43 xii	5
Š44 iv 27	34
Š44 v 21	111
Š44 vi 16	90
Š44 x	389
Š45 i 3	443
Š45 iii	442
Š45 iv	497
Š45 iv	635
Š45 viii 21	24
Š45 ix	304
Š45 x 10	676

 | DOI:10.1163/9789004461369_004

(*cont.*)

Date	No.
Š45 x 26	51
Š45 xi 17	9
Š45 xii	338
Š45 xii 7	115
Š45 xii 16	40
Š45 xii 17	76
Š46 i	163
Š46 i 17	53
Š46 i 17	125
Š46 ii	154
Š46 ii	279
Š46 ii	343
Š46 ii 12	45
Š46 ii 12	77
Š46 ii 15	141
Š46 ii 24	209
Š46 iii	263
Š46 iv	183
Š46 iv	520
Š46 iv 18	74
Š46 v	192
Š46 v 1	139
Š46 vi 14	47
Š46 vii 1	109
Š46 vii 21	101
Š46 viii	654
Š46 viii 9	85
Š46 x	170
Š46 x 16	28
Š46 x 24	33
Š46 xi 9	274
Š47 ii	88
Š47 ii	324
Š47 ii 14	100
Š47 ii 27	70

(*cont.*)

Date	No.
Š47 iii	403
Š47 iii 18	42
Š47 iv	269
Š47 iv 4	10
Š47 iv 18	71
Š47 v 19	82
Š47 vi	15
Š47 vi 2	644
Š47 vi 9	38
Š47 vi 16	244
Š47 vii 5	35
Š47 vii 19	645
Š47 vii 25	55
Š47 vii 25	131
Š47 viii 6	643
Š47 viii 9	245
Š47 viii 12	239
Š47 viii 16	13
Š47 viii 17	92
Š47 viii 17	242
Š47 viii 20	72
Š47 ix	347
Š47 ix	649
Š47 ix 7	247
Š47 ix 11	249
Š47 x 29	46
Š47 xi	201
Š47 xid	61
Š47 xi 2	69
Š47 xii 18	62
Š48 i 5	79
Š48 i 11	133
Š48 vi 15	56
Š48 vii 13	120
Š48 vii 14	11

(*cont.*)

Date	No.
Š48 viii	322
Š48 ix 27	44
Š48 x	59
Š48 xi	276
Š48 xi 22	299
Š48 xi 27	303
Š48 xii	287
Š - v	121
AS1 i	317
AS1 iii	344
AS1 iii 16	188
AS1 v 20	81
AS1 v 21	619
AS1 vi	583
AS1 vi 30	107
AS1 vii 22	240
AS1 vii --	175
AS1 viii 7	130
AS1 viii 7	301
AS1 viii 10	277
AS1 ix 16	186
AS1 ix 25	225
AS1 ix 26	231
AS1 x 9	178
AS1 x 10	73
AS1 x 19	134
AS1 x 28	359
AS1 x --	169
AS1 xi 7	135
AS1 xi 10	235
AS1 xi 18	290
AS1 xii 2	89
AS1 xii 17	117
AS1 xii 17	364
AS1 xii 24	679

(*cont.*)

Date	No.
AS1 xii 27	146
AS1-29	560
AS2 i 7	221
AS2 i 9	492
AS2 i 9	620
AS2 i 22	57
AS2 ii 4	97
AS2 ii 6	208
AS2 ii 8	591
AS2 ii 22	214
AS2 iii	425
AS2 iii 12	670
AS2 iii 27	271
AS2 iv 16	173
AS2 iv 27	640
AS2 v	323
AS2 v 5	211
AS2 v 7	241
AS2 v 9	641
AS2 v 9	666
AS2 v 10	199
AS2 v 18	230
AS2 v 23	680
AS2 v 30	673
AS2 vi	250
AS2 vi	412
AS2 vi 14	189
AS2 vi 29	210
AS2 vii	251
AS2 vii 16	446
AS2 vii 20	319
AS2 vii 26	116
AS2 viii 10	685
AS2 viii 14	503
AS2 viii 18	123

(*cont.*)

Date	No.
AS2 viii 24	226
AS2 viii 28	688
AS2 viii --	684
AS2 ix	521
AS2 ix 19	329
AS2 ix 21	161
AS2 ix 25	197
AS2 x	233
AS2 x 1	227
AS2 x 25	352
AS2 xi	157
AS2 xi 17	672
AS2 xi 20	512
AS2 xii	382
AS2 xii 27	118
AS3 i	355
AS3 i 23	224
AS3 ii 28	258
AS3 v	206
AS3 v 27	623
AS3 vi 10	200
AS3 vi 17	126
AS3 vii 28	365
AS3 viii	300
AS3 viii	499
AS3 ix	518
AS3 ix 25	479
AS3 x 4	198
AS3 x 8	213
AS3 x 11	181
AS3 x 11	196
AS3 x 16	182
AS3 x 22	662
AS3 x 28	655
AS3 xi 26	103

(*cont.*)

Date	No.
AS3 xii	267
AS3 xii 11	216
AS3 xii 27	353
AS4	280
AS4 i	366
AS4 i 1	215
AS4 i 11	589
AS4 i 18	341
AS4 ii 25	668
AS4 iii 26	528
AS4 iii 28	345
AS4 iv 7	238
AS4 iv 13	361
AS4 iv 24	234
AS4 iv 29	647
AS4 vi 6	108
AS4 vi 11	402
AS4 vi 18	636
AS4 vi 20	621
AS4 vi 21	633
AS4 vi 23	593
AS4 vi 23	632
AS4 vii 4	667
AS4 vii 8	639
AS4 vii 20	346
AS4 vii 24	677
AS4 viii 1	171
AS4 viii 1	600
AS4 viii 3	207
AS4 viii 8	237
AS4 viii 8	506
AS4 viii 14	232
AS4 viii 16	332
AS4 viii 24	527
AS4 viii 30	664

(*cont.*)

Date	No.
AS4 ix	308
AS4 ix	328
AS4 ix 1	504
AS4 ix 10	638
AS4 x	104
AS4 x 6	447
AS4 x 7	582
AS4 x 10	626
AS4 x 13	223
AS4 x 21	525
AS4 x 29	656
AS4 xi	414
AS4 xi 3	106
AS4 xi 8	278
AS4 xi 20	105
AS4 xii 5	310
AS4 xii 10	248
AS5 i	66
AS5 i 8	138
AS5 i 11	363
AS5 i 22	129
AS5 i 30	64
AS5 i 30	439
AS5 ii 3	22
AS5 iii 29	58
AS5 iv 25	83
AS5 iv 30	60
AS5 vi 1	30
AS5 vi 12	65
AS5 vi 12	67
AS5 vi 17	96
AS5 vii 25	43
AS5 viii 11	114
AS5 viii 13	91
AS5 ix 20	52

(*cont.*)

Date	No.
AS5 x	441
AS5 x	509
AS5 x	568
AS5 x 2	7
AS5 x 24	137
AS5 xi 25	127
AS5 xii	255
AS5 xii 25	54
AS5 xii 28	86
AS6 i 13	642
AS6 ii 2	220
AS6 iii 4	422
AS6 iii 6	599
AS6 iii 8	606
AS6 iii 12	675
AS6 iii 27	598
AS6 iv	281
AS6 iv 4	312
AS6 iv 4	298
AS6 iv 18	665
AS6 iv 26	618
AS6 iv 28	185
AS6 v	418
AS6 v 7	438
AS6 v 13	99
AS6 v 19	195
AS6 v 26	586
AS6 vi 1	128
AS6 vi 9	335
AS6 vi 13	204
AS6 vi 14	243
AS6 vi 30	176
AS6 vii	508
AS6 vii 22	351
AS6 vii 26	124

(*cont.*)

Date	No.
AS6 vii 27	657
AS6 viii 14	179
AS6 viii 21	212
AS6 viii 28	681
AS6 viii 30	203
AS6 ix 1	174
AS6 ix 1	659
AS6 ix 9	603
AS6 ix 17	325
AS6 x 4	486
AS6 x 9	349
AS6 x 23	229
AS6 x 25	140
AS6 xi	155
AS6 xi	456
AS6 xi 13	605
AS6 xi 24	166
AS6 xi 26	671
AS6 xii 13	217
AS6 xii 25	177
AS7	17
AS7 i	162
AS7 i 10	436
AS7 i 28	660
AS7 i 29	652
AS7 ii 1	93
AS7 ii 3	653
AS7 ii 21	663
AS7 ii 25	132
AS7 iii	516
AS7 iii 25	187
AS7 iii 25	342
AS7 iv 3	674
AS7 iv --	112
AS7 v 13	205

(*cont.*)

Date	No.
AS7 vi 5	413
AS7 vii 13	658
AS7 vii 14	648
AS7 vii 15	321
AS7 vii 17	360
AS7 vii 21	236
AS7 vii 29	669
AS7 viii	410
AS7 viii 1	218
AS7 viii 5	180
AS7 viii 17	333
AS7 ix	167
AS7 ix 7	202
AS7 ix 8	193
AS7 ix 26	625
AS7 x	576
AS7 x 12	191
AS7 x 18	164
AS7 xi	25
AS7 xi	455
AS7 xi 8	650
AS7 xi 9	651
AS7 xii 1+	306
AS7 xii 3	94
AS7 xii 18	194
AS7 xii 23	522
AS8 i	296
AS8 i 2	358
AS8 i 7	396
AS8 i 8	348
AS8 i 12	356
AS8 i 13	339
AS8 i 16	313
AS8 i 16	608
AS8 i 19	596

(*cont.*)

Date	No.
AS8 i 20	602
AS8 i 21	604
AS8 ii 2	337
AS8 ii 3	617
AS8 ii 13	190
AS8 ii 23	630
AS8 ii 25	219
AS8 ii 25	595
AS8 ii 26	514
AS8 ii 30	597
AS8 iii 6	490
AS8 iii 16	628
AS8 iii 18	613
AS8 iii 19	631
AS8 iii 27	400
AS8 iv	48
AS8 iv	498
AS8 iv	502
AS8 iv 9	615
AS8 iv 14	594
AS8 iv 17	616
AS8 iv 20+	98
AS8 v 2	228
AS8 v 12	682
AS8 v 24	610
AS8 iv/v 19	68
AS8 vi	524
AS8 vi 4	611
AS8 vi 12	517
AS8 vi 15	614
AS8 vii	523
AS8 vii	601
AS8 vii 12	609
AS8 vii 25	624
AS8 viii 10+	433

(*cont.*)

Date	No.
AS8 viii 13	320
AS8 viii 18	637
AS8 viii 20	678
AS8 viii 25	426
AS8 ix 1	102
AS8 ix 3	95
AS8 ix 8	588
AS8 ix 11	622
AS8 ix 19	530
AS8 ix 20	515
AS8 x 4	429
AS8 x 24	172
AS8 xi	87
AS8 xi 6	634
AS8 xi 14	354
AS8 xi 14	629
AS8 xi 23	592
AS8 xii	549
AS8 xii 29	607
AS8 --	383
AS9	3
AS9 i	336
AS9 i 8	275
AS9 ii 27	334
AS9 ii 30	4
AS9 iii	314
AS9 iii 2	326
AS9 iii 28	165
AS9 iv	158
AS9 iv	475
AS9 iv	572
AS9 iv 16	29
AS9 iv 16	160
AS9 iv 16	405
AS9 v	379

(*cont.*)

Date	No.
AS9 v	461
AS9 vii 27	452
AS9 ix 29	362
AS9 x 18	18
AS9 xi	478
AS9 xii 1	147
AS9 xii 12	415
AS9 xii 22	485
AS9 xii 29	149
AS9 xii 29	288
AS9 xiid 17	370
AS - ii	470
AS - ix 18	431
ŠS1 i 8	449
ŠS1 i 15	480
ŠS1 iii	406
ŠS1 iv 2	311
ŠS1 iv 19	423
ŠS1 v 4	372
ŠS1 v 13	445
ŠS1 vi	20
ŠS1 vi	567
ŠS1 vii 19	153
ŠS1 ix	432
ŠS1 ix 11	49
ŠS1 xi	331
ŠS1 xi 23	473
ŠS1 xii 1	612
ŠS1 xii 19	390
ŠS1 xii 23	444
ŠS1 xii 28	264
ŠS1 xii 29	587
ŠS1 xiid	548
ŠS1 xiid	575
ŠS1 xiid 9	144

(*cont.*)

Date	No.
ŠS1 xiid 16	557
ŠS1 xiid 17	385
ŠS2 i	152
ŠS2 i	535
ŠS2 i 5	687
ŠS2 ii	148
ŠS2 ii 24	487
ŠS2 iii	27
ŠS2 iii	553
ŠS2 iii	574
ŠS2 iii 24	686
ŠS2 iv	386
ŠS2 iv	580
ŠS2 viii	554
ŠS2 ix	391
ŠS2 x 11	384
ŠS2 x 24	561
ŠS2 x 25	590
ŠS2 x --	519
ŠS2 xi	417
ŠS2 xi 27	505
ŠS2 xii	392
ŠS3 i	16
ŠS3 i 1	571
ŠS3 i 6	380
ŠS3 i 8	488
ŠS3 i 24	543
ŠS3 i 29	467
ŠS3 ii 5	80
ŠS3 ii 5	110
ŠS3 iii	531
ŠS3 vi	421
ŠS3 vi 20	388
ŠS3 vii 1	556
ŠS3 viii	526

(*cont.*)

Date	No.
ŠS3 viii 17	565
ŠS3 viii 18	552
ŠS3 viii 25	546
ŠS3 ix	577
ŠS3 xi 5	450
ŠS3 xi 8	122
ŠS3 xi 21	573
ŠS3 xid 16	291
ŠS3 xii 9	75
ŠS4	12
ŠS4 i	293
ŠS4 i 22	63
ŠS4 iv 20	23
ŠS4 vi	377
ŠS4 vi	416
ŠS4 vii 2	460
ŠS4 vii 19	430
ŠS4 vii 22	481
ŠS4 viii 6	458
ŠS4 viii 21	37
ŠS4 ix	476
ŠS4 ix 12	474
ŠS4 xi	584
ŠS4 xi 9	136
ŠS5 ii 12	493
ŠS5 vi 2	26
ŠS5 ix 15	376
ŠS5 x 13	41
ŠS5 xi 28	471
ŠS6 iii 6	466
ŠS6 iv --	286
ŠS6 viii 28	272
ŠS7	36
ŠS7 i 20	408
ŠS7 ii 12	50

(*cont.*)

Date	No.
ŠS7 vii	464
ŠS7 vii	551
ŠS7 vii 6	437
ŠS7 vii 19	394
ŠS7 vii 21	19
ŠS7 viii 24	285
ŠS7 xii	39
ŠS8 iii 20	538
ŠS8 iv 28	14
ŠS8 v	378
ŠS8 v 18	448
ŠS8 viii 3	32
ŠS8 ix	31
ŠS8 ix	284
ŠS8 ix 1	482
ŠS8 ix 22	495
ŠS8 x	367
ŠS8 x	544
ŠS8 x 26	501
ŠS8 xi	578
ŠS9	398
ŠS9	539
ŠS9	564
ŠS9 i	420
ŠS9 i	532
ŠS9 i	579
ŠS9 i 11	542
ŠS9 iv	469
ŠS9 iv 15	540
ŠS9 v 4+	145
ŠS9 vii	541
ŠS9 vii	555
ŠS9 vii	566
ŠS9 vii 13	537
ŠS9 viii	558

(*cont.*)

Date	No.
ŠS9 viii	570
ŠS9 viii 14	536
ŠS9 ix 25	302
ŠS9 ix 26	6
ŠS9 x 13	533
ŠS9 x 13	534
ŠS9 x 16	459
ŠS9 xi 21	373
ŠS9 xii 13	483
šs - i	381
IS1	547
IS1	569
IS1 ii	563
IS1 iii 29	273
IS1 iv	435
IS1 iv	465
IS1 v 6	683
IS1 v/vi --	374
IS1 vi	318
IS1 vii 2	151
IS1 viii	350
IS1 viii 4	315
IS1 xi	559
IS1 x	295
IS1 xii	297
IS1 xii	375
IS1 xii 3	307
IS1 xiid	545
IS1 xiid	550
IS1 xiid	562
IS2 ii	484
IS2 v 8	168
IS2 vi	387
IS2 vi 12	491
IS2 vi 23	397

(*cont.*)

Date	No.
IS2 vii	159
IS2 x	581
IS2 x 1	472
IS2 x 4	270
IS2 xi 6	399
IS2 xi 16	21
IS2 xi 17	401
IS3 iii	393
-- i 22	340
-- iii	489
-- iii 24	468
-- iv	143
-- v	292
-- v 1	142
-- vi	440
-- vi 24	294
-- vii 4	246
-- viii	283
-- viii 27	84
-- ix	289
-- ix 6	369
-- x	409
-- xi	316
-- xi	627
-- xi --	507
-- xii	266
-- xii 18	113
-- -- 3	78
-- -- 7	529
-- -- 10	305
-- -- 12	646
-- -- 18	184
-- -- 19	252
-- -- 24	330
-- -- --	1

(*cont.*)

Date	No.
-- -- --	2
-- -- --	150
-- -- --	156
-- -- --	222
-- -- --	253
-- -- --	254
-- -- --	256
-- -- --	259
-- -- --	260
-- -- --	261
-- -- --	265
-- -- --	268
-- -- --	282
-- -- --	368
-- -- --	371
-- -- --	395
-- -- --	404
-- -- --	407
-- -- --	419
-- -- --	424
-- -- --	457
-- -- --	463
-- -- --	496
-- -- --	510
-- -- --	585
-- -- --	661

Catalogue of Seal Impressions

Seal holder	Seal impression	Text
A-hu-šu-ni	**A-hu-šu-ni**, dumu [ ]	576
Ab-ba-kal-la	Ab-ba-kal-la, dub-sar, dumu Lu$_2$-^{d}Nin-ĝir$_2$-su	420, 537, 538, 564, 578, 579
Bi$_2$-du$_{11}$-i$_3$-sa$_6$	**Bi$_2$-du$_{11}$-i$_3$-sa$_6$**, dumu Zu-[ ]	296
BU-la	**BU-la**, dub-sar, arad$_2$ ^{d}Nin-[ ]	400
Du$_{11}$-ga	**Du$_{11}$-ga** dub-sar, dumu Lu$_2$-^{d}Nin-ĝir$_2$-su, sipa na-gab$_2$-tum	295, 297, 532, 533, 540, 545, 547, 548, 563, 575
I-ri-ib	**I-ri-ib**, dumu SI.A-a, arad$_2$ lugal	314
I-zu-sa-bar	**I-zu-sa-bar**, dub-sar, arad$_2$ ^{d}[ ]	474
Li-bur-^{d}Šul-gi	**Li-bur-^{d}Šul-gi**, dub-sar, dumu Kal-la-mu	561
Lu$_2$-^{d}Da-mu	**Lu$_2$-^{d}Da-mu**, dub-sar, dumu [ ]	461
Lu$_2$-^{d}EN.ZU	**Lu$_2$-^{d}EN.ZU**, dumu Ur-sa$_6$-ga, sipa gu$_4$ niga	378
Lu$_2$-^{d}Nin-ĝir$_2$-su	**Lu$_2$-^{d}Nin-ĝir$_2$-su**, dub-sar, dumu Ur-sa$_6$-ga, sipa gu$_4$ niga	375
Lu$_2$-sa$_6$-ga	**Lu$_2$-sa$_6$-ga**, dub-sar, dumu Gu-za-ni kurušda	274
Lugal-amar-ku$_3$	**Lugal-amar-ku$_3$**, dub-sar, dumu Na-sa$_6$	458
Lugal-he$_2$-ĝal$_2$	**Lugal-he$_2$-ĝal$_2$**, dumu ^{d}En-lil$_2$-la$_2$, sipa gu$_4$ niga	649
Lugal-iti-da	^{d}Amar-^{d}EN.ZU, lugal kala-ga, lugal Uri$_5$^{ki}-ma, lugal an ub-da limmu$_2$-ba, **Lugal-iti-da**, dub-sar, dumu Ur-^{d}Dumu-zi-da, arad$_2$-zu	280
Lugal-ur$_2$-ra-ni	^{d}Šul-gi, nita kala-ga, lugal Uri$_5$^{ki}-ma, **Lugal-ur$_2$-ra-ni**, sipa ur, arad$_2$-zu	454
Ma-an-gi$_4$	**Ma-an-gi$_4$**, dumu Ur-sa$_6$-ga, muhaldim lugal	396

 | DOI:10.1163/9789004461369_005

(*cont.*)

Seal holder	Seal impression	Text
^{d}Nanna-ma-ba	**^{d}Nanna-ma-ba**, dub-sar, dumu U$_{2}$-na-ab-še-en$_{6}$	488
	^{d}Šu-^{d}EN.ZU, lugal kala-ga, lugal Uri$_{5}$^{ki}-ma, lugal an ub-da limmu$_{2}$-ba, **^{d}Nanna-ma-ba**, dub-sar, dumu U$_{2}$-na-ab-še-en$_{6}$, arad$_{2}$-zu	6, 151, 302, 315, 397, 408, 466, 472
^{d}Nin-mar^{ki}-ka	^{d}Šu-^{d}EN.ZU, lugal kala-ga, lugal Uri$_{5}$^{ki}-ma, lugal an ub-da limmu$_{2}$-ba, **^{d}Nin-mar^{ki}-ka**, sagi arad$_{2}$-zu	14
Nu-ur$_{2}$-^{d}EN.ZU	**Nu-ur$_{2}$-^{d}EN.ZU**, dub-sar	291
	^{d}Šu-^{d}EN.ZU, lugal kala-ga, lugal Uri$_{5}$^{ki}-ma, lugal an ub-da limmu$_{2}$-ba, **Nu-ur$_{2}$-^{d}EN.ZU**, dub-sar, dumu I-di$_{3}$-Er$_{3}$-ra, arad$_{2}$-zu	286, 307, 374, 376, 401, 465, 483, 491
	^{d}I-bi$_{2}$-^{d}EN.ZU, lugal kala-ga, lugal Uri$_{5}$^{ki}-ma, lugal an ub-da limmu$_{2}$-ba, **Nu-ur$_{2}$-^{d}EN.ZU**, dub-sar, dumu I-di$_{3}$-Er$_{3}$-ra, arad$_{2}$-zu	387, 683
Nu-ur$_{2}$-i$_{3}$-li$_{2}$	**Nu-ur$_{2}$-i$_{3}$-li$_{2}$**, dumu SI.A-a	284
Nu-ur$_{2}$-^{d}IŠKUR	**Nu-ur$_{2}$-^{d}IŠKUR**, dumu Šu-^{d}IŠKUR, kuš$_{7}$ lugal	147, 421, 487
PU$_{3}$.ŠA-a-bi$_{2}$	**PU$_{3}$.ŠA-a-bi$_{2}$**, lu$_{2}$ arad$_{2}$ Nin-kal-la	379
PU$_{3}$.ŠA-[ ]	**PU$_{3}$.ŠA-[ ]**, dumu Nu-hi-DINGIR	469
Ša$_{3}$-bi	**Ša$_{3}$-bi**, dub-sar, dumu Ba-sa$_{6}$	551
Šu-ad-mu	**Šu-ad-mu**, lu$_{2}$-[x], dumu Du$_{10}$-i$_{3}$-li$_{2}$	393
Šu-ku-bu-um	Geme$_{2}$-^{d}EN.ZU, dam Šul-gi, lugal Uri$_{5}$/^{ki}-ma, **Šu-ku-bu-um**, ra$_{2}$-[gaba], arad$_{2}$-[zu]	462
Ur-^{d}Ba-ba$_{6}$	^{d}Amar-^{d}EN.ZU, lugal kala-ga, lugal Uri$_{5}$^{ki}-ma, lugal an ub-da limmu$_{2}$-ba, **Ur-^{d}Ba-ba$_{6}$**, dub-sar arad$_{2}$-zu	3
Ur-^{d}En-lil$_{2}$-la$_{2}$	**Ur-^{d}En-lil$_{2}$-la$_{2}$**, dub-sar, dumu Lugal-ur$_{2}$-ra-ni	449
Ur-^{d}EN.ZU	**Ur-^{d}EN.ZU**, šagina, BAD$_{3}$.AN^{ki} nu-banda$_{3}$	162

(*cont.*)

Seal holder	Seal impression	Text
Ur-ku$_3$-nun-na	**Ur-ku$_3$-nun-na**, dub-sar, dumu Lu$_2$-^{d}Nin-ĝir$_2$-su sipa na-gab$_2$-tum	549, 552
	^{d}Šu-^{d}EN.ZU, lugal kala-ga, lugal Uri$_5$^{ki}-ma, lugal an ub-da limmu$_2$-ba, **Ur-ku$_3$-nun-na**, dub-sar, dumu Lu$_2$-^{d}Nin-ĝir$_2$-su kurušda, arad$_2$-zu	398, 419, 536, 539, 541, 544, 550, 555, 558, 559, 562, 566, 567, 569, 570, 581
Ur-mes	**Ur-mes**, dumu La-na kurušda	16, 148, 152, 380, 391, 467, 535, 543, 546, 553, 554, 556, 557, 565, 574, 577, 580, 585, 587, 612
Ur-^{d}Nanše	**Ur-^{d}Nanše**, dumu Gu-za-ni kurušda	403
Ur-^{d}Nin-ĝiš-zi-da	**Ur-^{d}Nin-ĝiš-zi-da**, dub-sar, dumu I$_3$-kal-la	313
Ur-^{d}Nin-sa-za	^{d}Amar-^{d}EN.ZU, lugal kala-ga, lugal Uri$_5$^{ki}-ma, lugal an ub-da limmu$_2$-ba, **Ur-^{d}Nin-sa-za**, aga$_3$-us$_2$, dumu Da-[ ], arad$_2$-zu	156
Ur-^{d}Šul-pa-e$_3$	^{d}Amar-^{d}EN.ZU, lugal kala-ga, lugal Uri$_5$^{ki}-ma, lugal an ub-da limmu$_2$-ba, **Ur-^{d}Šul-pa-e$_3$**, dub-sar, dumu Ur-^{d}Ha-ia$_3$, arad$_2$-zu	18, 149, 288, 370, 385, 390, 480
	^{d}Šu-^{d}EN.ZU, lugal kala-ga, lugal Uri$_5$^{ki}-ma, lugal an ub-da limmu$_2$-ba, **Ur-^{d}Šul-pa-e$_3$**, dub-sar, dumu Ur-^{d}Ha-ia$_3$, arad$_2$-zu	2, 153, 372, 373, 384, 448, 450, 459, 460, 482
Ur-tur	**Ur-tur** dub-sar, dumu Na-sa$_6$ kurušda	279

(*cont.*)

Seal holder	Seal impression	Text
[ ]	[ ], dub-sar, dumu [ ]	300
	[ ], dub-sar, dumu [x]-ne-ne	437
	[ ], lugal kala-ga, lugal Uri$_5$^{ki}-ma, lugal an ub-da limmu$_2$-ba, [ ], dub-sar, dumu Lugal-[ ], arad$_2$-zu	21
	^{d}Amar-^{d}EN.ZU, nita$_2$ kala-ga, lugal Uri$_5$^{ki}-ma, lugal an ub-da limmu$_2$-ba, [ ], dub-sar, dumu [ ], arad$_2$-zu	490
	^{d}Šu-^{d}EN.ZU, lugal kala-ga, [ ]	145
illegible		155, 272, 308, 388, 394, 468, 471, 473, 481, 485, 568, 571, 572, 573, 584

List of Texts Already Published

Museum No.	Publication
SM 1909.05.613	From the 21st Century BC, 419 32
SM 1909.05.631	MVN 11, W
SM 1911.03.004	MVN 11, 140
SM 1911.03.024	MVN 11, 141
SM 1911.03.025	MVN 11, 142
SM 1911.03.026	MVN 11, 143
SM 1911.03.028	MVN 11, 144
SM 1911.03.030	MVN 11, 145
SM 1911.03.031	MVN 11, 146
SM 1911.03.033	MVN 11, 147
SM 1911.03.037	MVN 11, 148
SM 1911.03.041	MVN 11, 149
SM 1911.03.045	MVN 11, 151
SM 1911.03.048	MVN 11, 152
SM 1911.03.049	MVN 11, 153
SM 1911.03.056	Fs Pettinato 160, 167 9, 171
SM 1911.03.062	MVN 11, 154
SM 1911.03.064	MVN 11, 155
SM 1911.03.079	MVN 11, 156
SM 1911.03.091	MVN 11, 158
SM 1911.03.092	OrAnt 16, 292 6
SM 1911.03.093	JCS 31, 172 C
SM 1911.03.097	MVN 11, 159
SM 1911.03.098	MVN 11, 160
SM 1911.03.099	MVN 11, 161
SM 1911.03.102	JCS 31, 175 H
SM 1911.03.108	Mes 12, 93 B
SM 1911.03.111	CM 26, 154
SM 1911.03.123	Mes 12, 94 C
SM 1911.06.020	MVN 11, 173
SM 1911.10.010	MVN 11, 176
SM 1911.10.013	MVN 11, 177

 | DOI:10.1163/9789004461369_006

(cont.)

Museum No.	Publication
SM 1911.10.014	MVN 11, 178
SM 1911.10.077	CM 26, 151
SM 1911.10.100	CM 26, 155
SM 1911.10.111	MVN 11, 179
SM 1911.10.112	MVN 11, 180
SM 1911.10.113	MVN 11, 181
SM 1911.10.116	MVN 11, 182
SM 1911.10.121	MVN 11, 183
SM 1911.10.122	MVN 11, 184
SM 1911.10.131	OrNS 46, 225
SM 1911.10.132	Mes 12, 95 E
SM 1911.10.134	RCU 52
SM 1911.10.136	MVN 11, 186
SM 1911.10.142	MVN 11, BB
SM 1911.10.160	MVN 11, 187
SM 1911.10.166	MVN 11, 188
SM 1911.10.171	CM 26, 140
SM 1911.10.172	MVN 11, 189
SM 1911.10.214	MVN 11, 191
SM 1911.10.225	BPOA 10, pl. 22 SM 1911.10.225
SM 1911.10.246	MVN 11, 192
SM 1911.10.264	MVN 11, 193
SM 1911.10.278	MVN 11, 194
SM 1911.10.281	MVN 11, CC
SM 1911.10.285	MVN 11, DD
SM 1911.10.297	MVN 11, 195
SM 1911.10.299	MVN 11, 196
SM 1911.10.305	MVN 11, 197
SM 1911.10.308	MVN 11, 198
SM 1911.10.312	MVN 11, 199
SM 1911.10.313	CM 26, 152
SM 1911.10.314	MVN 11, 200
SM 1911.10.322	MVN 11, 201
SM 1911.10.331	CM 26, 142
SM 1911.10.332	CM 26, 138

(*cont.*)

Museum No.	Publication
SM 1911.10.341	MVN 11, 202
SM 1911.10.348	MVN 11, 203
SM 1911.10.350	MCS 5, 59 HSM 7970*
SM 1911.10.354	BPOA 10, pl. 22 SM 1911.10.354
SM 1911.10.360	CM 26, 156
SM 1911.10.410	MVN 11, 205
SM 1911.10.419	MVN 11, 206
SM 1911.10.442	MVN 11, 207
SM 1911.10.443	MVN 11, 208
SM 1911.10.447	MVN 11, 209
SM 1911.10.460	JCS 28, 169
SM 1911.10.462	MVN 11, 210
SM 1911.10.464	MVN 11, 211
SM 1911.10.483	MVN 11, 212
SM 1911.10.491	CM 26, 139
SM 1911.10.494	MVN 11, 213
SM 1911.10.498	CM 26, 141
SM 1911.10.532	JCS 28, 166 2
SM 1911.10.566	MVN 11, 214
SM 1911.10.574	Priests & Officials p. 119 n. 48
SM 1911.10.577	ASJ 3, 91 1
SM 1918.01.004	MVN 11, 215
SM 1918.01.006	MVN 11, 217
SM 1995.03.056	JCS 23, 113 20
SM 1995.03.057	JCS 23, 112 19
SM 1995.03.059	JCS 23, 114 28
SM 1995.03.060	JCS 23, 112 14
SM 1995.03.063	JCS 23, 114 32
SM 1995.03.064	JCS 23, 112 18
SM 1995.03.065	JCS 23, 113 25
SM 1995.03.066	JCS 23, 114 26
SM 1995.03.067	JCS 23, 113 21
SM 1995.03.068	JCS 23, 113 24
SM 1995.03.069	JCS 23, 114 31
SM 1995.03.070	JCS 23, 112 17

(*cont.*)

Museum No.	Publication
SM 1995.03.071	JCS 23, 114 33
SM 1995.03.072	JCS 23, 112 15
SM 1995.03.080	JCS 23, 114 30
SM 1995.03.081	JCS 23, 114 29
SM 1995.03.082	JCS 23, 114 27
SM 1995.03.087	JCS 23, 113 23
SM 1995.03.089	JCS 23, 112 16
SM 1995.03.097	JCS 23, 113 22
SM 1995.09.003	CRRAI 45-2, 064
SM — (No. 07991)	MVN 11, EE
SM — (No. 08221)	MCS 7, 16 HSM 8221

Classification of Texts According to Text Formula

Formula	Bureau	Text
ba-zi	Abba-saga	43, 86, 160, 166, 177, 211, 221, 275, 305, 306, 321, 329, 356, 492, 504, 506, 512, 515, 517, 518, 521, 522, 528, 582, 592, 603, 610, 623, 637, 638, 681,
	Ahannishu	526
	Allamu	295, 419, 544, 579
	Aya-dingir	559
	Beli-azu	12
	Beli-ili	480
	Duga	29, 75, 144, 147, 372, 385, 390, 473, 487, 490, 541
	En-dingirmu	48, 98, 370
	Enlila	355, 505
	Enlil-zishagal	450, 474
	Ibni-Suen	294, 481
	Igi-Enlilshe	68, 452
	Intaea	6, 31, 37, 49, 54, 80, 103, 149, 151, 307, 384, 401, 472, 483, 488, 491, 525
	Ishme-ilum	550
	Lu-dingira	38
	Lu-saga	288
	Lugal-amarku	337, 514, 613
	Nalu	18, 20, 79, 89, 311, 415, 416, 449, 468, 479
	Nasa	10, 11, 13, 42, 82, 240, 299, 301, 303
	Puzur-Enlil	14, 32, 448, 459
	Shulgi-ili	2, 21
	Shu-Mama	400
	Tahish-atal	153, 485
	Ur-ezem	548
	Ur-kununa	41, 63, 145, 302, 373, 394, 397, 408, 430, 460, 465, 471, 482, 529
	Ur-mes	575
	Ur-Nanna	388
	Zubaga	95

 | DOI:10.1163/9789004461369_007

(*cont.*)

Formula	Bureau	Text
	[ ]	23, 168, 484
i_3-dab$_5$		
	Aba-Enlilgin	378, 532, 562
	Abba-saga	4, 58, 60, 64, 65, 67, 83, 87, 91, 94, 96, 97, 99, 102, 105, 114, 127, 129, 135, 138, 155, 158, 161, 162, 164, 165, 167, 171, 172, 173, 174, 176, 178, 179, 180, 181, 182, 185, 186, 187, 189, 191, 193, 194, 195, 196, 197, 198, 199, 200, 202, 203, 204, 205, 206, 207, 208, 210, 212, 213, 214, 215, 216, 217, 218, 220, 223, 224, 225, 226, 227, 228, 229, 230, 231, 232, 233, 234, 235, 236, 237, 238, 241, 243, 248, 271, 278, 298, 310, 319, 320, 325, 333, 334, 335, 339, 342, 345, 346, 348, 349, 351, 354, 358, 359, 360, 361, 364, 405, 429, 431, 433, 434, 438, 446, 447, 499, 502, 503, 523, 524, 527, 530, 572, 576, 586, 588, 589, 591, 593, 598, 599, 600, 605, 606, 607, 609, 611, 614, 618, 621, 622, 624, 625, 626, 629, 632, 633, 634, 636, 639, 640, 641, 642, 647, 648, 650, 651, 652, 653, 655, 656, 657, 658, 659, 660, 662, 663, 664, 665, 666, 667, 668, 669, 670, 671, 672, 673, 674, 675, 677, 682
	Ahuni	77, 409
	Ahu-Wer	152, 368, 476, 535
	Aya-dingir	16, 537
	Beli-azu	269, 561
	Duga	531, 549
	En-dingirmu	689
	Ibni-ilum	143, 156
	Intaea	93, 297, 350, 380, 391, 455, 467, 509, 519, 533, 534, 536, 540, 543, 546, 551, 552, 556, 563, 565, 570, 571, 587, 612, 661
	Ipqusha	201
	Kurbilak	557, 574, 590
	Lu-Ninshubur	649

(*cont.*)

Formula	Bureau	Text
	Lu-Suen	539
	Lugal-amarku	190, 219, 293, 594, 595, 596, 597, 602, 604, 608, 615, 616, 617, 628, 630, 631
	Lugal-itida	461
	Nanna-maba	36
	Nalu	73, 107, 163, 170, 264, 274, 326, 553, 577, 580
	Naram-ili	154, 322, 382, 389
	Nasa	15, 59, 88, 188, 276, 277, 287, 292, 317, 560, 583, 619, 646
	Nur-ili	284
	Puzur-Enlil	538, 558, 567
	Shulgi-aamu	66, 456, 680, 685
	Shulgi-ili	273, 566
	Shulgi-irimu	547
	Shu-Suen-bani	283
	Sugali	39
	Tab-ili	440
	Tahish-atal	148, 392, 601
	Ur-Baba	396, 568
	Ur-kununa	315, 508, 545, 581
	Ur-mes	584
	Ur-Nanshe	554, 585
mu-DU		
	Abba-saga	7, 22, 30, 52, 290, 332, 341, 402, 413, 436
	Enlila	192, 239, 244
	Intaea	19, 26, 272, 285, 286, 291, 374, 376, 458, 466, 573
	Nanshekam	304
	Nasa	5, 44, 61, 71, 85
	Ur-kununa	183
	--	8, 45, 47, 51, 119, 511, 520, 635
šu ba-ti		
	Abba-saga	157
	Ahuni	443
	Ahu-Wer	110, 112, 132, 353
	Beli-ili	136, 445

(*cont.*)

Formula	Bureau	Text
	En-dingirmu	133, 142, 676, 688
	Igi-Enlilshe	362
	Lu-dingira	55, 56, 57, 69, 72, 74, 81, 92, 100, 106, 113, 123, 126, 140, 146, 352, 678, 684
	Lu-Suen	375
	Nalu	109, 111, 115, 117, 120, 124, 125, 128, 130, 131, 134, 139, 141, 363, 679, 686
	Nasa	494
	Shu-Erra	118
	Shu-Idim	116
	Shukubum	121, 462
	Turam-Dagan	137
	Ur-Igalim	444
	Ur-Nanna	122
	Ur-kununa	270, 437
	Zubaga	108
zi-ga		
	Beli-azu	324
	Enlila	169, 175, 245, 620, 643
	Lu-dingira	28, 46, 62, 70
	Nalu	9, 33, 76, 90
	Nasa	222
	Shulgi-Lammamu	439
	Ur-Igalim	687
	Ur-kununa	209, 242, 246, 247, 249, 258, 262, 644, 645, 654
	Ur-Lugal-edin	101
	--	24, 34, 35, 40, 53, 150, 500
	[ ]	84
niĝ$_2$-ka$_9$(-ak)		
	Alid	516
	ĝiri$_3$ Intaea	250, 251
	Huru[x]	498
	Lugal-ezem	501
	Ur-mes	1

(*cont.*)

Formula	Bureau	Text
	Zazi	495
	--	497
[ ]		
	Abba-saga	300
	Naram-ili	453
	[ ]	78, 184, 254, 256, 259, 260, 261, 268, 282, 289, 305, 316, 395, 507
--		
	Intaea	157
	Shukubum	257
	--	3, 252, 253, 263, 267, 279, 318, 330, 340, 343, 365, 371, 404, 407, 420, 422, 427, 432, 435, 442, 454, 457, 463, 477, 496, 510, 513, 542, 564, 627
ki-be$_2$ gi$_4$-a	Intaea	493
	Ur-kununa	255

Texts Nos. 1–689

1: SM 1911.03.001 (-- -- --)

obv.

i (*beginning damaged*)

10-la$_2$-1 udu ĝiri$_3$ A-hu-wa-qar
ki-be$_2$ gi$_4$-a-ta
[U]ri$_5$^{ki}-ta
[40]+5 udu ki ensi$_2$ / Aš$_2$-nun-na^{ki}-ta
[x]+3 sila$_4$ u$_4$ 2-kam
[x si]la$_4$ u$_4$ 18-kam
[ĝiri$_3$] Ab-ba-kal-la
[4] udu ĝiri$_3$ U$_4$-lam-ma
[m]u-DU lugal-ta
[x m]aš$_2$ ki Ur-tur-ta
[x] sila$_4$ ki Šu-Eš$_{18}$-tar$_2$-ta
[x] niĝ$_2$-ka$_9$ Unug^{ki}-ga
[x]-zi-ta
[x ud]u ša$_3$ niĝ$_2$-ka$_9$ Unug/^{ki}
[x nu]-ur-ta
[ ]-ta

ii (*beginning damaged*)

537
ša$_3$-bi-ta
44 udu u$_4$ 1-kam
20-la$_2$-1 udu u$_4$ 2-kam
42 udu u$_4$ 16-kam
21 udu u$_4$ 17-kam
13 udu u$_4$ 18-kam
23 udu u$_4$ 20-la$_2$-1-kam
4 sila$_4$ bala Aš$_2$-nun-na^{ki}
4 sila$_4$ bala Babilim^{ki}
2 sila$_4$ bala ensi$_2$ nu-tuku
^{d}Inana šu-a-gi-na
4+[x] sila$_4$ mu ME-ni$_9$-ĝar-ta-še$_3$
[ĝir]i$_3$ Nu-ur$_2$-^{d}UTU

 | DOI:10.1163/9789004461369_008

180+[x]
zi-ga [ ]

rev.

iii
10 udu u$_4$ [x-kam]
4 udu u$_4$ [x-kam]
30 udu u$_4$ 20+[x]-kam
44
zi-ga lugal
1 maš$_2$ kišib A-ki-ma
1 maš$_2$ kišib A-hu-ni
1 maš$_2$ kišib PU$_3$.ŠA-Eš$_{18}$-tar$_2$
2 maš$_2$ kišib La-qi$_2$-ip
1 maš$_2$ kišib Lugal-me-lam$_2$
5 maš$_2$ la$_2$-ia$_3$ kišib A-hu-wa-qar
1 maš$_2$ kišib Pi$_5$-ša-/ah-DIĜIR
12
ša$_3$ kišib-ba
1 maš$_2$ DI.KU$_5$-i$_3$-li$_2$
1 maš$_2$ SUHUŠ-ki-in
3 maš$_2$ ša$_3$ 5 ^{d}Nanna-ma-ba
1 maš$_2$ La-te-ni{-NI}-iš
6
kin-gi$_4$-a[m$_3$]
4 udu Ur-^{d}Šul-[ ]
1 maš$_2$ Ur-^{d}[ ]
1 maš$_2$ Lu$_2$-^{d}[ ]
1 maš$_2$ Ĝiri$_3$-[ ]
(*damaged below*)

iv
[ ]
[ ]
14
[ ] šu ti-ĝa$_2$-dam
[1] udu Šu-ku-bu-um muhaldim
[1] udu A$_2$-da-da
[1] udu Ur-šu muhaldim
[1] udu ĝiri$_3$ Ur-^{d}Dumu-zi
4
[U$_4$]-lam-ma i$_3$-dab$_5$
72 udu Urim$_5$^{ki}-še$_3$
A-hu-ni i$_3$-dab$_5$

64 udu Hu-nu-nu-ur / i$_3$-dab$_5$
24 udu ma$_2$-a gub-ba
Za-zi i$_3$-dab$_5$
1 maš$_2$ ša$_3$ 7 A-la-mu / i$_3$-dab$_5$
165
ugu$_2$-a ba-a-ĝa$_2$-ar
šu-niĝin$_2$ 425
zi-ga-am$_3$
112 udu la$_2$-ia$_3$-am$_3$

[niĝ$_2$]-ka$_9$ Ur-mes
(*ending damaged*)

Obv. ii 13: This personal name is also attested in Princeton 2 120.
Rev. iv 4: Cf. Erm 15247 (unpub.).
Rev. iv 10: This personal name is also attested in Erm 14716 (unpub.) and TCL 2 5593.

2: SM 1911.03.002 (-- -- --)

obv.
[x g]u$_4$ niga [ ]
[x] gu$_4$ niga [x]
uzu a bala siskur$_2$ g[u-la]
1 gu$_4$ niga a-tu$_5$-a
^{d}Nin-tin-ug$_5$-ga
lugal ku$_4$-ra a$_2$-ĝi$_6$-ba-a
u$_4$ 1-kam
1 gu$_4$ niga 4-kam-us$_2$ ^{d}En-lil$_2$
1 gu$_4$ niga 4-kam-us$_2$ ^{d}Nin-lil$_2$
uzu a bala siskur$_2$ gu-la
ĝiri$_3$ PU$_3$.ŠA-Eš$_{18}$-tar$_2$ sagi
a$_2$-ĝi$_6$-ba-a u$_4$ 4-kam
(*beginning damaged*)

rev.
(*ending damaged*)
[x gu$_4$ niga 4-kam-u]s$_2$ ^{d}gu-za
[x gu$_4$ niga 4-ka]m-us$_2$ hur-saĝ-ga-lam-ma
[ša$_3$ e$_2$] ^{d}En-lil$_2$-la$_2$
[gu$_4$] niga 4-kam-us$_2$ 1 gu$_4$ niga
[x] gu$_4$ u$_2$ ^{d}Nin-lil$_2$
1 gu$_4$ niga ^{d}Nin-hur-saĝ
1 gu$_4$ niga ^{d}Inana

1 gu$_4$ niga ^{d}Nin-tin-ug$_5$-ga
eš$_3$-eš$_3$ e$_2$-u$_4$-[7]
lugal ku$_4$-ra u$_4$ 5-kam
1 gu$_4$ niga e$_2$ muhaldim mu kaš$_4$-ke$_4$-ne-še$_3$
^{d}Nanna-kam sukkal maškim
a$_2$-ĝi$_6$-ba-a u$_4$ 8-kam
1 gu$_4$ niga ^{d}En-lil$_2$
1 gu$_4$ niga ^{d}Nin-lil$_2$
uzu a bala siskur$_2$ gu-la
lugal ku$_4$-ra a$_2$-ĝi$_6$-ba-a
u$_4$ 9-kam
[ki ^{d}Šul]-gi-i$_3$-li$_2$-ta ba-zi
(*ending damaged*)

seal i ^{d}Šu-^{d}EN.ZU
lugal kala-ga
lugal Uri$_5$/^{ki}-ma
lugal an ub-da / limmu$_2$-ba

ii [Ur-^{d}Šul-pa-e$_3$]
dub-[sar]
dumu Ur-^{d}[Ha-ia$_3$]
arad$_2$-[zu]

3: SM 1911.03.003 ([AS9])

obv. (*beginning damaged*)
[2] udu niga 1 u[du]
[1] gukkal niga [ ]
A-hu-w[a-qar]
a$_2$-u$_4$-te-na [ ]
1 maš$_2$ Ur-dam u$_4$-d[a-tuš]
1 u$_8$ aslum$_x$(A.LUM) Bur-Ma-ma dam-gar$_3$
1 amar maš-da$_3$ nita$_2$ ^{d}En-lil$_2$-zi-ša$_3$-ĝal$_2$
12
mu-DU lugal
2 gu$_4$ niga 12 udu 1 maš$_2$ a$_2$-ĝi$_6$-ba-a
kaš-de$_2$-a ^{d}Inana Unug^{ki}
e$_2$ diĝir-[re-e]-ne-ke$_4$ ba-ab-dab$_5$
gu$_4$ udu ba[la] Ur-^{d}Li$_9$-si$_4$ ensi$_2$ / Umma^{ki}-ka ba-ši-ku$_5$
2 gu$_4$ 13 udu

mu-DU didli
====
šu-niĝin$_2$ 2 gu$_4$ niga 4 ^{anše}kunga$_2$ nita$_2$
šu-niĝin$_2$ 2 udu niga 1 udu aslum$_x$(A.LUM) niga
šu-niĝin$_2$ 1 gukkal niga 12 udu 2 sila$_4$
šu-niĝin$_2$ 1 u$_8$ aslum$_x$(A.LUM) 3 maš$_2$
rev. šu-niĝin$_2$ 1 amar maš-da$_3$ nita$_2$
30-la$_2$-1
ša$_3$-bi-ta
1 udu aslum$_x$(A.LUM) niga
1
Du$_{11}$-ga i$_3$-dab$_5$
1 u$_8$ aslum$_x$(A.LUM)
1
Ta$_2$-hi-iš-a-tal i$_3$-dab$_5$
2 udu niga 1 gukkal niga
3
En-diĝir-ĝu$_{10}$ i$_3$-dab$_5$
1 amar maš-da$_3$ nita$_2$
1
Lu$_2$-diĝir-ra i$_3$-dab$_5$
4 [^{anše}kunga$_2$] nita$_2$
4
Lu$_2$-bala-sa$_6$-ga kuš$_7$ i$_3$-dab$_5$
[1]+1 gu$_4$ niga 12 udu 2 sila$_4$ 3 maš$_2$
bala ensi$_2$ Umma^{ki}
[2] gu$_4$ 17 udu
[Du$_{11}$]-ga i$_3$-dab$_5$
(*below destroyed*)
seal [^{d}Amar-^{d}EN.ZU]
[lugal kala-ga]
lugal Uri$_5$^{ki}-ma
lugal an ub-da / limmu$_2$-ba
Ur-^{d}Ba-ba$_6$
dub-sar arad$_2$-zu

Rev. 18: The reconstruction of the date AS 9 is based on TAD 51 (AS9 i).

4: SM 1911.03.006 (AS9 ii 30)

obv. 1 ^{munus}a[š$_2$-gar$_3$ niga u$_4$ x-kam]
2 udu niga u$_4$ 13-kam
7 udu 1 sila$_4$ 1 ud$_5$
u$_4$ 18-kam
1 gukkal niga 1 udu LU$_2$.SU niga
1 u$_8$ LU$_2$.SU niga 3 maš$_2$-gal LU$_2$.SU niga
11 maš$_2$-gal LU$_2$.SU 2 [u]d$_5$ L[U$_2$.SU]
u$_4$ 20-la$_2$-1-kam
2 udu niga sig$_5$-us$_2$ 2 udu niga 3-kam-us$_2$
2 u$_8$ 2 sila$_4$
u$_4$ 20-kam
51 udu 2 maš$_2$-gal u$_4$ 21-kam
1 udu niga 2 gukkal 7 udu aslum$_x$(A.LUM)
2 sila$_4$ 2 maš$_2$-gal
u$_4$ 22-kam
2 udu niga 2 udu u$_4$ 23-kam
6 udu 5 maš$_2$-gal u$_4$ 24-kam
7 udu 2 maš$_2$-gal 1 maš$_2$
rev. u$_4$ 25-kam
3 udu u$_4$ 30-kam

šu-niĝin$_2$ 2 udu niga sig$_5$-us$_2$
šu-niĝin$_2$ 2 udu niga 3-kam-us$_2$
šu-niĝin$_2$ 5 udu niga
šu-niĝin$_2$ 1 udu LU$_2$.SU niga
šu-niĝin$_2$ 1 gukkal niga
šu-niĝin$_2$ 1 u$_8$ LU$_2$.SU niga
šu-niĝin$_2$ 3 maš$_2$-gal LU$_2$.SU niga
šu-niĝin$_2$ 1 ^{munus}aš$_2$-gar$_3$ niga
šu-niĝin$_2$ 76 udu 2 gukkal
šu-niĝin$_2$ 7 udu aslum$_x$(A.LUM) 5 sila$_4$
šu-niĝin$_2$ 2 u$_8$ 11 maš$_2$-gal
šu-niĝin$_2$ 11 maš$_2$-gal LU$_2$.SU 1 maš$_2$
šu-niĝin$_2$ 1 ud$_5$ 2 ud$_5$ LU$_2$.SU
134
ki Ab-ba-sa$_6$-ga-ta
Na-lu$_5$ i$_3$-dab$_5$
[iti šeš]-da-gu$_7$
[mu en ^{d}Nanna] Kar-zi-da/$^{[ki]}$ ba-huĝ

5: SM 1911.03.007 (Š43 xii)

obv. 5 kir$_{11}$ 12 ud$_5$
6 ^{munus}aš$_2$-gar$_3$ 2 maš$_2$
e$_2$-du$_6$-la niĝ$_2$-gur$_{11}$ Na-bi$_2$-i$_3$-l[li$_2$-š]u
168 kir$_{11}$ 3 udu
mu udu e$_2$-gal-ka u$_2$ gu$_7$-a / sar-ra-še$_3$
lu$_2$ Ma-al-ku^{ki}-ke$_4$-ne / in-su-ge-eš$_2$
8 u$_8$ 1 udu
1 ud$_5$ 1 maš$_2$
[ ] Za-ri$_2$-qum ugula-60-ka
[x] u$_8$ 1 udu
6 ud$_5$ 2 maš$_2$
e$_2$-du$_6$-la niĝ$_2$-gur$_{11}$ Dan-num$_2$-A-ka$_3$-/de$_3$^{ki} ha-za-num$_2$
mu dumu Ga-na-a-na-zu / udu e$_2$-gal ba-an-zuh-a
rev. (*beginning damaged*)
[ ] Šu-Ir-ha-an [ ]
[ ]
[ ]
(*damaged some lines*)
šu-niĝin$_2$ 20-la$_2$-1 [x]
šu-niĝin$_2$ 8 ^{munus}aš$_2$-gar$_3$
šu-niĝin$_2$ 5 maš$_2$
281
šu-niĝin 250-la$_2$-1 udu hi-a
šu-niĝin 32 maš$_2$ hi-a
e$_2$-du$_6$-la U$_3$-šu-da
mu-DU Na-sa$_6$ i$_3$-dab$_5$
iti še-KIN-ku$_5$
mu en ^{d}Nanna maš$_2$-e [i$_3$-pad$_3$]

6: SM 1911.03.008 (ŠS9 ix 26)

obv. (*mostly damaged*)
rev. u$_4$ 26-kam
ki In-ta-e$_3$-a-ta
ba-zi
ĝiri$_3$ ^{d}Nanna-ma-ba / dub-sar
iti ezem ^{d}Šu-^{d}[EN.ZU]
mu ^{d}Šu-^{d}EN.ZU / lugal Uri$_5$^{ki}-ma-ke$_4$ / e$_2$ ^{d}Šara$_2$ Umma^{ki}-ka / mu-du$_3$

left 36 udu
seal i ^{d}Šu-[^{d}EN.ZU]
lugal kala-ga
lugal Uri$_5$/^{ki}-ma
lugal an ub-/da limmu$_2$-ba
ii [^{d}Nanna-ma-ba]
dub-[sar]
dumu U$_2$-na-[ab-še]-/en$_6$
arad$_2$-[zu]

7: SM 1911.03.009 (AS5 x 2)

obv. 3 udu niga 1 sila$_4$ niga
Ṣe-ra-ra
1 sila$_4$ ^{d}Šara$_2$-kam ensi$_2$
1 sila$_4$ ^{d}UTU-ba-ni
1 sila$_4$ Šu-ru-uš-ki-in
1 sila$_4$ Al-la-mu sukkal
1 sila$_4$ Ur-^{d}En-gal-du-du
1 sila$_4$ Lu$_2$-^{d}Nanna / dumu Da-da-ge$_5$
1 maš$_2$ Lugal-dub-sar
4 maš$_2$-gal a-dara$_4$ niga 1 sila$_4$
Nir-i$_3$-da-ĝal$_2$
1 sila$_4$ Gu$_3$-de$_2$-a
rev. 1 maš$_2$ Ur-^{d}I[g-alim]
1 sila$_4$ Lugal-an-ne$_2$
2 udu 1 sila$_4$
Ur-ni$_9$-ĝar
1 sila$_4$ Ur-^{d}En-lil$_2$-la$_2$
1 sila$_4$ I-gi$_4$-ru-mah
1 maš$_2$ ^{d}Šul-gi-^{d}UTU^{ši}
1 sila$_4$ Hu-un-ha-WI
1 sila$_4$ Ur-^{d}Nin-gublaga
u$_4$ 2-kam
mu-DU
Ab-ba-sa$_6$-ga i$_3$-dab$_5$
iti ezem an-na
mu En-unu$_6$-gal ^{d}/Inana Unug^{ki} ba-huĝ
left 27

Rev. 20: The more frequently attested name is Hu-un-ha-ab-ur.

8: SM 1911.03.010 (Š43 vi 5)

obv. 30 gu$_4$ niga 3 lulim nita$_2$
10-la$_2$-1 lulim munus
6 udu 5 maš$_2$
7 ^{anše}kunga$_2$ nita$_2$
3 ^{anše}kunga$_2$ munus
Ur-^{d}EN.ZU
20 gu$_4$ 30 udu
70 maš$_2$
Ṣe-lu-uš-^{d}Da-gan
2 sila$_4$ Šeš-Da-da saĝĝa
1 sila$_4$ Lu$_2$-bala-sa$_6$-ga
1 sila$_4$ A$_2$-ti-mu
1 maš$_2$ Te-te
rev. 1 maš$_2$ SI.A-a nu-banda$_3$
1 maš$_2$ PU$_3$.ŠA-^{d}En-lil$_2$-la$_2$
1 sila$_4$ ensi$_2$ Ĝir$_2$-su^{ki}
1 sila$_4$ 1 amar maš-da$_3$
ensi$_2$ Nibru^{ki}
[1] amar maš-da$_3$ en ^{d}Inana
[1] sila$_4$ Ur-ni$_9$-ĝar
1 maš$_2$ Ur-mu
1 maš$_2$ Mu-ur$_2$-di$_2$-ga-ba
4 udu aslum$_x$(A.LUM) niga 2 sila$_4$
Šar-ru-um-i$_3$-li$_2$
2 amar HA am E$_2$-a-i$_3$-li$_2$
----
mu-DU iti a$_2$-ki-ti
mu en ^{d}Nanna maš-e i$_3$-pad$_3$
left u$_4$ 5-kam

Rev. 22: It is worth mentioning the variant spellings of the PN: Mu-ur$_2$-di$_2$-ga-ba, Mu-ur$_2$-di$_2$-gaba, and Mu-ur$_2$-di$_3$-ga-ba. This PN also appears in No. 155.

9: SM 1911.03.011 (Š45 xi 17)

obv. 3 udu niga 1 u$_8$ niga
^{d}En-lil$_2$
3 udu niga 1 u$_8$ niga
^{d}Nin-lil$_2$
siskur$_2$ ša$_3$ e$_2$-a

2 udu niga du$_6$-ku$_3$
1 u$_8$ niga ^{d}Nin-hur-saĝ
1 u$_8$ niga ^{d}Nusku
1 u$_8$ niga ^{d}Nin-urta
1 u$_8$ niga ^{d}Inana
1 maš$_2$ niga ^{d}Nin-sun$_2$
1 u$_8$ niga ^{d}Lugal-banda$_3$^{da}
1 u$_8$ niga ^{d}Nin-tin-ug$_5$-ga
siskur$_2$ ĝi$_6$
2 udu niga ^{d}En-lil$_2$
rev. 2 udu niga ^{d}Nin-lil$_2$
a-ra$_2$ 2-kam
2 udu niga ^{d}En-me-šar$_2$-ra
2 udu niga 2 maš$_2$ niga ^{ĝiš}kiri$_6$-mah
^{d}Nanše-ul$_4$-gal maškim
iti u$_4$ 17 ba-zal
====
šu-niĝin$_2$ 16 udu niga 8 u$_8$ niga / 3 maš$_2$ niga
zi-ga ki Na-lu$_5$
iti ezem Me-ki-ĝal$_2$
mu Ur-bi$_2$-lum^{ki} / ba-hul

10: SM 1911.03.012 (Š47 iv 4)

obv. 1 sila$_4$ niga An
1 sila$_4$ ^{d}Inana
mu-DU Arad$_2$-ĝu$_{10}$
1 sila$_4$ ^{d}En-lil$_2$
1 sila$_4$ ^{d}Nin-lil$_2$
mu-DU Šeš-Da-da saĝĝa
1 sila$_4$ ^{d}Nanna
mu-DU Šu-^{d}En-lil$_2$
1 sila$_4$ An
1 sila$_4$ ^{d}Inana
mu-DU U$_2$-u$_2$-mu
1 sila$_4$ ^{d}Utu
mu-DU ensi$_2$ Nibru^{ki}
1 maš$_2$ ^{d}Na-na-a
mu-DU Ur-^{d}En-lil$_2$-la$_2$

rev. zabar-dab$_5$ maškim
1 sila$_4$ mu-DU en ^{d}Inana
1 maš$_2$ gal niga LU$_2$.SU 1 maš$_2$ niga
mu-DU Ṣe-lu-uš-^{d}Da-gan
e$_2$ uz-ga
A-a-kal-la maškim
1 maš-da$_3$ Na-ra-am-i$_3$-li$_2$
1 amar anše edin-na nita$_2$ ga
zabar-dab$_5$
mu-DU E$_2$-a-i$_3$-li$_2$
Arad$_2$-ĝu$_{10}$ maškim
4 udu 20-la$_2$-1 u$_8$ 5 sila$_4$
2 ud$_5$ šu-gid$_2$ e$_2$ muhaldim-še$_3$
u$_4$ 4-kam
----
ki Na-sa$_6$-ta ba-zi
iti ki-siki ^{d}Nin-a-zu
mu us$_2$-sa Ki-maš^{ki} ba-hul

11: SM 1911.03.013 (Š48 vii 14)

obv. 1 sila$_4$ ^{d}En-lil$_2$
1 sila$_4$ ^{d}Nin-lil$_2$
mu-DU Šeš-Da-da saĝĝa
1 sila$_4$ niga ^{d}En-lil$_2$
mu-DU Ur-ni$_9$-ĝar / ka-guru$_7$
1 sila$_4$ ^{d}En-lil$_2$
1 maš$_2$ ^{d}Nin-lil$_2$
mu-DU en ^{d}Inana
zabar-dab$_5$ maškim
1 sila$_4$ e$_2$ uz-ga
mu-DU Ṣe-la-šu
Ur-^{d}Ba-ba$_6$ maškim
rev. [ ] udu hur-saĝ 3 u$_8$ hur-saĝ
1 dara$_4$ nita$_2$ 10 dara$_4$ munus
ba-ug$_7$ e$_2$ kišib-ba-še$_3$
mu-DU Nir-i$_3$-da-ĝal$_2$
10 gu$_4$ 4 ab$_2$ 32 udu
7 sila$_4$ 7 u8 1 kir$_{11}$
41 maš$_2$ 17 ud$_5$

7 ^{munus}aš$_2$-gar$_3$ šu-gid$_2$ e$_2$ muhaldim-še$_3$
u$_4$ 14-kam
----
ki Na-sa$_6$-ta ba-zi
iti ezem ^{d}Šul-gi
mu Ha-ar-ši^{ki} Ki-maš^{ki} Hu-ur$_5$-ti^{ki} u$_3$ ma-da-bi u$_4$ 1-a ba-hul

12: SM 1911.03.014 (ŠS4)

obv. 2 gu$_4$ niga ab$_2$ 2-ta ki-ba ĝa$_2$-ĝa$_2$
23 udu
Ur-^{d}Nanna i$_3$-dab$_5$
ki Be-li$_2$-a-zu-ta
ba-zi
rev. ====
mu ^{d}Šu-^{d}EN.ZU lugal Uri$_5$^{ki}-ma-ke$_4$ / bad$_3$ mar-tu Mu-ri-iq-Ti-id-ni-im mu-du$_3$
left 2 gu$_4$ 23 udu

13: SM 1911.03.015 (Š47 viii 16)

obv. 1 udu niga ^{d}En-lil$_2$
1 udu niga ^{d}Nin-lil$_2$
1 udu niga 1 sila$_4$
^{d}Inana
mu-DU kaš-de$_2$-a Ur-^{d}EN.ZU
zabar-dab$_5$ maškim
3 gu$_4$ 1 gu$_4$ mu-2
2 ab$_2$ 11 udu 18 u$_8$
1 ud$_5$ šu-gid$_2$ e$_2$ muhaldim
rev. 1 gu$_4$ ba-uš$_2$ e$_2$ kišib-ba-še$_3$
mu aga$_3$-us$_2$-e-ne-še$_3$
Ur-ni$_9$-ĝar šu ba-ti
u$_4$ 16-kam
====
ki Na-sa$_6$-ta ba-zi
iti šu-eš-ša
mu us$_2$-sa Ki-maš^{ki} ba-hul

Obv. 8-9: Cf. AUCT 1 882.

14: SM 1911.03.017 (ŠS8 iv 28)

obv. 1 gu$_4$ niga 4-kam-us$_2$
An-nu-ni-tum
niĝ$_2$-dab$_5$ ezem ku-ku
An-nu-ni-tum
e$_2$-na ku$_4$-ra
rev. [ĝiri$_3$ ^{d}Nin]-mar^{ki}/-[ka] sagi
u$_4$ 28-kam
ki PU$_3$.ŠA-^{d}En-lil$_2$-ta ba-zi
ša$_3$ Uri$_5$^{ki}-ma
====
iti u$_5$-bi$_2$^{mušen}-gu$_7$
mu ^{d}Šu-^{d}EN.ZU lugal / Uri$_5$^{ki}-ma-ke$_4$ ma$_2$-gur$_8$ mah / ^{d}En-lil$_2$ ^{d}Nin-lil$_2$-ra mu-ne-/dim$_2$
seal [^{d}Šu-^{d}EN.ZU]
[lugal kala-ga]
lugal Uri$_5$^{ki}-ma
lugal an ub-da limmu$_2$-ba
^{d}Nin-mar^{ki}-ka
sagi arad$_2$-z[u]

This text is a duplicate of Erm 14870 (CDLI No. P212171).
Obv. 3: For the expression ezem ku-ku and its variant ezem ku$_4$-ku$_4$ "festival of entering," see M. E. Cohen, *The Cultic Calendars of the Ancient Near East*, Bethesda, MD: CDL Press, 1993, pp. 138-39. Also see No. 273 (ezem DIĜIR-ku-ku).

15: SM 1911.03.018 (Š47 vi)

obv. 1 gu$_4$ gun$_3$-a
4 gu$_4$ mar-tu gun$_3$-a
6 ab$_2$ gun$_3$-a
2 ab$_2$
27 udu niga
1 gukkal ĝiš-du$_3$ niga
3 maš$_2$-gal niga
90 u$_8$ gi$_6$ LU$_2$.SU
30 u$_8$ babbar LU$_2$.SU
rev. 14 maš$_2$-gal
6 maš$_2$-gal babbar
5 maš$_2$-gal su$_4$
22 ud$_5$ babbar

27 ud$_5$ su$_4$
====
mu-DU lugal
ki Na-sa$_6$-ta
A-hu-ni i$_3$-dab$_5$
iti a$_2$-ki-ti
mu us$_2$-sa Ki-maš^{ki} u$_3$ Hu-ur$_5$-ti^{ki} ba-hul

16: SM 1911.03.019 (ŠS3 i)

obv. [ ] udu
83 u$_8$
63 maš$_2$ ĝiš-du$_3$
40-la$_2$-1 ud$_5$ maš$_2$ hi-a
10 ud$_5$ maš$_2$ nu-a
rev. ki!(ŠA$_3$) A-a-diĝir-ta
Ur-mes i$_3$-dab$_5$
====
iti maš-da$_3$-gu$_7$
mu us$_2$-sa ma$_2$ dara$_3$-[abzu ^{d}En-ki ba-a]b-du$_8$
seal Ur-mes
dumu La-na kurušda

17: SM 1911.03.020 (AS7)

obv. 30 ma-na siki gi
1 gu$_2$ 30 ma-na siki / gir$_2$-gul
a$_2$ ĝiš-ĝar-ra-aš
4 ma-na siki gi
5 2/3 ma-na 1 gin$_2$ / igi 6-ĝal$_2$ siki ud$_5$ babbar$_2$
8 1/2 sila$_3$ ni-ig-tum
rev. 8 ma-na ^{u2}U.EN
mu [ ] KA u$_8$ ud$_5$ / du$_3$-a 7 1/2-še$_3$
15 ma-na siki gi / mu-nesag-še$_3$
ki ^{d}Šul-gi-mi-šar
30 ma-na siki gir$_2$-gul
ki En-diĝir-ĝu$_{10}$
Ur-^{d}Nanše šu ba-ti
mu Hu-uh$_2$-nu-ri<ki> / ba-hul

Rev. 7: For the term ^{u2}U.EN, see JCS 52 16 no. 80, obv. 4; CUSAS 3 511, iii 68.

18: SM 1911.03.021 (AS9 x 18)

obv. 2 udu niga 4-kam us$_2$
4 udu niga ^{d}Nanna
[x] udu niga ^{d}Nin-[gal]
5 udu [niga] bara$_2$ An-na
2 [ ] sagi
2 [ ] sagi
2 [ ] sagi
ša$_3$ Uri$_5$^{ki}-ma
2 udu niga du$_6$-ur$_3$
1 u[du?]
rev. 3 udu niga ^{d}Nanna
1 udu niga dub-la$_2$-mah
2 udu niga ^{d}Nin-gal
1 udu niga ^{d}Da-mu
lugal ku$_4$-ra / siskur e$_2$ muhaldim mu [ ]
Arad$_2$-ĝu$_{10}$ maškim
ša$_3$ Ga-eš^{ki}
iti u$_4$ 18 ba-zal
ki Na-lu$_5$-ta ba-zi
ša$_3$ Uri$_5$^{ki}-ma
iti ezem an-na
mu en ^{d}Nanna Kar-/zi-da ba-huĝ
seal i [^{d}Amar-^{d}EN.ZU]
lugal kala-ga
lugal Uri$_5$^{ki}-ma
lugal an ub-[da limmu$_2$-ba]
ii Ur-^{d}[Šul-pa-e$_3$]
dub-sar
dumu Ur-^{d}Ha-ia$_3$
arad$_2$-zu

19: SM 1911.03.022 (ŠS7 vii 21)

obv. 3 udu niga sig$_5$-us$_2$
1 udu niga 3-kam-us$_2$
1 sila$_4$
1 amar maš-da$_3$ nita$_2$
Ur-mes ensi$_2$
1 sila$_4$ ^{d}UTU-ba-ni

1 sila$_4$ DIĜIR-dan
mu-DU lugal
rev. In-ta-e$_3$-a i$_3$-dab$_5$
ĝiri$_3$ Nu-ur$_2$-^{d}EN.ZU dub-/sar
u$_4$ 21-kam
iti a$_2$-ki-ti
mu ^{d}Šu-^{d}EN.ZU / lugal Uri$_5$^{ki}-ma-ke$_4$ / ma-da Za-ab-ša-li/^{ki} mu-hul
left 7 udu 1 maš-da$_3$

20: SM 1911.03.023 (ŠS1 vi)

obv. 6 udu niga sa$_2$-du$_{11}$ dub-la$_2$-mah
3 udu niga sa$_2$-du$_{11}$ ^{d}Nin-e$_2$-gal
2 udu sa$_2$-du$_{11}$ ^{d}En-ki-nin-/ul-gur$_3$
30 udu niga šu-a-gi-na
3 udu niga niĝ$_2$-diri
sa$_2$-du$_{11}$ ^{d}Šul-gi-ra
[x] udu niga šu-a-gi-na
[x u]du niga niĝ$_2$-diri
[sa$_2$-du$_{11}$] ^{d}Amar-^{d}EN.ZU
rev. [x udu] niga gu$_4$-e-us$_2$-sa
[ME-^{d}]Nisaba
[x] udu niga gu$_4$-e-us$_2$-sa
[Z]i-ha-tum
3 udu niga gu$_4$-e-us$_2$-sa
SI.A-tum
[ ] šu-a-gi-na iti 1-kam
[ki Na]-lu$_5$-ta ba-zi
[ĝi]ri$_3$ Lu$_2$-kar-zi-da / dub-sar
iti a$_2$-ki-ti
mu ^{d}Šu-^{d}EN.ZU lugal
left 90-la$_2$-1

Rev. 11: Cf. BPOA 7 2888 (šs 7); Princeton 1 16 (šs 1).

21: SM 1911.03.027 (IS2 xi 16)

obv. 3 udu niga 4-kam-us$_2$
^{d}Inana

2 udu niga 4-kam-us$_2$
An
^{d}EN.ZU-a-bu-šu / sagi maškim
[u$_4$]+16-kam
[ĝiri$_3$] PU$_3$.ŠA-^{d}En-lil$_2$
rev. ki ^{d}Šul-gi-i$_3$-li$_2$-/ta
ba-zi
ša$_3$ Unug^{ki}-ga
iti ezem an-na
mu en ^{d}Inana / Unug^{ki}-ga maš$_2$-e / i$_3$-pad$_3$
left 5 udu
seal i [ ]
lugal kala-ga
lugal Uri$_5$/^{ki}-ma
lugal an ub-/da limmu$_2$-ba
ii [ ]
[dub-sar]
dumu Lugal-[ ]
[arad$_2$-zu]

22: SM 1911.03.029 (AS5 ii 3)

obv. [1] sila$_4$ Lum-ma šabra
1 sila$_4$ Ur-mes ensi$_2$
3 šeg$_9$-bar nita$_2$
1 sila$_4$
Ša$_3$-ga-na-kum
1 sila$_4$ I$_3$-li$_2$-dan
1 sila$_4$ Ama-zi-mu
1 sila$_4$ Ha-ab-ru-ša
1 sila$_4$ A-hu-a
5 udu aslum$_x$(A.LUM) niga 1 maš$_2$-gal niga
rev. [1] sila$_4$
Nir-i$_3$-da-ĝal$_2$
1 gu$_4$ niga
10 udu 1 sila$_4$
I-ku-nu-um
u$_4$ 3-kam
mu-DU

Ab-ba-sa$_6$-ga i$_3$-dab$_5$
iti šeš-da-gu$_7$
mu En-unu$_6$-gal $^{[d]}$Inana Unug^{ki}-ga ba-huĝ
left 30-la$_2$-1

Obv. 10, rev. 13: Cf. OIP 121 178 (AS5 ii 3); P212159 (AS5 ii 3).

23: SM 1911.03.032 (ŠS4 iv 20)

obv. 126 udu u$_2$
32 maš$_2$ gal u$_2$
u$_4$ 8-kam
iti maš-da$_3$-gu$_7$
78 udu u$_2$
26 maš$_2$ gal u$_2$
u$_4$ 5-kam
iti šeš-da-gu$_7$
290 udu u$_2$
rev. 30 maš$_2$ gal u$_2$
u$_4$ 20-[kam]
iti u$_5$-b[i$_2$-gu$_7$]
e$_2$ eš$_3$ [ ]
Lugal-a$_2$-[zi-da i$_3$-dab$_5$]
ĝiri$_3$ [ ]
ki [PN-ta ba-zi]
mu ^{d}Šu-^{d}EN.ZU <lugal> / Uri$_5$^{ki}-ma-[ke$_4$] / bad$_3$ mar-tu Mu-ri-iq-/Ti-id-ni-im mu-du$_3$
left 582 udu

Rev. 14: Cf. SACT 1 179 (ŠS8).

24: SM 1911.03.034 (Š45 viii 21)

obv. 2 sila$_4$ ^{d}En-lil$_2$
2 sila$_4$ ^{d}Nin-lil$_2$
mu-DU Šeš-Da-da saĝĝa
1 amar maš-da$_3$ e$_2$ uz-ga
mu-DU Saĝ-^{d}Nanna-zu
1 sila$_4$ ^{d}Utu
mu-DU ensi$_2$ Nibru^{ki}

zabar-dab$_5$ maškim
7 ab$_2$ 1 gu$_4$ amar ga
311 u$_8$
82 udu
37 ud$_5$
rev. 13 [maš$_2$?]
šu-gid$_2$ e$_2$ muhaldim-[še$_3$]
3 dusu$_2$ nita$_2$
4 dusu$_2$ munus
5 udu 1 sila$_4$ ga 1 maš$_2$ ga
ba-ug$_7$ e$_2$ kišib-ba-še$_3$
2 dusu$_2$ munus ba-ug$_7$
mu ur-ra-še$_3$ DIĜIR-ba-ni / šu ba-ti
----
zi-ga u$_4$ 21-kam
iti šu-eš$_5$-ša
mu ^{d}Šul-gi lugal / Ur-bi$_2$-lum^{ki} Lu-lu-bu-um^{ki} / Si-mu-ru-um^{ki} u$_3$ Kara$_2$-har^{ki} aš-še$_3$ / sagdu-bi šu-bur$_2$-a bi$_2$-[ra]-/a

25: SM 1911.03.035 (AS7 xi)
obv. 600 sa gi
la$_2$-ia$_3$ su-ga gurum$_2$-ma / zadim-e-ne
ugula ^{d}Nanna-si-sa$_2$
ki Ur-bad$_3$-tibir$_x$(KU)-ra / dub-sar-ta
rev. mu-DU
A-bu-šu-ni
šu ba-an-ti
====
iti ezem Me-ki-ĝal$_2$
mu Hu-uh$_2$-nu-ri/^{ki} ba-hul

Obv. 4: This personal name is more frequently attested in the Girsu texts.

26: SM 1911.03.036 (ŠS5 vi 2)
obv. 4 udu niga
1 sila$_4$
Ur-^{d}Ba-ba$_6$ ensi$_2$
1 sila$_4$ ^{d}Šul-gi-ni-šu nu-banda$_3$

mu-DU lugal
In-ta-e$_3$-a
rev. i$_3$-dab$_5$
ĝiri$_3$ Nu-ur$_2$-^{d}EN.ZU dub-sar
u$_4$ 2-kam
iti ezem ^{d}Nin-a-zu
mu us$_2$-sa ^{d}Šu-^{d}EN.ZU lugal Uri$_5$^{ki}-ma-ke$_4$ bad$_3$ mar-tu Mu-ri-/iq-Ti-id-ni-im / mu-du$_3$
left 6 udu

27: SM 1911.03.038 (ŠS2 iii)

obv. 0.0.2 mun
0.0.1 zi$_3$-gazi
mu-du-lum-še$_3$
ša$_3$ e$_2$-gal-še$_3$
zi-ga
ša$_3$ Uri$_5$^{ki}-ma
[Lugal]-bad$_3$-iri-na / maškim
rev. [mu lugal]-bi / i$_3$-pad$_3$
====
iti u$_5$-bi$_2$-gu$_7$
mu ma$_2$-dara$_3$ abzu / ^{d}En-ki-ka ba-ab-du$_8$

Rev. 8: For the restored terms, see MVN 15 343.

28: SM 1911.03.039 (Š46 x 16)

obv. 1 ab$_2$
10-la$_2$-1 udu
7 u$_8$
10 maš$_2$-gal
33 ud$_5$
8 ud$_5$ su$_4$
šu-gid$_2$ e$_2$ muhaldim-še$_3$
rev. mu aga$_3$-us$_2$-e-/ne-še$_3$
iti u$_4$ 16 ba-zal
zi-ga
ki Lu$_2$-diĝir-ra
iti ezem An-na

mu Ki-maš^{ki} u$_3$ Hu-/ur-ti^{ki} ba-hul

29: SM 1911.03.040 (AS9 iv 16)

obv. 2 udu 8 u$_8$
mu kaš$_4$-ke$_4$-ne-še$_3$
8 udu 22 u$_8$
šu-gid$_2$
3 u$_8$ ba-ug$_7$
mu aga$_3$-us$_2$-e-ne-še$_3$
e$_2$ muhaldim
rev. Arad$_2$-ĝu$_{10}$ maškim
u$_4$ 16-kam
ki Du$_{11}$-ga-ta
ba-zi
ĝiri$_3$ ^{d}Nanna-ma-ba dub-sar
iti ki-siki ^{d}Nin-a-zu
mu en ^{d}Nanna Kar-/zi-da ba-huĝ
left 43

30: SM 1911.03.043 (AS5 vi 1)

obv. 1 gu$_4$ A-ab-ra-za-ak
4 gu$_4$ 3 udu
37 maš$_2$
Ku-u$_3$-tam
1 maš$_2$ A-hu-ni kuš$_7$
1 maš$_2$ PU$_3$.ŠA-Ka$_3$-ka$_3$ kuš$_7$
4 udu niga
1 sila$_4$ Gu$_3$-de$_2$-a ensi$_2$
rev. 1 sila$_4$ Eš$_{18}$-tar$_2$-il-šu
u$_4$ 1-kam
====
mu-DU lugal
Ab-ba-sa$_6$-ga i$_3$-dab$_5$
iti a$_2$-ki-ti
mu En-unu$_6$-gal / ^{d}Inana Unug^{ki} ba-huĝ
left 53

31: SM 1911.03.044 (ŠS8 ix)

obv. 37 udu LU$_2$.SU u$_2$
sa$_2$-du$_{11}$ Zi-ni-a-še$_3$
kišib Lugal-u$_4$-su$_{13}$-še$_3$ / šabra
ki In-ta-e$_3$-a-/ta ba-zi
rev. iti ezem ^{d}Šu-^{d}EN.ZU
mu ^{d}Šu-^{d}EN.ZU / lugal Uri$_5$^{ki}-ma-ke$_4$
ma$_2$-gur$_8$ mah
^{d}En-lil$_2$
^{d}Nin-lil$_2$-ra
mu-ne-dim$_2$
left 37 udu

32: SM 1911.03.046 (ŠS8 viii 3)

obv. 1 gu$_4$ niga 1 gu$_4$ u$_2$
a$_2$-u$_4$-te-na
^{d}En-lil$_2$ ^{d}Nin-lil$_2$
lugal ku$_4$-ra
u$_4$ 3-kam
ki PU$_3$.ŠA-^{d}En-lil$_2$-ta
rev. ba-zi
====
iti ezem ^{d}Šul-gi
mu ^{d}Šu-^{d}EN.ZU / lugal Uri$_5$^{ki}-ma-ke$_4$ / ma$_2$-gur$_8$ mah / ^{d}En-lil$_2$ ^{d}Nin-lil$_2$-ra / mu-ne-dim$_2$
seal ^{d}Šu-[^{d}EN.ZU]
lugal kala-ga
lugal Uri$_5$^{ki}-ma
lugal an ub-da [limmu$_2$-ba]
Ur-[^{d}Šul-pa-e$_3$]
dub-[sar]
dumu [Ur-^{d}Ha-ia$_3$]
[arad$_2$-zu]

33: SM 1911.03.047 (Š46 x 24)

obv. 2 udu niga ^{d}En-lil$_2$
2 udu niga ^{d}Nin-lil$_2$

1 ^{munus}aš$_2$-gar$_3$ niga ^{d}En-lil$_2$
1 ^{munus}aš$_2$-gar$_3$ niga ^{d}Nin-lil$_2$
a-ra$_2$ 2-kam
1 udu ni[ga ^{d}]Nusku
1 maš$_2$ gal [niga] ^{d}Nin-urta
1 maš$_2$ gal niga ^{d}Inana
1 maš$_2$ gal niga ^{d}Nin-sun$_2$
rev. 1 udu niga ^{d}Nin-tin-ug$_5$-/ga
^{d}Nanše-ul$_4$-gal maškim
iti u$_4$ 24 ba-zal

šu-niĝin$_2$ 6 udu niga 3 maš$_2$ gal niga / 2 ^{munus}aš$_2$-gar$_3$ niga
zi-ga ki Na-lu$_5$
iti ezem An-na
mu Ki-maš^{ki} u$_3$ Hu-/ur$_5$-ti^{ki} ba-hul

34: SM 1911.03.050 (Š44 iv 27)
obv. 4 maš-da$_3$
e$_2$ uz-ga
mu-DU E$_2$-a-i$_3$-li$_2$
A-a-kal-la maškim
1 gu$_4$
1 gu$_4$ mu-2
1 gu$_4$ mu-1
šu-gid$_2$ e$_2$ muhaldim-še$_3$
rev. ====
zi-ga u$_4$ 27-kam
iti ki-siki ^{d}Nin-a-zu
mu Si-mu-ru-um^{ki} / u$_3$ Lu-lu-bu^{ki} / a-ra$_2$ 10-la$_2$-1-kam-aš ba-hul

Rev. 5-8: Cf. SACT 1 135 (Š44 iv 27).

35: SM 1911.03.051 (Š47 vii 5)
obv. [1] sila$_4$ ^{d}Nin-a-zu
mu-DU Ša$_3$-kal-la
1 sila$_4$ ^{d}Nanna
1 sila$_4$ ^{d}Inana

[mu]-DU zabar-dab$_5$
[d]Nanše-ul$_4$-gal maškim
[1] gu$_4$ niga ^{d}Nanna
igi šu-nir-ra
1 ab$_2$ 5 udu
4 u$_8$ 3 maš$_2$
rev. 13 ud$_5$
šu-gid$_2$ e$_2$ muhaldim
mu aga$_3$-us$_2$-e-ne-še$_3$
Arad$_2$-ĝu$_{10}$ maškim
====
[zi-ga u$_4$ 5]-kam
[iti ezem ^{d}Šu]l-gi
[mu us$_2$-sa Ki]-maš^{ki} ba-hul

Rev. 17: For the restored year name, see OIP 115 459, 9 (Š47 vii 5).

36: SM 1911.03.052 (ŠS7)

obv. 3 udu niga 3-kam-us$_2$
51 udu niga
15 udu u$_2$
17 gukkal u$_2$
3 maš$_2$-gal u$_2$
ki ^{d}Nanna-ma-ba-ta
rev. A-ba-^{d}En-lil$_2$-gin$_7$
i$_3$-dab$_5$
mu ^{d}Šu-^{d}EN.ZU / lugal Uri$_5$^{ki}-/ke$_4$
ma-da Za-ab-ša-/li^{ki} mu-hul
left 89 udu

37: SM 1911.03.053 (ŠS4 viii 21)

obv. 8 udu u$_2$
2 maš$_2$-gal u$_2$
1 sila$_4$
Ba-la-la nar
Arad$_2$-ĝu$_{10}$ maškim
ša$_3$ mu-DU-ra-ta

rev. u$_4$ 21-kam
ki In-ta-e$_3$-a-ta [ba-zi]
ĝiri$_3$ Nu-ur$_2$-[^{d}EN.ZU dub]-sar
iti ezem ^{d}Šul-gi
mu ^{d}Šu-^{d}EN.ZU lugal-e
bad$_3$ mar-tu Mu-ri-iq-/Ti-id-ni-im mu-/du$_3$
left 11 udu

Obv. 1-3: Cf. Nisaba 30 67 (ŠS4 viii 21).

38: SM 1911.03.054 (Š47 vi 9)

obv. 2 udu niga
3 maš$_2$-gal niga
e$_2$ muhaldim-še$_3$
mu kaš$_4$-ke$_4$-ne-še$_3$
ĝiri$_3$ PU$_3$.ŠA-la-ba sukkal
Arad$_2$-ĝu$_{10}$ maškim
1 gu$_4$ niga
e$_2$ kišib-ba-še$_3$
rev. 1 udu niga
kak-gu-la$_2$-še$_3$
Kur-bi-la-ak maškim
iti u$_4$ 10-la$_2$-1 ba-zal
ša$_3$ Unug^{ki}-ga
ki Lu$_2$-diĝir-ra-ta
ba-zi
iti a$_2$-ki-ti
mu us$_2$-sa Ki-maš^{ki} / ba-hul

39: SM 1911.03.055 (ŠS7 xii)

obv. 6 ud$_5$ LU$_2$.SU u$_2$
20 ^{munus}aš$_2$-gar$_3$ LU$_2$.SU gaba
iti ezem ^{d}Nin-a-zu
27 ud$_5$ LU$_2$.SU u$_2$
iti ezem ^{d}Me-ki-ĝal$_2$
[ki] Su$_{11}$-ga-l[i]-/ta
rev. ^{d}Šul-gi-i$_3$-[li$_2$]

i$_3$-[dab$_5$]
mu ^{d}Šu-^{d}EN.ZU / lugal Uri$_5$^{ki}-/ma-ke$_4$
ma-da Za-ab-/ša-li^{ki} mu-/hul
left 53 udu

40: SM 1911.03.057 (Š45 xii 16)

obv. 1 sila$_4$ ^{d}Nusku
1 sila$_4$ ^{d}Nin-urta
mu-DU en ^{d}Inana
1 sila$_4$ ^{d}Inana
mu-DU Lugal-me-lam$_2$
1 sila$_4$ ^{d}En-lil$_2$
1 sila$_4$ ^{d}Nin-lil$_2$
mu-DU Šeš-da-da / saĝĝa
rev. zabar-dab$_5$ maškim
1 gu$_4$ 15 udu
4 u$_8$ 1 maš$_2$
šu-gid$_2$ e$_2$ muhaldim-še$_3$
====
zi-ga u$_4$ 16-kam
iti še-KIN-ku$_5$
mu Ur-bi$_2$-lum^{ki} / ba-hul

41: SM 1911.03.058 (ŠS5 x 13)

obv. 30 udu u$_2$
80 maš$_2$-gal u$_2$
70 ud$_5$ u$_2$
mu lu$_2$ maš$_2$-da-re-a-/ke$_4$-ne-še$_3$
ĝišbun$_2$ er$_2$ su$_3$-a
2 gu$_4$ u$_2$
50 maš$_2$-gal u$_2$
lugal Unug^{ki}-še$_3$ du-ni / ma$_2$-a ba-a-ĝa$_2$-ar
rev. e$_2$ muhaldim
Arad$_2$-ĝu$_{10}$ maškim
ša$_3$ Uri$_5$^{ki}-ma
u$_4$ 13-kam
ki Ur-ku$_3$-nun-na-ta ba-zi
ĝiri$_3$ Hu-la-al dub-sar

iti ezem mah
mu us$_2$-sa ^{d}Šu-^{d}EN.ZU / lugal Uri$_5$^{ki}-ma-ke$_4$
bad$_3$ mar-tu Mu-ri-iq-/Ti-id-ni-im mu-/du$_3$
left 2 gu$_4$ 230 udu

42: SM 1911.03.059 (Š47 iii 18)

obv. 1 sila$_4$ ^{d}Nusku
mu-DU ensi$_2$ Urum$_x$(UR$_2$×U$_2$)^{ki}
1 sila$_4$ ^{d}En-lil$_2$
mu-DU I$_3$-li$_2$-mi-ti
1 sila$_4$ ^{d}En-lil$_2$
mu-DU Ur-^{d}En-lil$_2$-la$_2$
1 sila$_4$ ^{d}Nin-lil$_2$
mu-DU Hu-un-ha-ab-/ur
rev. zabar-dab$_5$ maškim
1 gu$_4$ 1 ab$_2$ mu-3
šu-gid$_2$ e$_2$ muhaldim
[u$_4$] 18-kam
====
ki Na-sa$_6$-ta ba-zi
iti u$_5$-bi$_2$-gu$_7$ (*erased*)
mu us$_2$-sa Ki-maš^{ki} / ba-hul

For this text, cf. P212113 (Š47 iii 18).

43: SM 1911.03.060 (AS5 vii 25)

obv. 2 udu niga
1 maš$_2$-gal niga
1 ^{munus}aš$_2$-gar$_3$ niga
3 sila$_4$
A-bi$_2$-si$_2$-im-ti
Nu-hi-DIĜIR maškim
1 udu niga
rev. 1 ^{munus}aš$_2$-gar$_3$ niga
1 amar maš-da$_3$
e$_2$ uz-ga
A-a-kal-la maškim

ša$_3$ mu-DU-ra-ta
u$_4$ 25-kam
ki Ab-ba-sa$_6$-ga-ta
ba-zi
iti ezem ^{d}Šul-gi
mu En-unu$_6$-gal ^{d}/Inana ba-huĝ
left 10

For these animals, see MVN 13 425 (AS5 vii 25).

44: SM 1911.03.061 (Š48 ix 27)

obv. 4 udu niga 1 sila$_4$
I-di$_3$-^{d}EN.ZU
2 sila$_4$ ensi$_2$ Nibru^{ki}
1 sila$_4$ ensi$_2$ Adab$^{ki!(NA)}$
1 sila$_4$ A-da-lal$_3$
1 sila$_4$ zabar-dab$_5$
1 sila$_4$ Ur-^{d}Nin-gublaga
4 udu niga 1 sila$_4$
Nu-ur$_2$-Eš$_{18}$-tar$_2$
rev. 1 sila$_4$ Ur-^{d}EN.ZU
2 sila$_4$ Šu-^{d}En-lil$_2$
====
mu-DU Na-sa$_6$ i$_3$-dab$_5$
iti ezem mah
mu Ha-ar-ši^{ki} / u$_3$ Ki-maš^{ki} ba-hul
left u$_4$ 27-kam

Cf. MVN 2 163 (Š48 ix 27).

45: SM 1911.03.063 (Š46 ii 12)

obv. 4 udu 1 sila$_4$
Lugal-engar-du$_{10}$ šabra
1 sila$_4$ I-gi$_4$-ru-mah
2 Šeš-da-da saĝĝa
1 sila$_4$ Id-da-a
1 sila$_4$ Lu$_2$-sa$_6$-ga

rev. 1 maš$_2$
^{d}En-lil$_2$-la$_2$ kurušda
====
mu-DU
iti šeš-da-gu$_7$
mu us$_2$-sa Ur-bi$_2$-/lum^{ki} ba-hul
left u$_4$ 12-kam

46: SM 1911.03.065 (Š47 x 29)

obv. 5 udu niga
2 udu niga LU$_2$.SU.A
4 u$_8$ niga LU$_2$.SU.A
4 maš$_2$ gal babbar niga
kak-gu-la$_2$-še$_3$
Ur-ni$_9$-ĝar maškim
1 udu niga
rev. Ur-^{d}Lamma-$^{i3\text{-}si}$/Isin$_2^{ki}$
Kur-ĝiri$_3$-ni-še$_3$ maškim
iti u$_4$ 30-la$_2$-1 ba-zal
zi-ga
ki Lu$_2$-diĝir-ra
iti ezem an-na
mu us$_2$-sa Ki-maš^{ki} / ba-hul

Rev. 8: For the deification of Ur-Namma in Isin, see Kyoto 15, rev. 5 (Š47 xii 27).

47: SM 1911.03.066 (Š46 vi 14)

obv. 1 sila$_4$ A-bu-ni
1 sila$_4$ Ta-la-a
1 sila$_4$ Lu$_2$-^{d}Nanna
1 sila$_4$ Za-ak-li-li
2 udu niga Ṣe-lu-uš-/^{d}Da-gan
1 maš$_2$ Ur$_5$-sa$_6$-sa$_6$
3 udu 1 sila$_4$
rev. Šeš-kal-la ku$_3$-ĝal$_2$
2 udu niga 1 sila$_4$
ensi$_2$ Šuruppag^{ki}

	1 sila$_4$ Šu-Eš$_{18}$-tar$_2$
	11 dara$_4$ hur-saĝ
	E$_2$-a-i$_3$-li$_2$
	----
	mu-DU
	iti a$_2$-ki-ti
	mu Ki-maš^{ki} u$_3$ Hu-/ur$_5$-ti^{ki} ba-hul
left	u$_4$ 14-kam

Obv. 6: For this PN Ur$_5$-sa$_6$-sa$_6$, a possible variant of Ur-sa$_6$-sa$_6$, see also OIP 115 185 (Š46 vi 17); MVN 11 159 (Š47 v).

48: SM 1911.03.067 (AS8 iv)

obv.	17 udu
	2 gukkal
	1 u$_8$
	6 maš$_2$-gal
	1 ud$_5$
	ba-ug$_7$ mu ur-gi$_7$-ra-še$_3$
	I$_3$-lal$_3$-lum
rev.	šu ba-ti
	ša$_3$ Tum-ma-al
	ki En-diĝir-ĝu$_{10}$-ta
	ba-zi
	iti ki-siki ^{d}Nin-a-zu
	mu en Eridu^{ki} ba-huĝ
left	27

49: SM 1911.03.068 (ŠS1 ix 11)

obv.	2 udu niga
	16 udu aslum$_x$(A.LUM) niga
	2 u$_8$
	3 gukkal
	7 sila$_4$
	1 sila$_4$ gukkal
	2 maš$_2$
	ME-^{d}Ištaran
rev.	niĝ$_2$-dab$_5$ e$_2$-u$_4$-15

ša$_3$ mu-DU-ra-ta
u$_4$ 11-kam
ki In-ta-e$_3$-a-ta / ba-zi
ĝiri$_3$ Nu-ur$_2$-^{d}EN.ZU / dub-sar
iti ezem mah
mu ^{d}Šu-^{d}EN.ZU lugal
left 33

50: SM 1911.03.069 (ŠS7 ii 12)

obv. mu-DU nu-ub-tuku
u$_4$ 12-kam
ĝiri$_3$ ^{d}Nanna-ma-ba / dub-sar
iti maš-da$_3$-gu$_7$
rev. ====
mu ^{d}Šu-^{d}EN.ZU / lugal Uri$_5$^{ki}-/ma-ke$_4$
ma-da Za-ab-/ša-li^{ki}
mu-hul

51: SM 1911.03.070 (Š45 x 26)

obv. 1 sila$_4$ Saĝ-^{d}Nanna-zu
2 amar az
Arad$_2$-ĝu$_{10}$
2 u$_8$ sila$_4$ nu$_2$-a
2 ^{munus}aš$_2$-gar$_3$ 1 sila$_4$
Lugal-nir-ĝal$_2$
1 sila$_4$
rev. ensi$_2$ Gu$_2$-du$_8$-a^{ki}
2 sila$_4$ en ^{d}Inana
====
mu-DU
iti ezem An-na
mu Ur-bi$_2$-lum^{ki} / ba-hul
left u$_4$ 26-kam

Cf. BIN 3 612 (Š45 x 26).

52: SM 1911.03.071 (AS5 ix 20)

obv. 2 sila$_4$ Wa-ta$_2$-ru-um
1 sila$_4$ Šu-ru-uš-ki-in
1 sila$_4$ Lugal-an-ne$_2$
1 maš$_2$ Lugal-ezem nu-banda$_3$
1 sila$_4$ Da-da-ni
1 sila$_4$ E$_2$-a-ra-bi$_2$
u$_4$ 20-kam
rev. mu-DU
Ab-ba-sa$_6$-ga
i$_3$-dab$_5$
====
iti ezem mah
mu En-unu$_6$-gal / ^{d}Inana ba-huĝ
left 7

Obv. 1-4: For these animals, see PDT 1 22 (AS ix 20).

53: SM 1911.03.072 (Š46 i 17)

obv. 1 sila$_4$ An
mu-DU Nu-ur$_2$-i$_3$-li$_2$
1 sila$_4$ ^{d}Inana
mu-DU Ur-^{d}Nin-gublaga
1 sila$_4$ niga ^{d}Utu
mu-DU Id-da-a
zabar-dab$_5$ maškim
[4] gu$_4$ ĝiš Si-mu
[x] gu$_4$ ĝiš
rev. Gi-gag-za-la
E$_2$-a-i$_3$-li$_2$ maškim
2 gu$_4$ 21 udu 12 u$_8$
6 maš$_2$ 14 ud$_5$
šu-gid$_2$ e$_2$ muhaldim-še$_3$
1 amar maš-da$_3$ e$_2$ uz-ga
1 udu siskur$_2$ u$_2$-še$_3$
Na-ra-am-i$_3$-li$_2$ maškim

zi-ga u$_4$ 17-kam
iti maš-da$_3$-ku$_3$-gu$_7$
mu Ki-maš^{ki} u$_3$ Hu-ur$_5$-/ti^{ki} ba-hul

Obv. 1-6: Cf. BPOA 19 1084 (Š46 i 17).

54: SM 1911.03.073 (AS5 xii 25)

obv. [2] mu-2
[ ] udu
6 u$_8$
[x] maš$_2$
4 ud$_5$
ba-ug$_7$ e$_2$ muhaldim-še$_3$
rev. u$_4$ 25-kam
ki In-ta-e$_3$-a-/ta
ba-zi
iti še-KIN-ku$_5$
mu en ^{d}Inana / ba-huĝ
left 2 gu$_4$ 26 [udu]

55: SM 1911.03.074 (Š47 vii 25)

obv. 1 gu$_4$
1 gukkal niga
1 maš$_2$ gal niga LU$_2$.SU.A
2 udu
1 gukkal
1 udu gi$_6$ LU$_2$.SU.A
2 u$_8$
2 U$_8$+HUL$_2$
1 sila$_4$
rev. 1 u$_8$ gi$_6$ LU$_2$.SU.A
1 u$_8$ aslum$_x$(A.LUM)
2 ud$_5$
1 kir$_{11}$ gi$_6$
1 sila$_4$ ga gukkal

3 maš$_2$ ga
1 ^{munus}aš$_2$-gar$_3$ ga
ba-ug$_7$ u$_4$ 25-kam
ki Lu$_2$-diĝir-ra-ta
Ur-ni$_9$-ĝar šu ba-ti
iti ezem ^{d}Šul-gi
mu us$_2$-sa Ki-maš^{ki} ba-hul

56: SM 1911.03.075 (Š48 vi 15)

obv. 2 g[u$_4$] niga
2 udu niga
2 gukkal
1 udu aslum$_x$(A.LUM)
4 U$_8$+HUL$_2$
1 u$_8$ aslum$_x$(A.LUM)
2 U$_8$+HUL$_2$ babbar$_2$
4 u$_8$ LU$_2$.SU.A
1 sila$_4$ LU$_2$.SU.A
1 kir$_{11}$ aslum$_x$(A.LUM)
rev. 1 ud$_5$ babbar$_2$
1 kir$_{11}$ LU$_2$.SU.A
1 kir$_{11}$ gukkal
1 kir$_{11}$ ga
ba-ug$_7$ u$_4$ 15-kam
ki Lu$_2$-diĝir-ra-ta
Ur-ni$_9$-ĝar
šu [ba]-ti
iti [a$_2$-ki]-ti
mu [us$_2$-sa Ki-ma]š^{ki} ba-<hul> / mu-us$_2$-[sa]-bi

57: SM 1911.03.076 (AS2 i 22)

obv. 1 udu aslum$_x$(A.LUM) niga
1 gukkal niga
1 udu niga
1 u$_8$ niga
1 maš$_2$-gal niga
1 udu

2 u$_8$
4 sila$_4$
rev. 1 [ ]
2 sila$_4$ [ ]
1 kir$_{11}$ [ ]
ba-ug$_7$ u$_4$ 22-[kam]
ki Lu$_2$-diĝir-ra-ta
Ur-ni$_9$-ĝar
šu ba-ti
iti maš-da$_3$-gu$_7$
mu us$_2$-sa ^{d}Amar-^{d}EN.ZU / lugal

58: SM 1911.03.077 (AS5 iii 29)

obv. 22 udu
8 maš$_2$
u$_4$ 30-la$_2$-1-kam
ki Ab-ba-sa$_6$-ga-ta
In-ta-e$_3$-a
rev. i$_3$-dab$_5$
====
iti u$_5$-bi$_2$-gu$_7$
mu En-unu$_6$-gal / ^{d}Inana Unug^{ki} ba-huĝ
left 30

59: SM 1911.03.078 (Š48 x)

obv. 54 udu niga
4 gukkal niga
1 udu aslum$_x$(A.LUM) niga
3 maš$_2$-gal niga
2 ^{munus}aš$_2$-gar$_3$ niga
71 udu
2 sila$_4$
rev. 10 maš$_2$-gal
1 ^{munus}aš$_2$-gar$_3$
mu-DU lugal
ki Na-sa$_6$-ta
Na-lu$_5$ i$_3$-dab$_5$

iti ezem An-na
mu Ha-ar-ši^{ki} / u$_3$ Ki-maš^{ki} ba-hul

60: SM 1911.03.080 (AS5 iv 30)

obv. 236 udu niga
1 maš$_2$-gal niga
u$_4$ 30-kam
ki Ab-ba-sa$_6$-/ga-ta
rev. ^{d}Šul-gi-a-a-/ĝu$_{10}$
i$_3$-dab$_5$
====
iti ki-siki ^{d}Nin-a-zu
mu En-unu$_6$-gal / ^{d}Inana ba-huĝ
left 237

61: SM 1911.03.081 (Š47 xid)

obv. [x] sila$_4$
Šeš-Da-da saĝĝa
2 sila$_4$
ensi$_2$ Nibru^{ki}
1 sila$_4$
Nam-ha-ni
rev. 1 sila$_4$
Ur-sa$_6$-ga muhaldim
2 amar az zabar-dab$_5$
====
mu-DU Na-sa$_6$ i$_3$-dab$_5$
iti diri ezem Me-ki-ĝal$_2$ us$_2$-sa
mu us$_2$-sa Ki-maš^{ki} / ba-hul
left u$_4$ 7-kam

62: SM 1911.03.082 (Š47 xii 18)

obv. 1 u$_8$ sila$_4$ nu$_2$-a
mu-DU Ur-^{d}EN.ZU
e$_2$ uz-ga
A-a-kal-la maškim

1 udu niga
e$_2$ NI-da-gu$_2$ / lu$_2$-kin-gi$_4$-a
rev. lu$_2$ Ur-Kiš^{ki}-še$_3$
ĝiri$_3$ Lu$_2$-^{d}Da-mu sukkal
Arad$_2$-ĝu$_{10}$ maškim
iti u$_4$ 18 ba-zal
ša$_3$ (*erasure*)
zi-ga ki Lu$_2$-diĝir-[ra]
iti še-KIN-ku$_5$
mu us$_2$-sa Ki-maš^{ki} / ba-hul

Obv. 6: Cf. Kyoto 15, obv. 14 (e$_2$ Ku-du$_2$-ma lu$_2$-kin-gi$_4$-a lu$_2$ Šu-da-e^{ki}-še$_3$) and rev. 2-3 (e$_2$ NI-da-gu$_2$ lu$_2$-kin-gi$_4$-a lu$_2$ Ur-Kiš^{ki}-še$_3$).

63: SM 1911.03.083 (ŠS4 i 22)

obv. 10 ud$_5$ u$_2$ šu-gid$_2$
2 sila$_4$ ba-ug$_7$
e$_2$ muhaldim
mu lu$_2$ šuku-ra-/ke$_4$-ne-še$_3$
Arad$_2$-ĝu$_{10}$ maškim
rev. u$_4$ 22-kam
ki Ur-ku$_3$-nun-na-ta
ba-zi
ĝiri$_3$ Hu-la-al dub-sar
iti še-KIN-ku$_5$
mu ^{d}Šu-^{d}EN.ZU / lugal Uri$_5$^{ki}-ma-ke$_4$
bad$_3$ mar-tu Mu-ri-iq-/Ti-id-ni-im / mu-du$_3$
left 12 udu

64: SM 1911.03.084 (AS5 i 30)

obv. 1 dusu$_2$ munus mah$_2$
u$_4$ 30-kam
ki Ab-ba-sa$_6$-ga-/ta
Ze$_2$-ra-a i$_3$-dab$_5$
rev. ====
iti maš-da$_3$-gu$_7$
mu En-unu$_6$-gal / ^{d}Inana ba-huĝ
left 1

65: SM 1911.03.085 (AS5 vi 12)

obv. 1 gu$_4$
u$_4$ 12-kam
ki Ab-ba-sa$_6$-/ga-ta
Ur-tur
rev. i$_3$-dab$_5$
iti a$_2$-ki-ti
====
mu En-unu$_6$-gal / ^{d}Inana ba-huĝ
left 1

66: SM 1911.03.086 (AS5 i)

obv. 4 u$_8$ gi$_6$ LU$_2$.SU
ki ^{d}Šul-gi-a-a-ĝu$_{10}$-/ta
U$_2$-ta$_2$-mi-šar-ra-/am
i$_3$-dab$_5$
rev. ša$_3$ PU$_3$.ŠA-iš-^{d}Da-gan^{ki}
====
iti maš-da$_3$-gu$_7$
mu En-unu$_6$-gal / ^{d}Inana Unug^{ki} ba-/huĝ
left 4

67: SM 1911.03.087 (AS5 vi 12)

obv. 12 lulim nita$_2$
7 lulim munus
1 amar lulim munus ga
1 šeg$_9$-bar munus
1 ^{anše}si$_2$-si$_2$ munus
7 az
rev. u$_4$ 12-kam
ki Ab-ba-sa$_6$-ga-/ta
Lu$_2$-diĝir-ra i$_3$-dab$_5$
iti a$_2$-ki-ti
mu En-unu$_6$-gal / ^{d}Inana ba-huĝ
left 30-la$_2$-1

Obv. 1-6: For these animals, see SA 35 (AS5 vi 12).

68: SM 1911.03.089 (AS8 iv/v 19)

obv. [10]
u$_4$ [ ]
ĝiri$_3$ ^{d}Šul-gi-[dan]-/ga-da
1 udu ME-^{d}Nisaba lukur lugal
En-um-i$_3$-li$_2$ sukkal maškim
1 udu niga La-qi$_3$-[pu]-um
rev. lu$_2$ Ma-ri$_2$^{ki}
ĝiri$_3$ Šu-ab-ba sukkal
2 udu šu-gid$_2$ e$_2$ muhaldim
mu gar$_3$-du-ne-še$_3$
ĝiri$_3$ ^{d}Šul-gi-iri-ĝu$_{10}$
Arad$_2$-ĝu$_{10}$ maškim
iti u$_4$ 20-la$_2$-1 ba-zal
ki Igi-^{d}En-lil$_2$-še$_3$-[ta] / ba-zi
[iti x ^{d}]Nin-a-z[u]
[mu] en Eridu^{ki} ba-huĝ
left 14 udu

Obv. 6-rev. 7: Cf. MVN 18 715, 5 (AS8 iv/v).

69: SM 1911.03.094 (Š47 xi 2)

obv. 1 maš$_2$-gal niga
1 ud$_5$ niga LU$_2$.SU.A
1 udu
2 sila$_4$ ga gi$_6$
1 kir$_{11}$ ga LU$_2$.SU.A
1 maš$_2$ ga
2 maš$_2$ ga LU$_2$.SU.A
rev. 2 ^{munus}aš$_2$-gar$_3$ ga LU$_2$.SU.A
ba-ug$_7$ u$_4$ 2-kam
ki Lu$_2$-diĝir-ra-ta
Ur-ni$_9$-ĝar
šu ba-ti
iti ezem Me-ki-ĝal$_2$
mu us$_2$-sa Ki-maš^{ki} ba-/hul

70: SM 1911.03.095 (Š47 ii 27)

obv. 2 udu niga
3 maš$_2$-gal niga
mu-DU [ ]
1 gu$_4$ niga 2 udu niga
3 maš$_2$-gal niga
mu šagina u$_3$ nu-banda$_3$-/e-ne-še$_3$
25 u$_8$ LU$_2$.SU.A ni[ga]
rev. 5 [ ]
mu-DU [ ]
e$_2$ muhaldim-še$_3$
1 udu mu-DU Ur-^{d}EN.ZU
e$_2$ uz-ga
Arad$_2$-ĝu$_{10}$ maškim
[u$_4$] 27-kam
zi-ga ki Lu$_2$-diĝir-ra
iti šeš-da-gu$_7$
mu us$_2$-sa Ki-maš^{ki} / ba-hul

71: SM 1911.03.096 (Š47 iv 18)

obv. 1 sila$_4$
ensi$_2$ Urum$_x$(UR$_2$×U$_2$)^{ki}
1 sila$_4$
I$_3$-li$_2$-mi-ti
1 amar maš-da$_3$
I$_3$-li$_2$-mu
rev. 1 sila$_4$
Ur-^{d}En-lil$_2$-la$_2$
1 sila$_4$
Hu-un-ha-ab-ur
====
mu-DU Na-sa$_6$ i$_3$-dab$_5$
iti ki-siki ^{d}Nin-a-zu
mu us$_2$-sa Ki-maš^{ki} / ba-hul
left u$_4$ 18-kam

Cf. OIP 115 329 (Š47 iv 18), in which two persons, Ku-u$_3$ and a certain zabar-dab$_5$-official, delivering animals on this same day, are attested.

72: SM 1911.03.100 (Š47 viii 20)

obv. 1 gukkal niga
1 udu aslum$_x$(A.LUM)
3 udu LU$_2$.SU.A
7 U$_8$+HUL$_2$
1 u$_8$ LU$_2$.SU.A
4 maš$_2$-gal
1 ud$_5$
rev. 1 ud$_5$ LU$_2$.SU.A
1 sila$_4$ ga
1 kir$_{11}$ ga
ba-ug$_7$ u$_4$ 20-kam
ki Lu-diĝir-ra-ta
Ur-ni$_9$-ĝar šu ba-ti
iti šu-eš-ša
mu us$_2$-sa Ki-maš^{ki} u$_3$ / Hu-ur$_5$-ti^{ki} ba-hul

73: SM 1911.03.101 (AS1 x 10)

obv. 4 sila$_4$ ga
2 kir$_{11}$ ga
1 ^{munus}aš$_2$-gar$_3$ ga
u$_4$ 10-kam
u$_3$-tu-da
rev. e$_2$-udu-ka
ša$_3$ Nibru^{ki}
Na-lu$_5$ i$_3$-dab$_5$
iti ezem An-na
mu ^{d}Amar-^{d}EN.ZU / lugal

74: SM 1911.03.103 (Š46 iv 18)

obv. 1 gukkal niga
1 gukkal
2 u$_8$
1 U$_8$+HUL$_2$
1 maš$_2$-gal
1 maš$_2$-gal babbar$_2$
2 ud$_5$

rev. 1 maš$_2$ ga babbar$_2$
ba-ug$_7$ u$_4$ 18-kam
ki Lu$_2$-diĝir-ra-ta
Ur-ni$_9$-ĝar
šu ba-ti
iti ki-siki ^{d}Nin-a-zu
mu Ki-maš^{ki} u$_3$ Hu-ur$_5$-/ti^{ki} ba-hul

75: SM 1911.03.104 (ŠS3 xii 9)

obv. 5 udu u$_2$
ba-ug$_7$ e$_2$ muhaldim
mu aga$_3$-us$_2$-e-ne-še$_3$
Arad$_2$-ĝu$_{10}$ maškim
u$_4$ 9-kam
rev. ki Du$_{11}$-ga-ta
ba-zi
ĝiri$_3$ Hu-la-al / dub-sar
iti še-KIN-ku$_5$
mu ^{d}Šu-^{d}EN.ZU / lugal-e Si-ma-num$_2$/$^{[ki]}$ mu-hul

76: SM 1911.03.105 (Š45 xii 17)

obv. 2 udu niga
^{d}En-lil$_2$
2 udu niga
^{d}Nin-lil$_2$
^{d}Nanše-ul$_4$-gal / maškim
rev. iti u$_4$ 17 ba-zal
zi-ga
ki Na-lu$_5$
iti še-KIN-ku$_5$
mu Ur-bi$_2$-lum/^{ki} ba-hul

77: SM 1911.03.106 (Š46 ii 12)

obv. 2 gu$_4$ niga saĝ-gu$_4$
4 gu$_4$ niga
eš$_3$-eš$_3$ e$_2$-u$_4$-15
iti u$_4$ 12 ba-zal

zi-ga
rev. ki A-hu-ni
Na-sa$_6$ i$_3$-dab$_5$
====
iti šeš-da-gu$_7$
mu us$_2$-sa Ur-/bi$_2$-lum^{ki} ba-hul

78: SM 1911.03.107 (-- -- 3)

obv. 2 udu niga sa$_2$-d[u$_{11}$]
1 maš$_2$-gal niga
u$_4$ 3-kam
Nin-ĝu$_{10}$ ĝa$_2$-udu-še$_3$ / e$_3$-a-še$_3$
iti-ta u$_4$ 10+5+[x ba]-/ra-[zal]
rev. (*all damaged*)

Obv. 4: Cf. DoCu 299, R13 (Š47 ix 20). Nin-ĝu$_{10}$ may not be a PN but rather “my mistress” or “my queen,” which may correspond to nin-ĝa$_2$ in Umma texts.

79: SM 1911.03.109 (Š48 i 5)

obv. 2 udu niga 1 U$_8$+HUL$_2$ niga
2 sila$_4$ ^{d}En-lil$_2$
2 udu niga 1 U$_8$+HUL$_2$ niga
2 sila$_4$ ^{d}Nin-lil$_2$
^{d}En-lil$_2$-zi-ša$_3$-ĝal$_2$ / sagi maškim
rev. iti u$_4$ 5 ba-zal
ki Na-lu$_5$-ta
ba-zi
iti maš-da$_3$-gu$_7$
mu Ha-ar-ši^{ki} / u$_3$ Ki-maš^{ki} / ba-hul

80: SM 1911.03.110 (ŠS3 ii 5)

obv. 1 amar maš-da$_3$ munus
^{d}En-lil$_2$
1 amar maš-da$_3$ munus
^{d}Nin-lil$_2$
lugal ku$_x$(KWU147)-ra

ša$_3$ mu-DU-ra-ta
u$_4$ 5-kam
rev. ki In-ta-e$_3$-a-/ta ba-zi
ĝiri$_3$ Nu-ur$_2$-^{d}EN.ZU / dub-sar
iti šeš-da-gu$_7$
mu us$_2$-sa ma$_2$ dara$_3$-/abzu ^{d}En-ki-ka / ba-ab-du$_8$
left 2

81: SM 1911.03.112 (AS1 v 20)

obv. 1 gu$_4$
2 amar gir ga gun$_3$-a
1 maš$_2$-gal niga sig$_5$
1 u$_8$ niga
1 sila$_4$ niga
1 U$_8$+HUL$_2$
1 sila$_4$ ga
rev. ba-ug$_7$ u$_4$ 20-kam
ki Lu$_2$-diĝir-ra-ta
Ur-ni$_9$-ĝar
šu ba-ti
iti ezem ^{d}Nin-a-zu
mu ^{d}Amar-^{d}EN.ZU / lugal

82: SM 1911.03.113 (Š47 v 19)

obv. 2 sila$_4$ e$_2$ uz-ga
mu-DU en ^{d}Inana
Lu$_2$-^{d}Ba-ba$_6$ maškim
1 sila$_4$ ^{d}En-lil$_2$
mu-DU Lu$_2$-diĝir-ra / šabra
1 sila$_4$ ^{d}Nin-lil$_2$
mu-DU Ur-^{d}Nin-gal
rev. zabar-dab$_5$ maškim
4 u$_8$ 1 ud$_5$
šu-gid$_2$ e$_2$ muhaldim-še$_3$
u$_4$ 20-la$_2$-1-kam
----
ki Na-sa$_6$-ta ba-zi

iti ezem ^{d}Nin-a-zu
mu us$_2$-sa Ki-maš^{ki} / ba-hul

Obv. 5: Cf. PDT 2 1061 (Š47 v 19).

83: SM 1911.03.114 (AS5 iv 25)

obv. 15 gu$_4$
u$_4$ 25-kam
ki Ab-ba-sa$_6$-/ga-ta
Ur-tur
rev. i$_3$-dab$_5$
iti ki-siki ^{d}Nin-/a-zu
mu En-unu$_6$-/gal ^{d}Inana ba-huĝ
left 15

84: SM 1911.03.115 (-- viii 27)

obv. 2 uz-tur
2 tu-gur$_4$^{mušen}
iti-ta u$_4$ 25 ba-ra-zal
1 uz-tur
iti-ta u$_4$ 26 ba-ra-/zal
rev. [ ]
[iti]-ta u$_4$ 27 / ba-ra-zal
[ ]
zi-ga [ ]
iti šu-eš$_5$-ša
mu us$_2$-sa [ ]

85: SM 1911.03.116 (Š46 viii 9)

obv. 4 gu$_4$ šu-gi$_4$
2 ab$_2$ šu-gi$_4$
ki Bu-qu$_2$-šum / šabra-ta
mu-DU
rev. Na-sa$_6$
i$_3$-dab$_5$
====

iti šu-eš$_5$-ša
mu Ki-maš^{ki} u$_3$ Hu-/ur$_5$-ti^{ki} ba-hul
left u$_4$ 10-la$_2$-1-kam

86: SM 1911.03.117 (AS5 xii 28)

obv. 1 sila$_4$ ^{d}En-ki
1 sila$_4$ ^{d}Dam-gal-/nun-na
mu-DU Arad$_2$-ĝu$_{10}$
Pa$_2$-pa$_2$-an-še-en / maškim
rev. u$_4$ 28-kam
ki Ab-ba-sa$_6$-ga-/ta
ba-zi
iti še-KIN-ku$_5$
mu en ^{d}Inana / ba-huĝ
left 2

Obv. 1-2: For these animals, see Amorites 18, rev. iii 8' (AS5 xii 28).

87: SM 1911.03.118 (AS8 xi)

obv. 2 gu$_4$ šu-gid$_2$
ki Ab-ba-sa$_6$-/ga-ta
Ur-tur
i$_3$-dab$_5$
rev. iti ezem Me-ki-ĝal$_2$
mu en Eridu^{ki} / ba-huĝ
====

88: SM 1911.03.120 (Š47 ii)

obv. 1 ^{anše}si$_2$-si$_2$ / nita$_2$
2 ^{anše}si$_2$-si$_2$ munus
ša$_3$ nam-ra-ak
ki Na-sa$_6$-ta
rev. Šu-^{d}Idim
i$_3$-dab$_5$
----

iti šeš-da-gu$_7$
mu us$_2$-sa Ki-maš/^{ki} ba-hul

Cf. BPOA 19 1104 (Š47 ii).

89: SM 1911.03.121 (AS1 xii 2)

obv. 2 udu niga
2 maš$_2$-gal niga
a-tu$_5$-a / ^{d}Nin-tin-ug$_5$-ga
^{d}Nanše-ul$_4$-gal / maškim
rev. iti u$_4$ 2 ba-zal
ki Na-lu$_5$-ta
ba-zi
iti še-KIN-ku$_5$
mu ^{d}Amar-^{d}EN.ZU / lugal
left 4

90: SM 1911.03.122 (Š44 vi 16)

obv. 4 udu niga 1 maš$_2$-gal niga
^{d}Nin-lil$_2$
1 udu niga 1 maš$_2$-gal niga
du$_6$-ku$_3$
2 udu niga ^{d}EN.ZU
rev. ^{d}Nanše-ul$_4$-gal / maškim
iti u$_4$ 16 ba-zal
zi-ga ki Na-lu$_5$
iti a$_2$-ki-ti
mu Si-mu-ru-um^{ki} / Lu-lu-bu^{ki} a-ra$_2$ / 10-la$_2$-1-kam-aš ba-hul

91: SM 1911.03.124 (AS5 viii 13)

obv. 108 udu
5 sila$_4$
84 maš$_2$-gal
u$_4$ 13-kam
ki Ab-ba-sa$_6$-/ga-ta
rev. In-ta-e$_3$-a

i$_3$-dab$_5$
====
iti šu-eš$_5$-ša
mu En-unu$_6$-/gal ^{d}Inana ba-huĝ
left 198!(197)

This text is a duplicate of OIP 121 254 (AS 5 viii 13). For these animals, see KM 89225 (AS 5 viii 13).

92: SM 1911.03.125 (Š47 viii 17)

obv. 1 udu niga
1 ud$_5$ niga LU$_2$.SU.A
2 udu
2 U$_8$+HUL$_2$
1 u$_8$
1 u$_8$ LU$_2$.SU.A
1 sila$_4$ gukkal
rev. 1 sila$_4$ ga
1 maš$_2$ ga
ba-ug$_7$ u$_4$ 17-kam
ki Lu$_2$-diĝir-ra-ta
Ur-ni$_9$-ĝar
šu ba-ti
iti šu-eš$_5$-ša
mu us$_2$-sa Ki-maš^{ki} / ba-hul

93: SM 1911.03.126 (AS7 ii 1)

obv. 10-la$_2$-1 ab$_2$ mu-2
1 gu$_4$ mu-2
u$_4$ 1-kam
ki In-ta-e$_3$-a-/ta
rev. Ur-tur i$_3$-dab$_5$
====
iti šeš-da-gu$_7$
mu Hu-uh$_2$-nu-ri/^{ki} ba-hul
left 10

94: SM 1911.03.127 (AS7 xii 3)

obv. 1 gu$_4$
30 ab$_2$
u$_4$ 3-kam
ki Ab-ba-sa$_6$-/ga-ta
rev. In-ta-e$_3$-a / i$_3$-dab$_5$
====
iti še-KIN-ku$_5$
mu Hu-uh$_2$-nu-/ri^{ki} ba-hul
left 31 gu$_4$

95: SM 1911.03.128 (AS8 ix 3)

obv. 1 udu niga
Šul-ĝa$_2$-a-ad lu$_2$ Zi-da-ah-ri^{ki}
ĝiri$_3$ ^{d}Nanna-kam sukkal
Arad$_2$-ĝu$_{10}$ maškim
rev. iti u$_4$ 3 ba-zal
ki Zu-ba-ga-ta
ba-zi
ĝiri$_3$ Ad-da-kal-/la dub-sar
iti ezem mah
mu en Eridu^{ki} ba-huĝ
left 1 udu

96: SM 1911.03.129 (AS5 vi 17)

obv. 4 udu
10 sila$_4$
2 maš$_2$
u$_4$ 17-kam
ki Ab-ba-sa$_6$-/ga-ta
rev. In-ta-e$_3$-a
i$_3$-dab$_5$
====
iti a$_2$-ki-ti
mu En-unu$_6$-/gal ^{d}Inana ba-huĝ
left 16

This text is a duplicate of OIP 121 223 (AS vi 17). For these animals, see MVN 13 848 (AS 5 vi 17).

97: SM 1911.03.130 (AS2 ii 4)

obv. 1 maš$_2$
u$_4$ 4-kam
ki Ab-ba-sa$_6$-ga-/ta
^{d}Šul-gi-a-a-ĝu$_{10}$ / i$_3$-dab$_5$
rev. iti šeš-da-gu$_7$
mu Ur-bi$_2$-lum^{ki} / ba-hul
====
left 1

98: SM 1911.03.131 (AS8 iv 20+)

obv. 3 ud[u]
4 [u$_8$]
3 ma[š$_2$ gal]
šu-gid$_2$ [e$_2$ muhaldim]
mu gar$_3$-du-[e-ne-še$_3$]
^{d}Nanna-[kam maškim]
rev. iti u$_4$ 20+[(x)] [ba-zal]
ša$_3$ EN.[LIL$_2$^{ki}]
ki En-di[ĝir-ĝu$_{10}$-ta]
ba-z[i]
iti ki-siki [^{d}Nin-a-zu]
mu en Eridu[^{ki} / ba-huĝ]
left 10

99: SM 1911.03.132 (AS6 v 13)

obv. 1 udu aslum$_x$(A.LUM) niga
u$_4$ 13-kam
ki Ab-ba-sa$_6$-ga-/ta
Tu-ra-am-^{d}Da-gan
rev. i$_3$-dab$_5$
====

iti ezem ^{d}Nin-/a-zu
mu Ša-aš-ru^{ki} / ba-hul

Cf. AUCT 2 241 (AS6 v 13).

100: SM 1911.03.133 (Š47 ii 14)

obv. 1 eme$_6$
1 amar eme$_6$ ga
1 maš$_2$ a-dara$_4$
1 ud$_5$ a-dara$_4$
1 az
ba-ug$_7$
rev. u$_4$ 14-kam
ki Lu$_2$-diĝir-ra-ta
Ur-ni$_9$-ĝar
šu ba-ti
iti šeš-da-gu$_7$
mu us$_2$-sa Ki-maš^{ki} / Hu-ur$_5$-ti^{ki} / ba-hul

101: SM 1911.03.134 (Š46 vii 21)

obv. [ ] udu niga gu$_4$-e-us$_2$-sa
[ ] babbar
[uz-t]ur
[ ] mušen
[ba-ug$_7$ e$_2$-gal]-la ba-an-ku$_x$(KWU147)
[iti-ta u$_4$] 21 ba/-ra-zal
rev. zi-ga
Ur-^{d}Lugal-edin-/ka
iti ezem ^{d}Šul-gi
mu Ki-maš^{ki} u$_3$ / Hu-ur$_5$-ti^{ki} ba-hul

102: SM 1911.03.135 (AS8 ix 1)

obv. 1 gukkal
u$_4$ 1-kam
ki Ab-ba-sa$_6$-/ga-ta
U$_2$-ta$_2$-mi-šar-ra-am

rev. i$_3$-dab$_5$
====
iti ezem mah
mu en Eridu/^{ki} ba-huĝ

103: SM 1911.03.136 (AS3 xi 26)

obv. 3 gu$_4$
3 ab$_2$
5 udu
šu-gid$_2$ e$_2$ muhaldim-še$_3$
u$_4$ 26-kam
rev. ki In-ta-e$_3$-a-/ta
ba-zi
iti ezem Me-ki-ĝal$_2$
mu ^{d}gu-za ^{d}En-/lil$_2$-la$_2$ ba-dim$_2$

104: SM 1911.03.137 (AS4 x)

obv. 2 tug$_2$ uš-bar
tug$_2$ sa gi$_4$-a
ki I-din-Er$_3$-ra / ^{lu2}azlag$_2$-ta
mu-DU
rev. Nu-ur$_2$-^{d}EN.ZU
šu ba-ti
----
iti ezem An-na
mu En-mah-gal-/an-na en ^{d}Nanna / ba-huĝ

105: SM 1911.03.138 (AS4 xi 20)

obv. 6 gu$_4$
1 sila$_4$
3 maš$_2$
u$_4$ 20-kam
ki Ab-ba-sa$_6$-/ga-ta
rev. In-ta-e$_3$-/a i$_3$-dab$_5$
====
iti ezem Me-ki-ĝal$_2$

[mu] en ^{d}Nanna / ba-huĝ
left 10

106: SM 1911.03.139 (AS4 xi 3)

obv. 1 ud$_5$ a-dara$_4$
3 maš$_2$ ga a-dara$_4$
1 maš-da$_3$
ba-ug$_7$ u$_4$ 3-kam
ki Lu$_2$-diĝir-ra-ta
rev. ^{d}Šul-gi-iri-ĝu$_{10}$
šu ba-ti
====
iti ezem Me-ki-ĝal$_2$
mu En-mah-gal-/an-na en ^{d}Nanna / ba-huĝ
left 5

107: SM 1911.03.140 (AS1 vi 30)

obv. 2 sila$_4$ ga
1 kir$_{11}$ ga
u$_4$ 30-la$_2$-1-kam
1 sila$_4$ ga
2 kir$_{11}$ ga
u$_4$ 30-kam
rev. u$_3$-tu-da
e$_2$-udu-ka
ša$_3$ Nibru^{ki}
Na-lu$_5$ i$_3$-dab$_5$
iti a$_2$-ki-ti
mu ^{d}Amar-^{d}EN.ZU / lugal

108: SM 1911.03.141 (AS4 vi 6)

obv. 1 udu niga
3 udu
1 guk[kal]
1 u$_8$
1 maš$_2$-gal

rev. ba-ug$_7$ u$_4$ 6-kam
ki Zu-ba-ga-ta
^{d}Šul-gi-iri-ĝu$_{10}$
šu ba-ti
iti a$_2$-ki-ti
mu en ^{d}Nanna / ba-huĝ
left 7 udu

109: SM 1911.03.142 (Š46 vii 1)

obv. 2 udu
1 u$_8$
1 maš$_2$
ba-ug$_7$
u$_4$ 1-kam
rev. ki Na-lu$_5$-ta
Ur-ni$_9$-ĝar
šu ba-ti
iti ezem ^{d}Šul-gi
mu Ki-maš^{ki} u$_3$ / Hu-ur$_5$-ti^{ki} ba-/hul

110: SM 1911.03.143 (ŠS3 ii 5)

obv. 1 udu niga gu$_4$-e-us$_2$-sa
1 maš$_2$ ga
ba-ug$_7$ u$_4$ 5-kam
ki A-hu-We-er-ta
^{d}Šul-gi-iri-ĝu$_{10}$
rev. šu ba-ti
ĝiri$_3$ Ur-uš-gid$_2$-/da
====
iti šeš-da-gu$_7$
mu us$_2$-sa ma$_2$ ^{d}En-ki / ba-ab-du$_8$
left 2 udu

111: SM 1911.03.144 (Š44 v 21)

obv. 10-la$_2$-1 udu
2 maš$_2$

ba-ug$_7$
u$_4$ 21-kam
ki Na-lu$_5$-[ta]
rev. Ur-ni$_9$-ĝar
šu ba-ti
iti ezem ^{d}Nin-a-/zu
mu Si-mu-ru-um^{ki} / Lu-lu-bu^{ki} a-ra$_2$ / 10-la$_2$-1-kam-aš ba-hul

112: SM 1911.03.145 (AS7 iv --)

obv. [x] udu
[x] u$_8$
[x] sila$_4$
ba-ug$_7$ u$_4$ [x-kam]
[k]i A-hu-We-[er-ta]
rev. ^{d}Šul-gi-iri-ĝu$_{10}$
šu ba-ti
iti ki-si[ki ^{d}Nin-a-zu]
mu [Hu-uh$_2$-nu-]ri^{ki} / ba-hul
left [x] udu

113: SM 1911.03.146 (-- xii 18)

obv. 1 maš$_2$ ga a-dara$_4$
ba-uš$_2$
u$_4$ 18-kam
ki Lu$_2$-diĝir-ra-[ta]
[^{d}Šul]-gi-iri-ĝu$_{10}$
rev. [šu] ba-[ti]
====
iti še-KIN-[ku$_5$]
mu [ ]
left 1

114: SM 1911.03.147 (AS5 viii 11)

obv. 1 dusu$_2$ nita$_2$
u$_4$ 11-kam
ki Ab-ba-sa$_6$-ga-/ta
Šu-Er$_3$-ra

rev. i$_3$-dab$_5$
====
iti šu-eš$_5$-ša
mu En-unu$_6$-gal / ^{d}Inana Unug^{ki} ba-huĝ
left 1

115: SM 1911.03.148 (Š45 xii 7)

obv. 3 udu
1 u$_8$
1 sila$_4$ ga
ba-ug$_7$ u$_4$ 7-kam
rev. ki Na-lu$_5$-ta
Ur-ni$_9$-ĝar
šu ba-ti
iti še-KIN-ku$_5$
mu Ur-bi$_2$-/lum^{ki} ba-hul

116: SM 1911.03.149 (AS2 vii 26)

obv. 1 šeg$_9$-bar
ba-uš$_2$
u$_4$ 26-kam
ki Šu-^{d}Idim-ta
rev. Ur-ni$_9$-ĝar
šu ba-ti
iti ezem ^{d}Šul-gi
mu ^{d}Amar-^{d}EN.ZU / lugal-e Ur-[bi$_2$]-/lum^{ki} [mu-hul]

117: SM 1911.03.150 (AS1 xii 17)

obv. 2 udu
1 sila$_4$
ba-ug$_7$
u$_4$ 17-kam
ki Na-lu$_5$-ta
rev. Ur-ni$_9$-ĝar
šu ba-ti
iti še-KIN-ku$_5$
mu ^{d}Amar-^{d}EN./ZU lugal

118: SM 1911.03.151 (AS2 xii 27)

obv. 1 dusu$_2$ munus
ba-uš$_2$
u$_4$ 27-kam
ki Šu-Er$_3$-ra-ta
rev. Ur-ni$_9$-ĝar
šu ba-ti
====
iti še-KIN-ku$_5$
mu ^{d}Amar-^{d}EN.ZU / lugal-e Ur-bi$_2$-lum/^{ki} mu-hul

119: SM 1911.03.152 (Š43 iii 9)

obv. 3 gu$_4$
3 ab$_2$ 1 sila$_4$
E$_2$-ki um-mi-a
1 sila$_4$
rev. Ma-an-ba
====
mu-DU
iti u$_5$-bi$_2$-gu$_7$
mu en ^{d}Nanna / maš-e i$_3$-pad$_3$
left u$_4$ 10-la$_2$-1-kam

Obv. 3: Cf. MVN 2 157.

120: SM 1911.03.153 (Š48 vii 13)

obv. 3 udu
2 gukkal
2 u$_8$
4 U$_8$+HUL$_2$
1 maš$_2$-gal
rev. ba-ug$_7$ u$_4$ 13-kam
ki Na-lu$_5$-ta
Ur-ni$_9$-ĝar
šu ba-ti
iti ezem ^{d}Šul-gi
mu Ha-ar-ši^{ki} / ba-hul

121: SM 1911.03.154 (Š - v)

obv. 46 gukkal
2 sila$_4$
ba-ug$_7$
ki Ba-a-ta
Šu-ku-bu-um / šu ba-ti
rev. iti ezem ^{d}Nin-/a-zu
====
[mu ^{d}Šul]-gi / lugal-e
[ ]^{ki} mu-/hul

122: SM 1911.03.155 (ŠS3 xi 8)

obv. 1 ab$_2$
1 amar gu$_4$ ga
1 udu
1 udu aslum$_x$(A.LUM)
2 maš$_2$-gal
2 u$_8$
rev. 1 kir$_{11}$
ba-ug$_7$ u$_4$ 8-kam
ki Ur-^{d}Nanna-ta
^{d}Šul-gi-iri-ĝu$_{10}$
šu ba-ti
iti ezem Me-ki-ĝal$_2$
mu Si-ma-num$_2$/^{ki} ba-hul
left 2 gu$_4$ 7 udu

123: SM 1911.03.156 (AS2 viii 18)

obv. 1 maš$_2$-gal niga
2 udu
1 u$_8$
1 sila$_4$
1 sila$_4$ ga
ba-ug$_7$ u$_4$ 18-kam
rev. ki Lu$_2$-diĝir-ra-ta
Ur-ni$_9$-ĝar
šu ba-ti

iti šu-eš$_5$-ša
mu ^{d}Amar-^{d}EN.ZU / lugal-e Ur-bi$_2$-/lum^{ki} mu-hul
left 6

124: SM 1911.03.157 (AS6 vii 26)

obv. 1 u$_8$
ba-uš$_2$
u$_4$ 26-kam
ki Na-lu$_5$-ta
rev. ^{d}Šul-gi-/iri-ĝu$_{10}$
šu ba-ti
iti ezem ^{d}Šul-gi
mu Ša-aš-ru^{ki} / ba-hul

125: SM 1911.03.158 (Š46 i 17)

obv. 3 udu
1 u$_8$
1 maš$_2$ ga
ba-ug$_7$ u$_4$ 17-kam
ki Na-lu$_5$-ta
rev. Ur-ni$_9$-ĝar
šu ba-ti
iti maš-da$_3$-gu$_7$
mu us$_2$-sa Ur-/bi$_2$-lum^{ki} ba-/hul

126: SM 1911.03.160 (AS3 vi 17)

obv. 1 ^{munus}aš$_2$-gar$_3$ niga sig$_5$-us$_2$
1 u$_8$
ba-ug$_7$ u$_4$ 17-kam
ki Lu$_2$-diĝir-ra-ta
rev. ^{d}Šul-gi-iri-ĝu$_{10}$
šu ba-ti
iti a$_2$-ki-ti
mu ^{d}gu-za / ^{d}En-lil$_2$-la$_2$ ba-dim$_2$
left 2

127: SM 1911.03.161 (AS5 xi 25)

obv. 1 udu aslum$_x$(A.LUM) ĝiš-du$_3$ / niga
u$_4$ 25-kam
ki Ab-ba-sa$_6$-/ga-ta
rev. ^{d}Šul-gi-a-a-/ĝu$_{10}$ i$_3$-dab$_5$
----
iti ezem Me-ki-ĝal$_2$
mu En-unu$_6$-/gal ^{d}Inana ba-huĝ
left 1 udu

128: SM 1911.03.162 (AS6 vi 1)

obv. 2 udu
1 maš$_2$
2 kir$_{11}$ ga
ba-ug$_7$
u$_4$ 1-kam
rev. ki Na-lu$_5$-ta
^{d}Šul-gi-iri-ĝu$_{10}$
šu ba-ti
iti a$_2$-ki-ti
mu Ša-aš-ru^{ki} / ba-hul

129: SM 1911.03.163 (AS5 i 22)

obv. 4 sila$_4$
1 maš$_2$
u$_4$ 22-kam
ki Ab-ba-sa$_6$-ga-/ta
In-ta-e$_3$-a
rev. i$_3$-dab$_5$
====
iti maš-da$_3$-gu$_7$
mu En-unu$_6$-gal / ^{d}Inana Unug^{ki} / ba-huĝ
left 5

130: SM 1911.03.164 (AS1 viii 7)

obv. 1 udu
1 sila$_4$ ga

ba-ug$_7$
u$_4$ 7-kam
rev. ki Na-lu$_5$-ta
Ur-ni$_9$-ĝar
šu ba-ti
iti šu-eš-ša
mu ^{d}Amar-^{d}EN./ZU lugal

131: SM 1911.03.165 (Š47 vii 25)

obv. 2 udu
1 u$_8$
ba-ug$_7$
u$_4$ 25-kam
rev. ki Na-lu$_5$-ta
Ur-ni$_9$-ĝar
šu ba-ti
iti ezem ^{d}Šul-/gi
mu us$_2$-sa Ki-maš/^{ki} ba-hul

132: SM 1911.03.166 (AS7 ii 25)

obv. 1 amar gir ga
4 udu
2 u$_8$
1 sila$_4$
1 sila$_4$ ga
ba-ug$_7$ u$_4$ 25-kam
rev. ki A-hu-We-er-ta
^{d}Šul-gi-iri-ĝu$_{10}$
šu ba-ti
iti šeš-da-gu$_7$
mu Hu-uh$_2$-nu-ri/^{ki} ba-hul
left 1 gu$_4$ 8 udu

133: SM 1911.03.167 (Š48 i 11)

obv. 1 U$_8$+HUL$_2$
1 maš$_2$-gal

ba-ug$_7$
u$_4$ 11-kam
ša$_3$ Tum-ma-al/^{ki}
rev. ki En-diĝir-ĝu$_{10}$-ta
Ur-ni$_9$-ĝar
šu ba-ti
====
iti maš-da$_3$-gu$_7$
mu Ha-ar-ši^{ki} / ba-hul

134: SM 1911.03.168 (AS1 x 19)

obv. 1 udu
ba-uš$_2$
u$_4$ 20-la$_2$-1-kam
ki Na-lu$_5$-ta
rev. Ur-ni$_9$-ĝar
šu ba-ti
iti ezem An-na
mu ^{d}Amar-^{d}EN./ZU lugal

135: SM 1911.03.169 (AS1 xi 7)

obv. 1 gu$_4$
1 ab$_2$ mu-2
2 udu
3 gukkal
u$_4$ 7-kam
ki Ab-ba-sa$_6$-ga-/ta
rev. Lu$_2$-diĝir-ra
i$_3$-dab$_5$
====
iti ezem Me-ki-ĝal$_2$
mu ^{d}Amar-^{d}EN.ZU / lugal
left 7

136: SM 1911.03.170 (ŠS4 xi 9)

obv. 1 udu
1 maš$_2$

2 ud$_5$
1 sila$_4$
ba-ug$_7$
rev. u$_4$ 9-kam
ki Be-li$_2$-i$_3$-li$_2$-ta
^{d}Šul-gi-iri-ĝu$_{10}$
šu ba-ti
iti ezem An-na
mu bad$_3$ mar-tu ba-du$_3$
left 5

137: SM 1911.03.171 (AS5 x 24)

obv. 1 dara$_4$ nita$_2$
ba-uš$_2$ ša$_3$ libir
u$_4$ 24-kam
ĝiri$_3$ Niĝ$_2$-mu-mu-kal-le
ki Tu-ra-am-^{d}Da-/gan-ta
rev. ^{d}Šul-gi-iri-/ĝu$_{10}$
šu ba-ti
iti ezem An-na
mu En-unu$_6$-gal / ^{d}Inana ba-huĝ
left 1 udu

138: SM 1911.03.172 (AS5 i 8)

obv. 6 sila$_4$
u$_4$ 8-kam
ki Ab-ba-sa$_6$-ga-/ta
rev. In-ta-e$_3$-a
i$_3$-dab$_5$
iti maš-da$_3$-gu$_7$
mu us$_2$-sa En-/mah-gal-an-na en / ^{d}Nanna ba-huĝ
left 6

Obv. 1: Cf. BIN 3 538 (AS 5 i 8).

139: SM 1911.03.173 (Š46 v 1)

obv. 1 udu niga
1 udu
2 sila$_4$ ga
ba-ug$_7$ u$_4$ 1-kam
rev. ki Na-lu$_5$-ta
Ur-ni$_9$-ĝar
šu ba-ti
iti ezem ^{d}Nin-a-zu
mu us$_2$-sa Ur-/bi$_2$-lum^{ki} / ba-hul

140: SM 1911.03.174 (AS6 x 25)

obv. 1 lulim munus
1 az
ba-ug$_7$
u$_4$ 25-kam
rev. ki Lu$_2$-diĝir-ra-ta
^{d}Šul-gi-iri-ĝu$_{10}$
šu ba-ti
iti ezem An-na
mu Ša-aš-ru^{ki} / ba-hul
left 2

141: SM 1911.03.175 (Š46 ii 15)

obv. 2 udu
2 u$_8$
1 ^{munus}aš$_2$-gar$_3$
ba-ug$_7$ u$_4$ 15-kam
rev. ki Na-lu$_5$-ta
Ur-ni$_9$-ĝar
šu ba-ti
iti šeš-da-gu$_7$
mu Ki-maš^{ki} u$_3$ Hu-/ur$_5$-ti^{ki} ba-hul

142: SM 1911.03.176 (-- v 1)

obv. 1 udu
1 sila$_4$

ba-ug$_7$ u$_4$ 1-kam
ki En-diĝir-ĝu$_{10}$-ta
rev. ^{d}Šul-gi-iri-ĝu$_{10}$
šu ba-ti
iti ezem ^{d}Nin-/a-zu
left 2

143: SM 1911.04.001 (-- iv)

obv. 1 ^{anše}si$_2$-si$_2$
Ib-ni-DIĜIR
i$_3$-dab$_5$
iti ki-siki ^{d}Nin-a-zu
rev. ====

144: SM 1911.04.002 (ŠS1 xiid 9)

obv. 6 udu 1 amar maš-da$_3$
ba-ug$_7$ e$_2$ muhaldim
u$_4$ 10-la$_2$-1-[kam]
2 amar ma[š-da$_3$]
2 amar [ ]
šu-g[id$_2$]
rev. u$_4$ 11-kam
==== (*seal*)
ki Du$_{11}$-ga-ta
ba-zi
iti diri še-KIN-ku$_5$
mu ^{d}Šu-^{d}EN.ZU / lugal
seal ^{d}Šu-^{d}EN.ZU
lugal kala-ga
lugal Uri$_5$^{ki}-ma
lugal an ub-da limmu$_2$-ba
Ur-^{d}Šul-pa-e$_3$
dub-sar
dumu Ur-^{d}Ha-ia$_3$
[arad$_2$-zu]

145: SM 1911.04.004 (ŠS9 v 4+)

obv. 1 gu$_4$ mu-3
5 u$_8$ u$_2$
4 ud$_5$ u$_2$
šu-gid$_2$ e$_2$ muhaldim
mu aga$_3$-us$_2$ u$_3$ lu$_2$ / šuku-ra-ke$_4$-ne-še$_3$
[Id]-ni-id sukkal maškim
rev. [u$_4$ x]+4-kam
[ki Ur]-ku$_3$-nun-na-ta
ba-zi
ĝiri$_3$ ^{d}Nanna-ma-ba
u$_3$ Hu-la-al
iti ki-siki ^{d}Nin-a-zu
mu ^{d}Šu-^{d}EN.ZU / lugal Uri$_5$[^{ki}-ma]-ke$_4$ / e$_2$ ^{d}Šara$_2$ Um[ma^{ki}]-/ka
mu-[du$_3$]
left 1 gu$_4$ 9 [udu]
seal ^{d}Šu-^{d}EN.ZU
lugal kala-ga
[ ]

Obv. 6: Cf. Ripon 1; MVN 2 154, i 4, 21 (IS2 xii 2-15).

146: SM 1911.04.005 (AS1 xii 27)

obv. 1 udu niga
1 u$_8$ niga
1 udu
1 u$_8$
1 sila$_4$
1 ud$_5$
3 sila$_4$ ga
rev. 3 kir$_{11}$ ga
ba-ug$_7$
u$_4$ 27-kam
ki Lu$_2$-diĝir-ra-ta
Ur-ni$_9$-ĝar
šu ba-ti
iti še-KIN-ku$_5$
mu ^{d}Amar-^{d}EN.ZU / lugal

147: SM 1911.04.006 (AS9 xii 1)

obv.	10-la$_2$-1 udu
	10 u$_8$
	1 ud$_5$
	ba-ug$_7$ e$_2$ muhaldim
	mu aga$_3$-us$_2$-e-ne-še$_3$
	u$_4$ 1-kam
	ki Du$_{11}$-ga-ta
rev.	ba-zi
	ĝiri$_3$ Nu-ur$_2$-^{d}IŠKUR / dub-sar
	iti še-KIN-ku$_5$
	mu en ^{d}Nanna / Kar-zi-da ba-huĝ
left	20
seal	Nu-ur$_2$-^{d}IŠKUR
	dumu Šu-^{d}IŠKUR
	kuš$_7$ lugal

148: SM 1911.04.012 (ŠS2 ii)

obv.	4 [udu]
	1 maš$_2$
	šu-gid$_2$
	<ki> Tah-ša-tal-ta
	Du$_{11}$-ga i$_3$-dab$_5$
rev.	kišib Ur-mes
	====
	iti šeš-da-gu$_7$
	mu ma$_2$-dara$_3$ / abzu [^{d}En-ki ba-du$_3$]
seal	Ur-mes
	dumu La-na kurušda

149: SM 1911.04.014 (AS9 xii 29)

obv.	2 [x]
	^{d}En-lil$_2$
	1 maš-da$_3$ munus
	^{d}Nin-lil$_2$
	u$_4$ 30-la$_2$-1-kam
rev.	ki In-ta-e$_3$-/a-ta ba-zi

====
iti še-KIN-ku$_5$
mu en ^{d}Nanna / Kar-zi-da ba-huĝ
seal ^{d}Amar-^{d}EN.ZU
lugal kala-ga
lugal Uri$_5$^{ki}-ma
lugal an ub-da limmu$_2$-ba
Ur-^{d}Šul-pa-e$_3$
dub-sar
dumu Ur-^{d}Ha-ia$_3$
arad$_2$-zu

150: SM 1911.04.015 (-- -- --)

obv. (*beginning damaged*)
[xx] dah
[xx] ta
(*ending damaged*)
rev. 1 gu$_4$ kišib Er$_3$-ra-ba-[ni]
20
ša$_3$-bi-ta
5 gu$_4$ Ur-e$_2$-an-na
1 gu$_4$ Ba-ba-ti
2 gu$_4$ DIĜIR-dan
1 gu$_4$ Lugal-dub-sar
1 gu$_4$ A-da-lal$_3$
4 gu$_4$ Ur-ku$_3$-nun-na
2 gu$_4$ Ur-^{d}Lamma
16
zi-ga-am$_3$
4 gu$_4$ ib$_2$-tak$_4$

151: SM 1911.10.002 (IS1 vii 2)

obv. 2 sila$_4$ niga / sig$_5$-us$_2$
^{d}Nanna
lugal ku$_4$-ra
u$_4$ 2-kam
ki In-ta-e$_3$-a-ta

rev. ba-zi
ĝiri$_3$ ^{d}Nanna-ma-/ba dub-sar
iti a$_2$-ki-ti
mu ^{d}I-bi$_2$-/^{d}EN.ZU lugal
left 2 udu
seal i [^{d}Šu-^{d}EN.ZU]
lugal kala-ga
lugal Uri$_5$/^{ki}-ma
lugal [an ub-da limmu$_2$-ba]
ii [^{d}Nanna-ma-ba]
[dub-sar]
dumu U$_2$-na-ab-[še-en$_6$]
[arad$_2$-zu]

152: SM 1911.10.003 (ŠS2 i)

obv. 5 sila$_4$
5 maš$_2$
ki A-hu-We-er-ta
Du$_{11}$-ga i$_3$-dab$_5$
rev. kišib Ur-mes
ĝiri$_3$ Ur-^{d}Lugal-/banda$_3$^{da}
iti maš-da$_3$-gu$_7$
mu ma$_2$-dara$_4$ abzu / ^{d}En-ki-ka ba-ab-du$_8$
seal Ur-mes
dumu La-na kurušda

153: SM 1911.10.004 (ŠS1 vii 19)

obv. 1 udu niga sig$_5$-[us$_2$]
1 udu niga 3-kam-[us$_2$]
1 maš$_2$ gal niga [2/3-kam-us$_2$]
^{d}En-lil$_2$
1 udu niga sig$_5$-us$_2$
1 udu niga 4-kam-us$_2$
1 maš$_2$ gal niga 3-kam-us$_2$
^{d}Nin-lil$_2$
rev. lugal ku$_4$-ra
iti u$_4$ 20-la$_2$-1 ba-zal

ki Tah-ša-tal-ta
ba-zi
iti ezem ^{d}Šul-gi
mu ^{d}Šu-^{d}EN.ZU / lugal
seal [^{d}Šu-^{d}EN.ZU]
lugal kala-ga
lugal Uri$_5$^{ki}-ma
lugal an ub-da limmu$_2$-ba
Ur-^{d}Šul-pa-e$_3$
dub-sar
dumu Ur-^{d}Ha-ia$_3$
[arad$_2$-zu]

154: SM 1911.10.006 (Š46 ii)

obv. 34 dusu$_2$ / munus
2 dusu$_2$ munus / mu-2
2 dusu$_2$ munus / amar [ga]
rev. mu-DU lugal
ĝiri$_3$ I-gi$_4$-ru-/mah
ki Na-ra-am-i$_3$-/li$_2$-ta
Lugal-an-na-ab-tum$_2$
i$_3$-dab$_5$
iti [šeš]-da-gu$_7$
m[u u]s$_2$-sa Ur-/bi$_2$-lum^{ki} ba-hul

This text is a duplicate of PDT 1 23 (Š46 ii).

155: SM 1911.10.007 (AS6 xi)

obv. 1 sila$_4$
ki Ab-ba-sa$_6$-/ga-ta
Mu-ur$_2$-di$_3$-gaba
i$_3$-dab$_5$
rev. iti ezem Me-ki-ĝal$_2$
==== (*seal*)
mu Ša-aš-ru^{ki} / ba-hul
seal (*illegible*)

156: SM 1911.10.008 (-- -- --)

obv. 1 sila$_4$
ki Ib-ni-DIĜIR-/ta
Ur-^{d}Nin-sa-za / i$_3$-dab$_5$
rev. ==== (*seal*)
seal i ^{d}Amar-^{d}EN.ZU
lugal kala-ga
lugal Uri$_5$/^{ki}-ma
lugal an ub-/da limmu$_2$-ba
ii Ur-^{d}Nin-sa-[za]
aga$_3$-us$_2$
dumu Da-[ ]
arad$_2$-[zu]

157: SM 1911.10.009 (AS2 xi)

obv. 2 gu$_4$
1 ab$_2$
1 amar gir mu-1
ba-ug$_7$
ki Ab-ba-sa$_6$-ga-/ta
Ur-ni$_9$-ĝar-ke$_4$
rev. [šu ba]-ti
====
iti ezem Me-ki-ĝal$_2$
mu ^{d}Amar-^{d}EN.ZU / lugal-e Ur-bi$_2$-lum^{ki} / mu-hul

158: SM 1911.10.011 (AS9 iv)

obv. 40 udu
20 maš$_2$-[gal]
e$_2$ ^{d}Al-[la]-/tum-m[a]
ki Ab-ba-sa$_6$-/ga-[ta]
[PN]
rev. [i$_3$-dab$_5$]
====
iti ki-siki ^{d}[Nin-a-zu]
mu en ^{d}[Nanna] / Kar-zi-da / ba-huĝ
left 60

159: SM 1911.10.012 (IS2 vii)

obv. 2 udu mu udu niga-še$_3$
ša$_3$ Uri$_5$^{ki}-ma
ĝiri$_3$ PU$_3$.ŠA-^{d}En-lil$_2$ / dumu Lugal-iti-da
ki In-ta-e$_3$-a-/ta
rev. gaba-ri
kišib Ab-ba-kal-la
====
iti a$_2$-ki-ti
mu en ^{d}Inana / maš$_2$-e i$_3$-pad$_3$

160: SM 1911.10.015 (AS9 iv 16)

obv. 2 udu 1 sila$_4$
Kur-ti-lum ra$_2$-gaba
ĝiri$_3$ Edin-e-ki-aĝ$_2$ / sukkal
Ur-^{d}Amar-^{d}EN.ZU / maškim
ša$_3$ mu-DU-ra-ta
rev. u$_4$ 16-kam
ki Ab-ba-sa$_6$-ga-/ta ba-zi
ĝiri$_3$ Nu-ur$_2$-^{d}EN.ZU / dub-sar
iti ki-siki ^{d}Nin-a-zu
mu en ^{d}Nanna / Kar-zi-da ba-huĝ
left 3

161: SM 1911.10.016 (AS2 ix 21)

obv. 4 dur$_3$
6 eme$_6$
8 šeg$_9$-bar nita$_2$
13 šeg$_9$-bar munus
15 udu hur-sag
20 u$_8$ hur-sag
rev. u$_4$ 21-kam
ki Ab-ba-sa$_6$-/ga-ta
Lu$_2$-diĝir-ra i$_3$-dab$_5$
iti ezem mah
mu ^{d}Amar-^{d}EN.ZU / lugal-e Ur-bi$_2$-/lum^{ki} mu-hul
left 66

162: SM 1911.10.017 (AS7 i)

obv. 1 sila$_4$
ki Ab-ba-sa$_6$-/ga-ta
Ur-^{d}En-gal-du-<du>
rev. i$_3$-dab$_5$
ĝiri$_3$ Lu$_2$-ša-lim
==== (*seal*)
iti maš-da$_3$-gu$_7$
mu us$_2$-sa Ša-aš-/ru^{ki} ba-hul
seal Ur-^{d}EN.ZU
šagina
BAD$_3$.AN^{ki} nu-banda$_3$

Seal 3: Cf. RA 13 21 7; Trouvaille 74.

163: SM 1911.10.018 (Š46 i)

obv. 170+[2 udu]
30 u$_8$
57 maš$_2$
šu-gid$_2$
ki Na-lu$_5$-ta
rev. mu-DU
Ur-ku$_3$-nun-na
i$_3$-dab$_5$
====
iti maš-da$_3$-gu$_7$
mu us$_2$-sa Ur-bi-/lum^{ki} ba-[hul]
left 260-la$_2$-1

164: SM 1911.10.019 (AS7 x 18)

obv. 1 gu$_4$
u$_4$ 18-kam
ki Ab-ba-sa$_6$-ga-/ta
Ur-šu-ga-lam-/ma
rev. i$_3$-dab$_5$
====

iti ezem An-na
mu Hu-uh$_2$-nu-ri/^{ki} ba-hul
left 1

165: SM 1911.10.020 (AS9 iii 28)

obv. 1 gu$_4$
u$_4$ 28-kam
ki Ab-ba-sa$_6$-/ga-ta
^{d}En-lil$_2$-la$_2$
i$_3$-dab$_5$
rev. ====
iti u$_5$-bi$_2$-gu$_7$
mu en ^{d}Nanna / Kar-zi-da ba-huĝ
left 1

166: SM 1911.10.021 (AS6 xi 24)

obv. 1 ud$_5$ maš$_2$ nu-a
1 sila$_4$
mu-DU Nir-i$_3$-da-ĝal$_2$
e$_2$ uz-ga
Ur-^{d}Ba-ba$_6$ maškim
1 udu gi$_6$ niga 1 gukkal niga
2 maš$_2$-gal niga 10-la$_2$-1 sila$_4$
A-bi$_2$-si$_2$-im-ti
rev. Šu-^{d}Nin-šubur / maškim
u$_4$ 24-kam
ki Ab-ba-sa$_6$-ga-/ta ba-zi
iti ezem Me-ki-ĝal$_2$
mu Ša-aš-ru^{ki} ba-/hul
left 15

For these animals, see CT 32 10 BM 103412 (= Nisaba 8 36), rev. i 6-17 (AS6 xi 24).

167: SM 1911.10.022 (AS7 ix)

obv. 35 udu niga gu$_4$-/e-us$_2$-sa
25 maš$_2$-gal niga / gu$_4$-e-[us$_2$-sa]

155 [ ]
95 [ ]
rev. ki Ab-ba-sa$_6$-ga-[ta]
En-diĝir-ĝu$_{10}$ i$_3$-dab$_5$
iti ezem mah
mu Hu-uh$_2$-nu-ri/^{ki} ba-hul
left 300+[10]

168: SM 1911.10.023 (IS2 v 8)

obv. 1 ab$_2$ u$_2$
šu-gid$_2$ e$_2$ muhaldim
mu lu$_2$ šuku-ra-ke$_4$-/ne-še$_3$
Arad$_2$-ĝu$_{10}$ maškim
u$_4$ 8-kam
rev. [ki PN]-ta
[ba]-zi
====
u$_3$
iti ki-siki ^{d}Nin-a-zu
mu en ^{d}Inana / Unug^{ki}-ga maš$_2$-e / i$_3$-pad$_3$
left 1 gu$_4$

169: SM 1911.10.024 (AS1 x --)

obv. 1 gu$_4$ e$_2$ muhaldim u$_4$ 3-kam
1 gu$_4$ u$_4$ 6-kam
1 gu$_4$ u$_4$ 12-kam
14 gu$_4$ 2 ab$_2$ u$_4$ 13-kam
2 gu$_4$ u$_4$ 18-kam
1 gu$_4$ u$_4$ 20-la$_2$-1-kam
11 gu$_4$ [u$_4$ x]-kam
(*ending damaged*)
rev. (*beginning damaged*)
šu-niĝin$_2$ 58 gu$_4$
šu-niĝin$_2$ 20 ab$_2$
zi-ga ki ^{d}En-lil$_2$-la$_2$
iti ezem An-na
mu ^{d}Amar-^{d}EN.ZU / lugal
left 78

170: SM 1911.10.025 (Š46 x)

obv. 157 udu
50 u$_8$
107 maš$_2$
[x]+3 ud$_5$
[x] sila$_4$ gaba
[ki N]a-lu$_5$-ta
rev. [Ur]-ku$_3$-nun-na
i$_3$-dab$_5$
====
iti ezem An-na
mu Ki-maš^{ki} / ba-hul
left 300+[x [udu]

171: SM 1911.10.026 (AS4 viii 1)

obv. 4 udu ĝiš-du$_3$ LU$_2$.SU.A
2 u$_8$ LU$_2$.SU
2 maš$_2$-gal LU$_2$.SU
u$_4$ 1-kam
ki Ab-ba-sa$_6$-ga-/ta
rev. A-hu-We-er i$_3$-dab$_5$
====
iti šu-eš$_5$-ša
mu En-mah-gal-an-/na en ^{d}Nanna / ba-huĝ
left 8

172: SM 1911.10.027 (AS8 x 24)

obv. 2 gu$_4$ šu-gid$_2$
u$_4$ 24-kam
ki Ab-ba-sa$_6$-ga-/ta
^{d}En-lil$_2$-la$_2$
rev. i$_3$-dab$_5$
====
iti ezem An-na
mu en Eridu^{ki} / ba-huĝ
left 2

173: SM 1911.10.028 (AS2 iv 16)

obv. 12 maš$_{2}$-gal gun$_{3}$-a
1 ^{munus}aš$_{2}$-gar$_{3}$ niga
u$_{4}$ 16-kam
mu-DU lugal
ki Ab-ba-sa$_{6}$-ga-/ta
rev. Lu$_{2}$-diĝir-ra
i$_{3}$-dab$_{5}$
iti ki-siki ^{d}Nin-a-/zu
mu ^{d}Amar-^{d}EN.ZU / lugal-e Ur-bi$_{2}$-/lum^{ki} mu-hul
left 13

174: SM 1911.10.029 (AS6 ix 1)

obv. 24 gu$_{4}$ niga
36 gu$_{4}$
3 ab$_{2}$
108 udu
31 udu LU$_{2}$.SU
120 maš$_{2}$-gal
rev. u$_{4}$ 1-kam
ki Ab-ba-sa$_{6}$-ga-/ta
Šu-Ma-ma
i$_{3}$-dab$_{5}$
iti ezem mah
mu Ša-aš-ru^{ki} / ba-hul
left 63 gu$_{4}$ 260-la$_{2}$-1 udu

175: SM 1911.10.030 (AS1 vii --)

obv. 3 gu$_{4}$
2 ab$_{2}$ mu-2
bala ensi$_{2}$ / Šuruppag^{ki}
u$_{4}$ [x-kam]
zi-[ga]
rev. ki ^{d}En-lil$_{2}$-[la$_{2}$]
====
iti ezem ^{d}Šul-/gi
mu ^{d}Amar-^{d}EN./ZU lugal
left 5

176: SM 1911.10.031 (AS6 vi 30)

obv. 30 udu
1 ud$_5$ maš$_2$ nu-a
u$_4$ 30-kam
ki Ab-ba-sa$_6$-ga-/ta
In-ta-e$_3$-a
rev. [i$_3$]-dab$_5$
====
iti a$_2$-ki-ti
mu Ša-aš-ru^{ki} / ba-hul
left 31

177: SM 1911.10.032 (AS6 xii 25)

obv. 3 udu
8 [x]
2 [x]
A-bi$_2$-si$_2$-[im-ti]
mu-DU u$_4$ [ ]
Šu-^{d}Nin-šubur / maškim
rev. u$_4$ 25-kam
ki Ab-ba-sa$_6$-/ga-ta
ba-zi
====
iti še-KIN-ku$_5$
mu Ša-aš-ru^{ki} ba-/hul
left 13

Obv. 5: Cf. mu-DU u$_4$ nu$_2$-a-ka-na ki-ba ba-na-a-ĝa$_2$-ar (P102197), or mu-DU u$_4$-sakar (P416441).

178: SM 1911.10.033 (AS1 x 9)

obv. 13 gu$_4$ niga
4 gu$_4$
u$_4$ 10-la$_2$-1-kam
ki Ab-ba-sa$_6$-ga-/ta
rev. Ur-šu-ga-lam-/ma
i$_3$-dab$_5$
iti ezem An-na
mu ^{d}Amar-^{d}EN.ZU / lugal

left 17

179: SM 1911.10.034 (AS6 viii 14)

obv. 12 ud$_5$ LU$_2$.SU
u$_4$ 14-kam
ki Ab-ba-sa$_6$-/ga-ta
Tu-ra-am-^{d}/Da-gan
rev. i$_3$-dab$_5$
====
iti šu-eš$_5$-ša
mu Ša-aš-ru^{ki} / ba-hul
left 12

180: SM 1911.10.035 (AS7 viii 5)

obv. 1 ^{munus}aš$_2$-gar$_3$ ša-ru-mi-/um
u$_4$ 5-kam
ki Ab-ba-sa$_6$-ga-/ta
Ta$_2$-hi-iš-a-tal
rev. i$_3$-dab$_5$
====
iti šu-eš$_5$-ša
mu Hu-uh$_2$-nu-ri/^{ki} ba-hul
left 1

181: SM 1911.10.036 (AS3 x 11)

obv. 12 udu
5 sila$_4$
8 maš$_2$
u$_4$ 11-kam
ki Ab-ba-sa$_6$-/ga-ta
rev. In-ta-e$_3$-a
i$_3$-dab$_5$
====
iti ezem An-na
mu ^{d}gu-za ^{d}En-/lil$_2$-la$_2$ ba-dim$_2$
left 25

182: SM 1911.10.037 (AS3 x 16)

obv. 4 udu niga
1 sila$_4$ niga
u$_4$ 16-kam
ki Ab-ba-sa$_6$-ga-/ta
Na-lu$_5$
rev. i$_3$-dab$_5$
====
iti ezem An-na
mu ^{d}gu-za ša$_3$-/hul$_2$-la ^{d}En-lil$_2$-la$_2$ / ba-dim$_2$
left 5

183: SM 1911.10.038 (Š46 iv)

obv. 10 u$_8$
ki I-di$_3$-^{d}EN.ZU-/ta
mu-DU
Ur-ku$_3$-nun-na
rev. i$_3$-dab$_5$
====
mu-DU
iti ki-siki ^{d}Nin-a-zu
mu Ki-maš^{ki} ba-hul

184: SM 1911.10.039 (-- -- 18)

obv. 22 gu$_4$
4 ab$_2$
8 udu
10 sila$_4$
171 maš$_2$ gal
1 maš$_2$
u$_4$ 18-kam
rev. (*all damaged*)
left 210+[6]

185: SM 1911.10.040 (AS6 iv 28)

obv. 3 sila$_4$
1 maš$_2$

u$_{4}$ 28-kam
ki Ab-ba-sa$_{6}$-/ga-ta
rev. In-ta-e$_{3}$-a / i$_{3}$-dab$_{5}$
iti ki-siki ^{d}Nin-/a-zu
mu Ša-aš-ru/^{ki} ba-hul
left 4

186: SM 1911.10.041 (AS1 ix 16)

obv. 2 gu$_{4}$ niga
10-la$_{2}$-1 gu$_{4}$
1 udu
1 sila$_{4}$
10-la$_{2}$-1 maš$_{2}$
rev. u$_{4}$ 16-kam
ki Ab-ba-sa$_{6}$-ga-/ta
A-hu-ni i$_{3}$-dab$_{5}$
iti ezem mah
mu ^{d}Amar-^{d}EN.ZU / lugal
left 22

187: SM 1911.10.042 (AS7 iii 25)

obv. 2 udu niga
u$_{4}$ 25-kam
ki Ab-ba-sa$_{6}$-/ga-ta
Šu-Ma-ma
rev. i$_{3}$-dab$_{5}$
====
iti u$_{5}$-bi$_{2}$-gu$_{7}$
mu Hu-uh$_{2}$-nu-ri/^{ki} ba-hul
left 2

188: SM 1911.10.043 (AS1 iii 16)

obv. 4 udu niga
1 sila$_{4}$ niga
u$_{4}$ 14-kam
3 udu niga

2 udu
u$_4$ 16-kam
rev. mu-DU
ki Na-sa$_6$-ta
A-hu-ni i$_3$-dab$_5$
====
iti u$_5$-bi$_2$-gu$_7$
mu ^{d}Amar-^{d}EN.ZU / lugal

189: SM 1911.10.044 (AS2 vi 14)

obv. 2 udu niga
u$_4$ 14-kam
ki Ab-ba-sa$_6$-ga-/ta
Na-lu$_5$ i$_3$-dab$_5$
rev. iti a$_2$-ki-ti
mu ^{d}Amar-^{d}EN.ZU / lugal-e Ur-bi$_2$-/lum^{ki} mu-hul
====
left 2

190: SM 1911.10.045 (AS8 ii 13)

obv. 6 ud$_5$ hur-saĝ
u$_4$ 13-kam
ki Lugal-amar-ku$_3$-ta
Ta$_2$-hi-iš-a-tal
i$_3$-dab$_5$
rev. ====
iti šeš-da-gu$_7$
mu En-nun-e-/^{d}Amar-^{d}EN.ZU-ra-/ki-aĝ$_2$ en / Eridu^{ki} ba-huĝ
left 6

191: SM 1911.10.046 (AS7 x 12)

obv. 5 gu$_4$
16 udu
2 maš$_2$-gal
u$_4$ 12-kam
ki Ab-ba-sa$_6$-ga-/ta

rev. In-ta-e$_3$-a
i$_3$-dab$_5$
====
iti ezem An-na
mu Hu-uh$_2$-/nu-ri^{ki} ba-hul
left 5 gu$_4$ 18 udu

192: SM 1911.10.047 (Š46 v)

obv. [x-la$_2$]-1 gu$_4$
4 ab$_2$
a$_2$-ĝi$_6$ il$_2$-la
ki Ur-sukkal-ta
mu-DU
rev. ^{d}En-lil$_2$-la$_2$
i$_3$-dab$_5$
====
iti ezem ^{d}Nin-a-/zu
mu [Ki]-maš^{ki} ba-/hul

193: SM 1911.10.048 (AS7 ix 8)

obv. 7 udu lu$_2$-ulu$_3$-um
16 maš$_2$-gal LU$_2$.SU
u$_4$ 8-kam
ki Ab-ba-sa$_6$-/ga-ta
rev. Na-lu$_5$ i$_3$-dab$_5$
====
iti ezem mah
mu Hu-uh$_2$-nu-/ri^{ki} ba-hul
left 23

194: SM 1911.10.049 (AS7 xii 18)

obv. 7 [udu]
1 maš$_2$-gal
u$_4$ 18-kam
ki Ab-ba-sa$_6$-ga-/ta
Na-lu$_5$

rev. i$_3$-dab$_5$
====
iti še-KIN-ku$_5$
mu Hu-uh$_2$-nu-/ri^{ki} ba-hul
left 8

195: SM 1911.10.050 (AS6 v 19)

obv. 1 maš$_2$
u$_4$ 20-la$_2$-1-kam
ki Ab-ba-sa$_6$-/ga-ta
In-ta-e$_3$-a
rev. i$_3$-dab$_5$
iti ezem ^{d}Nin-/a-zu
mu Ša-aš-ru/^{ki} ba-hul
left 1

196: SM 1911.10.051 (AS3 x 11)

obv. 3 udu niga
u$_4$ 11-kam
ki Ab-ba-sa$_6$-/ga-ta
Na-lu$_5$
rev. i$_3$-dab$_5$
====
iti ezem An-na
mu ^{d}gu-za / ^{d}En-lil$_2$-la$_2$ ba-/dim$_2$
left 3

197: SM 1911.10.052 (AS2 ix 25)

obv. 3 gu$_4$ niga
5 gu$_4$
158 udu
20 maš$_2$-gal
u$_4$ 25-[kam]
ki Ab-ba-sa$_6$-ga-/ta
rev. Lu$_2$-diĝir-ra / i$_3$-dab$_5$
====

	iti ezem mah
	mu ^{d}Amar-^{d}EN.ZU / lugal-e Ur-bi$_2$-/lum^{ki} mu-hul
left	186

198: SM 1911.10.053 (AS3 x 4)

obv.	2 u$_8$ 1 gukkal
	12 sila$_4$
	5 maš$_2$
	u$_4$ 4-kam
	ki Ab-ba-sa$_6$-/ga-ta
rev.	In-ta-e$_3$-a
	i$_3$-dab$_5$
	iti ezem An-na
	mu gu-za / ^{d}En-lil$_2$-la$_2$ ba-/dim$_2$
left	20

199: SM 1911.10.054 (AS2 v 10)

obv.	3 gu$_4$
	1 ab$_2$
	šu-gid$_2$
	e$_2$ muhaldim-še$_3$
	u$_4$ 10-kam
rev.	ki Ab-ba-sa$_6$-/ga-ta ba-zi
	iti ezem ^{d}Nin-a-zu
	mu ^{d}Amar-^{d}EN.ZU / lugal-e Ur-bi$_2$-/lum^{ki} mu-hul
left	4

200: SM 1911.10.057 (AS3 vi 10)

obv.	3 udu
	20 [x]
	(*ending damaged*)
rev.	(*beginning damaged*)
	u$_4$ 10-kam
	ki Ab-ba-sa$_6$-/ga-ta ba-zi
	iti a$_2$-ki-ti
	mu ^{d}gu-za ^{d}En-/lil$_2$-la$_2$ ba-dim$_2$
left	30

201: SM 1911.10.058 (Š47 xi)

obv. 2 gu$_4$
ki Ip-qu$_2$-ša-ta
^{d}En-lil$_2$-la$_2$ / i$_3$-dab$_5$
iti ezem Me-ki-ĝal$_2$
rev. ====
mu us$_2$-sa Ki-maš^{ki} / ba-hul
====

202: SM 1911.10.059 (AS7 ix 7)

obv. 1 udu aslum$_x$(A.LUM)
1 u$_8$ gukkal
u$_4$ 7-kam
ki Ab-ba-sa$_6$-ga-ta
Ta$_2$-hi-iš-a-tal
rev. i$_3$-dab$_5$
====
iti ezem mah
mu Hu-uh$_2$-nu-/ri^{ki} ba-hul
left 2

203: SM 1911.10.060 (AS6 viii 30)

obv. 2 gu$_4$
3 sila$_4$
1 maš$_2$
u$_4$ 30-kam
ki Ab-ba-sa$_6$-/ga-ta
rev. In-ta-e$_3$-a
i$_3$-dab$_5$
====
iti šu-eš$_5$-ša
mu Ša-aš-ru^{ki} / ba-hul
left 2 gu$_4$ 4 udu

204: SM 1911.10.061 (AS6 vi 13)

obv. 4 udu 11 sila$_4$
42 u$_8$ 10-la$_2$-1 kir$_{11}$ gub

1 maš$_2$ 5 maš$_2$ gub
u$_4$ 13-kam
ki Ab-ba-sa$_6$-/ga-ta
rev. In-ta-e$_3$-a / i$_3$-dab$_5$
iti a$_2$-ki-ti
mu Ša-aš-ru^{ki} / ba-hul
left 72

205: SM 1911.10.062 (AS7 v 13)

obv. 1 sila$_4$
u$_4$ 13-kam
ki Ab-ba-sa$_6$-ga-/ta
In-ta-e$_3$-a
rev. i$_3$-dab$_5$
====
iti ezem ^{d}Nin-a-zu
mu Hu-uh$_2$-/nu-ri^{ki} ba-hul
left 1

206: SM 1911.10.063 (AS3 v)

obv. 2 dusu$_2$ nita$_2$ / šu-gid$_2$
nam-ra-ak kur mar-tu
ki Ab-ba-sa$_6$-ga-/ta
rev. Šu-Er$_3$-ra
i$_3$-dab$_5$
====
iti ezem ^{d}Nin-a-zu
mu ^{d}gu-za ^{d}En-lil$_2$-la$_2$ / ba-dim$_2$

207: SM 1911.10.064 (AS4 viii 3)

obv. 3 gu$_4$
17 maš$_2$-gal / LU$_2$.SU
u$_4$ 3-kam
ki Ab-ba-sa$_6$-/ga-ta

rev. ^{d}Šul-gi-[a-a]-/ĝu$_{10}$ i$_{3}$-[dab$_{5}$]
iti šu-eš$_{5}$-ša
mu En-mah-gal-an-na en ^{d}/Nanna ba-huĝ
left 20

Cf. Ontario 1 110 (AS4 viii 3).

208: SM 1911.10.065 (AS2 ii 6)

obv. 1 am gu$_{4}$
u$_{4}$ 6-kam
ki Ab-ba-sa$_{6}$-ga-/ta
^{d}Šul-gi-a-a-ĝu$_{10}$
rev. i$_{3}$-dab$_{5}$
====
iti šeš-da-gu$_{7}$
mu Ur-bi$_{2}$-lum/^{ki} ba-hul
left 1

209: SM 1911.10.066 (Š46 ii 24)

obv. 40-la$_{2}$-1 udu
kaš-de$_{2}$-a / ^{d}En-lil$_{2}$-la$_{2}$
u$_{4}$ Ki-maš^{ki} ba-/hul-a
u$_{4}$ 24-kam
rev. zi-ga
bala A-mur-^{d}EN.ZU
ki Ur-ku$_{3}$-nun-na
====
iti šeš-da-gu$_{7}$
mu us$_{2}$-sa Ur-/bi$_{2}$-lum^{ki} ba-hul

210: SM 1911.10.067 (AS2 vi 29)

obv. 8 maš-da$_{3}$
u$_{4}$ 30-la$_{2}$-1-kam
ki Ab-ba-sa$_{6}$-ga-ta
Lu$_{2}$-^{d}Nanna / šabra i$_{3}$-dab$_{5}$
iti a$_{2}$-ki-ti

rev. mu ^{d}Amar-^{d}EN.ZU / lugal-e Ur-bi$_{2}$-/lum^{ki} mu-hul
====
left 8

211: SM 1911.10.068 (AS2 v 5)

obv. 3 gu$_{4}$
2 ab$_{2}$
1 gu$_{4}$ mu-1
šu-gid$_{2}$
e$_{2}$ muhaldim-še$_{3}$
u$_{4}$ 5-kam
rev. ki Ab-ba-sa$_{6}$-/ga-ta ba-zi
====
iti ezem ^{d}Nin-a-zu
mu ^{d}Amar-^{d}EN.ZU / lugal-e Ur-bi$_{2}$-/lum^{ki} mu-hul
left 6

212: SM 1911.10.069 (AS6 viii 21)

obv. 81 udu
u$_{4}$ 21-kam
ki Ab-ba-sa$_{6}$-/ga-ta
En-diĝir-ĝu$_{10}$
i$_{3}$-dab$_{5}$
rev. ====
iti šu-eš$_{5}$-ša
mu Ša-aš-ru^{ki} / ba-hul
left 81 udu

213: SM 1911.10.070 (AS3 x 8)

obv. 11 sila$_{4}$
2 maš$_{2}$
u$_{4}$ 8-kam
ki Ab-ba-sa$_{6}$-ga-ta
In-ta-e$_{3}$-a
rev. i$_{3}$-dab$_{5}$
====

iti ezem An-na
mu gu-za ^{d}/En-lil$_2$-la$_2$ ba-dim$_2$
left 13

214: SM 1911.10.071 (AS2 ii 22)

obv. 2 udu niga
u$_4$ 22-kam
ki Ab-ba-sa$_6$-/ga-ta
Na-lu$_5$
rev. i$_3$-dab$_5$
iti šeš-da-gu$_7$
mu ^{d}Amar-^{d}EN.ZU / lugal-e
Ur-bi$_2$-lum/^{ki} mu-hul

215: SM 1911.10.072 (AS4 i 1)

obv. 1 kir$_{11}$ niga
1 ^{munus}aš$_2$-gar$_3$ niga
u$_4$ 1-kam
ki Ab-ba-sa$_6$-/ga-ta
rev. Na-lu$_5$ i$_3$-dab$_5$
====
iti maš-da$_3$-gu$_7$
mu us$_2$-sa ^{d}/gu-za ^{d}En-lil$_2$-la$_2$ / ba-dim$_2$
left 2

216: SM 1911.10.073 (AS3 xii 11)

obv. 1 ^{munus}aš$_2$-gar$_3$ niga
u$_4$ 11-kam
ki Ab-ba-sa$_6$-ga-/ta
A-hu-We-er i$_3$-dab$_5$
rev. ====
iti še-KIN-ku$_5$
mu ^{d}gu-za ^{d}En-/lil$_2$-la$_2$ ba-dim$_2$
left 1

217: SM 1911.10.074 (AS6 xii 13)

obv. 3 gu$_4$ niga
u$_4$ 13-kam
ki Ab-ba-sa$_6$-/ga-ta
A-hu-We-er
rev. i$_3$-dab$_5$
====
iti še-KIN-ku$_5$
mu Ša-aš-ru^{ki} / ba-hul
left 3 gu$_4$

218: SM 1911.10.075 (AS7 viii 1)

obv. 1 sila$_4$
u$_4$ 1-kam
ki Ab-ba-sa$_6$-/ga-ta
In-ta-e$_3$-a
rev. i$_3$-dab$_5$
====
iti šu-eš$_5$-ša
mu Hu-uh$_2$-/nu-ri^{ki} ba-hul
left 1

This text is a duplicate of OIP 121 340 (AS7 viii 1).

219: SM 1911.10.076 (AS8 ii 25)

obv. 2 udu aslum$_x$(A.LUM)
u$_4$ 25-kam
ki Lugal-amar-ku$_3$-ta
U$_2$-ta$_2$-mi-šar-/ra-[am]
rev. i$_3$-dab$_5$
====
iti šeš-da-gu$_7$
mu en-nun-e-/^{d}Amar-^{d}EN.ZU-ra-/ki-aĝ$_2$ en Eridu/^{ki} ba-huĝ
left 2

220: SM 1911.10.078 (AS6 ii 2)

obv. 5 sila$_4$
u$_4$ 2-kam

ki Ab-ba-sa$_6$-/ga-ta
In-ta-e$_3$-a
rev. i$_3$-dab$_5$
iti šeš-da-gu$_7$
mu Ša-aš-ru/^{ki} ba-hul
left 5

221: SM 1911.10.079 (AS2 i 7)

obv. 1 amar maš-da$_3$
e$_2$ uz-ga
mu-DU Da-da / u$_3$-kul
Ur-^{d}Ba-ba$_6$ maškim
rev. 1 amar maš-da$_3$ ba-uš$_2$
e$_2$ kišib-ba-še$_3$
u$_4$ 7-kam
ki Ab-ba-sa$_6$-ga-ta / ba-zi
iti maš-da$_3$-gu$_7$
mu Ur-bi$_2$-lum^{ki} / ba-hul
left 2

222: SM 1911.10.080 (-- -- --)

obv. 1 udu niga Saĝ-da-na
1 udu IŠ ša$_3$ e$_2$-gal-ta
1 udu Maš-da-de$_2$-a
dam ensi$_2$-ka-/ta
rev. 3 udu niga sa$_2$-du$_{11}$
ĝiri$_3$ ^{d}Nin-šubur-/an-dul$_3$
2 udu niga Saĝ-da-na
ĝiri$_3$ A$_2$-na-na

Ur-^{d}Dumu-zi-da / kurušda nin i$_3$-dab$_5$
zi-ga Na-sa$_6$

223: SM 1911.10.081 (AS4 x 13)

obv. 5 gukkal
u$_4$ 13-kam

ki Ab-ba-sa$_6$-ga-/ta
A-hu-We-er
rev. i$_3$-dab$_5$
====
iti ezem An-na
mu En-mah-gal-/an-na en ^{d}Nanna / ba-huĝ
left 5

224: SM 1911.10.082 (AS3 i 23)

obv. 2 gu$_4$
u$_4$ 23-kam
ki Ab-ba-sa$_6$-ga-/ta
Lu$_2$-diĝir-ra
i$_3$-dab$_5$
rev. ====
iti maš-da$_3$-gu$_7$
mu ^{d}gu-za / ^{d}En-lil$_2$-la$_2$ ba-dim$_2$
left 2

225: SM 1911.10.083 (AS1 ix 25)

obv. 7 udu niga
1 sila$_4$ niga
ki Ab-ba-sa$_6$-ga-/ta
Na-lu$_5$ i$_3$-dab$_5$
rev. u$_4$ 25-kam
====
iti ezem mah
mu ^{d}Amar-^{d}EN./ZU lugal
left 8

226: SM 1911.10.084 (AS2 viii 24)

obv. 1 dusu$_2$ munus
u$_4$ 24-kam
ki Ab-ba-sa$_6$-/ga-ta
Šu-Er$_3$-ra
i$_3$-dab$_5$
rev. ====

iti šu-eš$_5$-ša
mu ^{d}Amar-^{d}EN.ZU / lugal-e
Ur-bi$_2$-lum^{ki} / mu-hul
left 1

227: SM 1911.10.085 (AS2 x 1)

obv. 17 udu niga
2 sila$_4$ niga
2 ^{munus}aš$_2$-gar$_3$ niga
u$_4$ 1-kam
ki Ab-ba-sa$_6$-ga-/ta
rev. Na-lu$_5$ i$_3$-dab$_5$
====
iti ezem An-na
mu ^{d}Amar-^{d}EN.ZU / lugal-e Ur-bi$_2$-/lum^{ki} mu-hul
left 21

228: SM 1911.10.086 (AS8 v 2)

obv. 18 udu
1 maš$_2$-gal
u$_4$ 2-kam
ki Lugal-amar-ku$_3$-ta
Na-lu$_5$
rev. i$_3$-dab$_5$
====
iti ezem ^{d}Nin-a-/zu
mu En-nun-e-^{d}Amar-^{d}EN.ZU-/ra-ki-aĝ$_2$ en Eridu^{ki} / ba-huĝ
left 20-la$_2$-1

229: SM 1911.10.087 (AS6 x 23)

obv. 10-la$_2$-1 sila$_4$
u$_4$ 23-kam
ki Ab-ba-sa$_6$-/ga-ta
In-ta-e$_3$-a
rev. i$_3$-dab$_5$
====

iti ezem An-na
mu Ša-aš-ru^{ki} / ba-hul
left 10-la$_2$-1 udu

230: SM 1911.10.088 (AS2 v 18)

obv. 2 udu niga
10 maš$_2$-gal
u$_4$ 18-kam
ki Ab-ba-sa$_6$-ga-/ta
rev. ^{d}Šul-gi-a-a-ĝu$_{10}$ i$_3$-dab$_5$
iti ezem ^{d}Nin-/a-zu
mu ^{d}Amar-^{d}EN.ZU / lugal-e Ur-bi$_2$-/lum^{ki} mu-hul
left 12

This text is a duplicate of P235687 (AS2 v 18). For these animals, see OLP 8 8 3 (AS 2 v 18).

231: SM 1911.10.089 (AS1 ix 26)

obv. 2 amar az
ki Ab-ba-sa$_6$-/ga-ta
Lu$_2$-diĝir-ra / dumu Arad$_2$-hul$_3$-la
rev. i$_3$-dab$_5$
u$_4$ 26-kam
====
iti ezem mah
mu ^{d}Amar-^{d}EN.ZU / lugal
left 2

232: SM 1911.10.090 (AS4 viii 14)

obv. 4 gu$_4$ niga 1 gu$_4$
u$_4$ 14-kam
ki Ab-ba-sa$_6$-ga-/ta
A-hu-We-er
rev. i$_3$-dab$_5$
====

iti šu-eš$_5$-ša

mu En-mah-gal-/[an]-na en ^{d}Nanna / ba-huĝ

left 5

233: SM 1911.10.091 (AS2 x)

obv. 5 dusu$_2$ nita$_2$

2 dusu$_2$ nita$_2$ / mu-2

2 dusu$_2$ munus

šu-gid$_2$

ki Ab-ba-sa$_6$-/ga-ta

rev. Šu-Er$_3$-ra / i$_3$-dab$_5$

====

iti ezem An-na

mu ^{d}Amar-^{d}EN./ZU lugal-e Ur-/bi$_2$-lum^{ki} / mu-hul

left 10-la$_2$-1

234: SM 1911.10.092 (AS4 iv 24)

obv. 1 gu$_4$

1 sila$_4$

u$_4$ 24-kam

ki Ab-ba-sa$_6$-/ga-ta

rev. A-hu-We-er / i$_3$-dab$_5$

iti ki-siki ^{d}Nin-/a-zu

mu En-mah-gal-/an-na en ^{d}Nanna / ba-huĝ

left 2

235: SM 1911.10.093 (AS1 xi 10)

obv. 1 gu$_4$ niga

5 udu

u$_4$ 10-kam

ki Ab-ba-sa$_6$-/ga-ta

rev. ^{d}Šul-gi-/a-a-ĝu$_{10}$ i$_3$-dab$_5$

====

iti ezem Me-ki-ĝal$_2$

mu ^{d}Amar-^{d}EN.ZU / lugal

left 6

236: SM 1911.10.094 (AS7 vii 21)

obv. 3 sila$_4$
u$_4$ 21-kam
ki Ab-ba-sa$_6$-ga-/ta
In-ta-e$_3$-a
rev. i$_3$-dab$_5$
====
iti ezem ^{d}Šul-gi
mu Hu-uh$_2$-nu-ri/^{ki} ba-hul
left 3

237: SM 1911.10.095 (AS4 viii 8)

obv. 4 udu niga
u$_4$ 8-kam
ki Ab-ba-sa$_6$-/ga-ta
rev. En-diĝir-ĝu$_{10}$ i$_3$-dab$_5$
====
iti šu-eš$_5$-ša
mu En-mah-gal-/an-na en ^{d}Nanna / ba-huĝ
left 4

This text is a duplicate of Nisaba 8 307 (AS4 viii 8).

238: SM 1911.10.096 (AS4 iv 7)

obv. 3 sila$_4$
u$_4$ 7-kam
ki Ab-ba-sa$_6$-/ga-ta
In-ta-e$_3$-[a]
rev. i$_3$-dab$_5$
iti ki-siki ^{d}Nin-/a-zu
mu en ^{d}Nanna / ba-huĝ
left 3

This text is a duplicate of BPOA 7 2685 (AS4 iv 7).

239: SM 1911.10.097 (Š47 viii 12)

obv. 1 gu$_4$

u$_4$ 12-kam
mu-DU lugal
^{d}En-lil$_2$-la$_2$
rev. i$_3$-dab$_5$
====
iti šu-eš-ša
mu us$_2$-sa Ki-maš/^{ki} ba-hul

240: SM 1911.10.098 (AS1 vii 22)

obv. 1 sila$_4$
^{d}En-lil$_2$
1 sila$_4$ ^{d}Nin-lil$_2$
ku$_6$-da ku$_x$(KWU147)-ra
rev. Hi-ir-zum sagi / maškim
u$_4$ 22-kam
====
šu-niĝin$_2$ 2 sila$_4$
bala
ki Na-sa$_6$-ta ba-zi
iti ezem ^{d}Šul-gi
mu ^{d}Amar-^{d}EN.ZU / lugal
left 2

241: SM 1911.10.099 (AS2 v 7)

obv. 1 gukkal
u$_4$ 7-kam
ki Ab-ba-sa$_6$-/ga-ta
^{d}Šul-gi-/a-a-ĝu$_{10}$
rev. i$_3$-dab$_5$
====
iti ezem ^{d}Nin-a-/zu
mu ^{d}Amar-^{d}EN.ZU / lugal-e Ur-bi$_2$-/lum^{ki} mu-hul
left 1

242: SM 1911.10.101 (Š47 viii 17)

obv. 12 udu

20-la$_2$-1 u$_8$
3 maš$_2$
1 ud$_5$
e$_2$ muhaldim
rev. 1 maš$_2$ Šu-^{d}IŠKUR
u$_4$ 17-kam
zi-ga ki Ur-ku$_3$-nun-na
iti šu-eš$_5$-ša
mu us$_2$-sa Ki-maš^{ki} / ba-hul

243: SM 1911.10.102 (AS6 vi 14)

obv. 1 sila$_4$
u$_4$ 14-kam
ki Ab-ba-sa$_6$-ga-ta
In-ta-e$_3$-a
rev. i$_3$-dab$_5$
====
iti a$_2$-ki-ti
mu Ša-aš-ru^{ki} / ba-hul
left 1

244: SM 1911.10.103 (Š47 vi 16)

obv. 1 gu$_4$
u$_4$ 16-kam
mu-DU lugal
^{d}En-lil$_2$-la$_2$
rev. i$_3$-dab$_5$
====
iti a$_2$-ki-ti
mu us$_2$-sa Ki-maš/^{ki} ba-hul

245: SM 1911.10.104 (Š47 viii 9)

obv. 10 gu$_4$
4 ab$_2$
e$_2$ muhaldim
u$_4$ 10-la$_2$-1-kam

zi-ga
rev. ki ^{d}En-lil$_2$-la$_2$
iti šu-eš-ša
mu us$_2$-sa / Ki-maš^{ki} ba-hul(IGI./UR)

246: SM 1911.10.105 (-- vii 4)

obv. 38 udu
3 u$_8$
15 maš$_2$
34 ud$_5$
rev. e$_2$ muhaldim
u$_4$ 4-kam
zi-ga
ki Ur-ku$_3$-nun-na
iti ezem ^{d}Šul-/gi

247: SM 1911.10.106 (Š47 ix 7)

obv. 11 udu
20-la$_2$-1 u$_8$
3 maš$_2$
8 ud$_5$
e$_2$ muhaldim
rev. [u$_4$] 7-kam
zi-ga
ki Ur-ku$_3$-nun-na
iti ezem mah
mu us$_2$-sa Ki-maš/^{ki} ba-hul

Obv. 1-4: For these animals, see BIN 3 511 (Š47 ix 7).

248: SM 1911.10.107 (AS4 xii 10)

obv. 4 udu niga gu$_4$-e-/us$_2$-sa
u$_4$ 10-kam
ki Ab-ba-sa$_6$-ga-/ta
rev. Na-lu$_5$ i$_3$-dab$_5$
====

iti še-KIN-ku$_5$
mu en ^{d}Nanna / ba-huĝ
left 4

249: SM 1911.10.108 (Š47 ix 11)

obv. 11 sila$_4$
52 u$_8$
3 maš$_2$
6 ud$_5$
e$_2$ muhaldim
rev. u$_4$ 11-kam
zi-ga
ki Ur-ku$_3$-nun-na
iti ezem mah
mu us$_2$-sa Ki-maš/^{ki} ba-hul

250: SM 1911.10.109 (AS2 vi)

obv. [33] gu$_4$
16 ab$_2$
410-la$_2$-1 udu
495 u$_8$
458 maš$_2$
357 ud$_5$
1768
ib$_2$-tak$_4$
3 gu$_4$ ki ^{d}Utu-ul$_4$-gal-/ta
====
saĝ-niĝ$_2$-gur$_{11}$-ra-kam
ša$_3$-bi-ta
36 gu$_4$
16 ab$_2$
rev. 52
kišib ^{d}En-lil$_2$-la$_2$
391 udu
496 u$_8$
468 maš$_2$
356 ud$_5$
1711

kišib Ur-ku$_3$-nun-na
----
zi-ga-am$_3$
la$_2$-ia$_3$ 7 u$_8$
la$_2$-ia$_3$ 1 ud$_5$
====
[ib$_2$-tak$_4$] niĝ$_2$-ka$_9$-ak
ĝiri$_3$ In-ta-e$_3$-a
iti a$_2$-ki-ti
mu ^{d}Amar-^{d}EN.ZU lugal-e / [Ur-bi$_2$-lu]m^{ki} mu-hul
left ĝiri$_3$ In-ta-e$_3$-a

251: SM 1911.10.110 (AS2 vii)

obv. 71 gu$_4$ niga
63 gu$_4$
7 ab$_2$
605 udu
720 u$_8$
422 maš$_2$
403 ud$_5$
2291
ib$_2$-tak$_4$
1 gu$_4$ 20 udu ki In-ta-e$_3$(UD./DU)-a-ta
====
saĝ-niĝ$_2$-gur$_{11}$-ra-kam ša$_3$-bi-ta
64 gu$_4$
7 ab$_2$
71
rev. kišib ^{d}En-lil$_2$-la$_2$
25 gu$_4$ niga
Ur-šu-ga-lam-ma en$_3$-/bi tar-re-dam
3 gu$_4$ niga zabar-dab$_5$
ĝiri$_3$ Ba-za
60 gu$_4$ niga 633 udu
720 u$_8$ 421 maš$_2$
403 ud$_5$
2180
kišib Ur-ku$_3$-nun-na
35 gu$_4$ niga e$_2$ gu$_4$ niga-še$_3$

zi-ga lugal
====
zi-ga-am$_3$
la$_2$-ia$_3$ 8 gu$_4$ niga
ib$_2$-tak$_4$ niĝ$_2$-ka$_9$-ak
iti ezem ^{d}Šul-gi
mu ^{d}Amar-^{d}EN.ZU lugal-e / Ur-bi$_2$-lum^{ki} mu-hul
left ĝiri$_3$ In-ta-e$_3$-a

252: SM 1911.10.114 (-- -- 19)

obv. 110-la$_2$-1 maš$_2$ gal
3 gu$_4$ niga
Tah-hi-ša-tal i$_3$-dab$_5$
15 udu 10 maš$_2$ gal

Na-lu$_5$ i$_3$-dab$_5$
10 gu$_4$ niga 11 gu$_4$
1 gu$_4$ (erased)

Ur-tur i$_3$-dab$_5$
11 udu šu-la$_2$-a
ĝiri$_3$ KA.KA-u$_2$
----
62 udu 3 maš$_2$ gal mu Lu$_2$-^{d}Nanna-še$_3$
ĝiri$_3$ Ur-^{d}Nanše
2 gu$_4$ niga Lu$_2$-^{d}Nanna šabra
5 gu$_4$ niga Lu$_2$-Ma$_2$-gan-na ab$_2$ 2-ta
3 gu$_4$ niga A-bu-DIĜIR ab$_2$ 2
2 gu$_4$ niga ensi$_2$ Šuruppag^{ki} ab$_2$ 2
2 gu$_4$ niga I-di$_3$-^{d}Da-gan ab$_2$ 2
2 gu$_4$ niga mu i$_3$-bi-lum / Igi-^{d}En-lil$_2$-še$_3$
102 udu bar-ĝal$_2$ Unug^{ki}-še$_3$
10 maš$_2$ Lu$_2$-Ma$_2$-gan-na
21 udu 5 maš$_2$ šu-gid$_2$
10-la$_2$-1 gu$_4$ [ ] / Uri$_5$^{ki}-ma
rev. 203 gu$_4$ / 420 udu
ša$_3$-bi-ta
14 16 gu$_4$ niga 1 ab$_2$ niga

41 gu$_4$ 10 ab$_2$
15 udu 10 maš$_2$ gal
67 gu$_4$ 25 udu
Zu-ba-ga i$_3$-dab$_5$
14 16 gu$_4$ niga 1 ab$_2$ niga
42 gu$_4$ 4 ab$_2$
16 udu 10 maš$_2$ gal

Igi-^{d}En-lil$_2$-še$_3$ i$_3$-dab$_5$
3 gu$_4$ niga
U$_2$-ta$_2$-mi-šar-am i$_3$-dab$_5$
left u$_4$ 20-la$_2$-1

253: SM 1911.10.115 (-- -- --)

obv. 20 gu$_4$ niga ab$_2$-2-ta ki-ba ĝa$_2$-ĝa$_2$
16 gu$_4$
ki Ur-šu-ga-lam-ma-ta
32 gu$_4$ niga ab$_2$-2-ta ki-ba ĝa$_2$-ĝa$_2$
5 gu$_4$
[x gu$_4$ niga ab$_2$-2-ta] ki-ba ĝa$_2$-ĝa$_2$
[ ] 5 sila$_4$
(*ending damaged*)
rev. [ ] 7 udu
[x]+5 maš$_2$
[ ]-^{d}Utu i$_3$-dab$_5$
3 ab$_2$ 83 udu
8 sila$_4$ 10 maš$_2$
Gu$_3$-de$_2$-a i$_3$-dab$_5$
4 ab$_2$ 2 udu
1 sila$_4$
Ur-^{d}Ba-ba$_6$ i$_3$-dab$_5$
20 ab$_2$ 112 udu
3 sila$_4$ 51 maš$_2$
Ip-hur i$_3$-dab$_5$
46 ab$_2$ 236 udu
13 sila$_4$ 340-la$_2$-1 maš$_2$
Lu$_2$-^{d}Utu i$_3$-dab$_5$
1 ab$_2$ 2 udu
24 maš$_2$

Šu-E$_2$-a i$_3$-dab$_5$
23 ab$_2$ 41 udu
23 sila$_4$ 70 maš$_2$
Šu-^{d}Dumu-zi i$_3$-dab$_5$
3 udu 10 maš$_2$ gu-za-la$_2$ / nu-tuku

šu-niĝin$_2$ 156 ab$_2$ 916 udu
šu-niĝin$_2$ 51 sila$_4$ 550-la$_2$-1 maš$_2$

254: SM 1911.10.117 (-- -- --)

obv.

i [x] gu$_4$ niga
[x] ab$_2$ mu-2 niga
[x]+8 gu$_4$
4 ab$_2$ mu-2
1 dusu$_2$ munus mu-/2
307 udu niga
284 udu
231 sila$_4$
25 u$_8$
8 kir$_{11}$
26 ud$_5$ maš$_2$ nu-a
13 ud$_5$
10 ^{munus}aš$_2$-gar$_3$
206 maš$_2$
bala-a zi-ga
11 udu niga
mu mu-du-lum / u$_3$ uzu-had$_2$-še$_3$
10 sila$_4$
gu-gu-tum-še$_3$
====
šu-niĝin$_2$ 50 gu$_4$ niga
šu-niĝin$_2$ 32 gu$_4$
šu-niĝin$_2$ 1 dusu$_2$
šu-niĝin$_2$ 318 udu niga
šu-niĝin$_2$ 558 / udu
ii šu-niĝin$_2$ 255 maš$_2$
1214 ====
ša$_3$-bi-ta

3 gu$_4$ niga
2 gu$_4$
3 ab$_2$ mu-2
43 udu niga
34 udu
37 sila$_4$
3 kir$_{11}$
4 ^{munus}aš$_2$-gar$_3$
20-la$_2$-1 maš$_2$
bala u$_4$ 4 šabra / ^{d}En-ki gu$_4$ udu-bi / ki In-ni-ta
25 gu$_4$ niga
3 ab$_2$ mu-2 niga
17 gu$_4$
1 dusu$_2$ munus mu-/2
170-la$_2$-1 udu niga
126 udu
157 sila$_4$
15 u$_8$
16 ud$_5$ maš$_2$ nu-a
[ ] maš$_2$
iii bala u$_4$ 16 šabra / ^{d}Nanna
5 gu$_4$ niga
1 ab$_2$ mu-2 niga
3 gu$_4$
32 udu niga
44 udu
18 sila$_4$
5 u$_8$
6 ud$_5$
11 maš$_2$
bala u$_4$ 3 šabra / ^{d}Nin-gal
4 gu$_4$ niga
1 ab$_2$ mu-2 niga
2 gu$_4$
27 udu niga
33 udu
18 sila$_4$
5 u$_8$
3 ud$_5$ maš$_2$ nu-a
11 maš$_2$

bala u$_4$ 2 1/2 šabra / An-na
4 gu$_4$ niga
1 ab$_2$ mu-2 niga
2 gu$_4$
27 udu niga
32 udu
5 sila$_4$
3+[x] kir$_{11}$
rev.
iv 3 ud$_5$ maš$_2$ nu-a
[ ] ud$_5$
[ ] maš$_2$
[bala u$_4$ x] šabra
(*some lines damaged*)
[ ] maš$_2$
[bala u$_4$ x] šabra / ^{d}En-ki
====
v (*all damaged*)
vi (*beginning damaged*)
u$_4$ [ ]
iti [ ]
mu [ ]

255: SM 1911.10.118 (AS5 xii)

obv. 80 udu Gu$_3$-de$_2$-a
200 sila$_4$ Ur-^{d}[ ]-ta
[x]+46 udu ki DU$_{10}$-i$_3$-li$_2$-ta
[x]+7 udu ki U-bar-ta
[x]+2 udu mu-DU lugal
[x] sila$_4$ ki sipa-e-ne-ta
492
[ša$_3$-bi]-ta
[x]+24 udu e$_2$ muhaldim-še$_3$
[x] udu Uri$_5$^{ki}-[ma]
[x] udu zi-ga lu[gal]
[ ] ĝiri$_3$ Ur-[ ]
[ ]
(*ending damaged*)

rev. (*beginning damaged*)
====
ki-be$_2$ gi$_4$-a
Ur-ku$_3$-nun-na
iti še-KIN-ku$_5$
mu [En]-unu$_6$-gal ^{d}/Inana ba-huĝ

256: SM 1911.10.119 (-- -- --)

obv. (*beginning damaged*)
i 30 udu An-ne$_2$-mu
1 udu Bi$_2$-zi
16 udu Lu$_2$-^{d}Utu
11 udu Uš-mu
1 udu Za-ti-ru-um
2 udu Lugal-ezem / gala
2 udu Lu$_2$-diĝir-ra / nagar!(GU)
1 udu Ur-PAP.PAP
[ ] Ur-^{d}IŠKUR unu$_3$
[ ] Lu$_2$-sa$_6$-ga
(*ending damaged*)
ii (*beginning damaged*)
1 udu Ur-^{d}[ ]
1 udu Ra-[ ]
1 udu UN-[ ]
1 udu DIĜIR-[ ]
1 udu Lu$_2$-[ ]
1 udu Da-[ ]
3 udu Ur-[ ]
2 udu [ ]
(*ending damaged*)
rev. (*all damaged*)

257: SM 1911.10.120 (Š33 ii)

obv. 1 gu$_2$ uruda
ki Šu-ku$_8$-bu-um-ma-t[a]
E$_2$-saĝ-da-na
Nibru^{ki}-ka-še$_3$
i$_3$-im-de$_6$-a

[x] ^{d}Nin-hur-saĝ-ka / ba-an-ku$_{x}$(KWU147)-ra
[ ]-ba saĝ 1 ma-na
[ ] gin$_{2}$ i$_{3}$-ĝal$_{2}$
rev. ĝiri$_{3}$ ^{d}Utu-ul$_{4}$-gal
u$_{3}$ Ṣe-bi
ša$_{3}$ Iri-saĝ-rig$_{7}$/^{ki}
----
iti šeš-da-gu$_{7}$
mu us$_{2}$-sa a-ra$_{2}$ [3-kam-aš] / [Si-mu-ru]-um^{ki} ba-[hul]

258: SM 1911.10.123 (AS3 ii 28)

obv. 10-la$_{2}$-1 udu 3 [sila$_{4}$] 3 maš$_{2}$ e$_{2}$ muhaldim
u$_{4}$ [x]-kam
2 udu $^{[d]}$Šul-gi
5 udu 5 sila$_{4}$ e$_{2}$ muhaldim
u$_{4}$ 6-kam
2 udu Si-mu
u$_{4}$ 7-kam
2 sila$_{4}$ 16 ud$_{5}$ e$_{2}$ muhaldim
u$_{4}$ 8-kam
6 udu 4 sila$_{4}$ 10-la$_{2}$-1 ud$_{5}$
e$_{2}$ muhaldim u$_{4}$ 10-la$_{2}$-1-kam
5 udu 5 maš$_{2}$ e$_{2}$ [muhaldim]
u$_{4}$ 10-[kam]
5 udu 10 u$_{8}$ e$_{2}$ [muhaldim]
u$_{4}$ 11-[kam]
5 udu 5 m[aš$_{2}$ e$_{2}$ muhaldim]
u$_{4}$ [x-kam]
15 udu [e$_{2}$ muhaldim]
u$_{4}$ [x-kam]
rev. (*beginning damaged*)
[x] udu [ ]
3 u$_{8}$ 2 [ ]
u$_{4}$ 10+[x-kam]
4 udu 6 sila$_{4}$ [u$_{4}$ x-kam]
3 sila$_{4}$ u$_{4}$ 10+[x-kam]
2 udu Uri$_{5}$^{ki}-[ma]
15 u$_{8}$ 5 sila$_{4}$ u$_{4}$ 20+[x-kam]

10 u$_8$ 10 ud$_5$ u$_4$ 28-kam
30-la$_2$-1 udu sa$_2$-du$_{11}$ ^{d}Gu-la
30-la$_2$-1 udu ba-ug$_7$ kišib DIĜIR-ba-ni
5 udu sa$_2$-du$_{11}$ Inim-^{d}Nanna

šu-niĝin$_2$ [x] udu 115 u$_8$
šu-niĝin$_2$ [x maš$_2$] 110-la$_2$-1 ud$_5$
[zi-ga ki Ur-ku$_3$]-nun-na
iti šeš-[da]-gu$_7$
mu gu-za [^{d}En-lil$_2$-la$_2$] ba-dim$_2$
left 360

259: SM 1911.10.124 (-- -- --)

obv.
i (*beginning damaged*)
[x] udu niga [ ]
^{d}Nin-[ ]
[x udu] niga 1 sila$_4$
$^{[d]}$Nin-PA
[x] udu niga 1 sila$_4$
[ka$_2$] ĝi$_6$-par$_4$
[x udu] niga 1 sila$_4$
[k]a i$_7$ ku$_3$-ga
[x] udu niga 1 sila$_4$
[k]un i$_7$ ku$_3$-ga
[x sil]a$_4$ An
[x si]la$_4$ ^{d}Uraš
(*ending damaged*)
ii (*beginning damaged*)
1 gu$_4$ niga 2 [ ]
1 sila$_4$ ^{d}En-[ ]
1 udu An

ša$_3$ Eridu$^{[ki]}$
1 gu$_4$ niga 2 udu niga [ ]
1 sila$_4$ ^{d}Nin-[ ]
1 gu$_4$ niga 2 udu niga [ ]
1 sila$_4$ AN [ ]
1 udu niga 1 udu [ ]
(*ending damaged*)

rev.

iii [ ]

1 gu$_4$ niga 2 [ ]

1 sila$_4$ [ ]

1 udu NI-DA-[ ]

1 gu$_4$ niga 2 udu niga [ ]

1 sila$_4$ ^{d}Nanna

1 gu$_4$ niga 2 udu niga [ ]

1 sila$_4$ ^{d}Nin-[ ]

ša$_3$ Uri$_5$$^{[ki]}$

====

šu-niĝin$_2$ 5 gu$_4$ niga [ ]

(*ending damaged*)

iv [ša$_3$]^{ki}

[šu-niĝin$_2$ x] gu$_4$ niga 6 udu niga

[šu-niĝin$_2$] 5 udu 3 sila$_4$

[ša$_3$] Uri$_5$^{ki}

====

[x]+1 gu$_4$ niga

(*ending damaged*)

260: SM 1911.10.125 (-- -- --)

obv.

i (*all damaged*)

ii (*beginning damaged*)

[ ]-ru-/um^{ki}

====

iii (*beginning damaged*)

[x] gu$_4$ ni[ga]

4 udu niga sig$_5$

20 udu

SUHUŠ-ki-in

3 gu$_4$ niga

rev.

iv 30 udu

Šu-Eš$_{18}$-tar$_2$

2 gu$_4$ niga
20 udu

(*ending damaged*)
v 3 gu$_4$ niga
30 udu

Ur-ni$_9$-ĝar-/ka$_2$-^{d}Šara$_2$
[x] gu$_4$ niga
(*ending damaged*)
vi [Ṣe]-lu-uš-/[$^{(d)}$D]a-gan
[ ] niga
[ ] udu
(*ending damaged*)

Rev. v 3: Cf. Ur-ni$_9$-ĝar-ni$_3$-lagar lunga (BPOA 1 791, 2); Ur-ni$_9$-ĝar-A-pi$_4$-sal$_4$^{ki} (BPOA 7 1584, 4).

261: SM 1911.10.126 (-- -- --)
obv.
i (*beginning damaged*)
2 udu u$_2$
[eri]n$_2$ Zag-tum^{ki}

[ ] Šeš-kal-la
[x] udu u$_2$
[ ]-^{d}IŠKUR
ii (*beginning damaged*)
10 [ ]-ti-a
10 udu u$_2$ U$_3$-ze$_2$-e
nu-banda$_3$-me
10 gu$_4$ u$_2$
100 udu u$_2$
erin$_2$ Lu-lu-bu^{ki}
rev.
iii 10 gu$_4$ u$_2$ / 500 udu u$_2$
ugula Ri-im-DIĜIR
380 udu u$_2$
Lu$_2$-kala-ga

20 udu u$_2$ Dan-^{d}Šul-gi
10 udu u$_2$ Ša-ab-ša-mi$_2$-um
10 udu u$_2$ Ša-ki-im-[ ]
(*ending damaged*)
iv [x] gu$_4$ u$_2$ 30 udu u$_2$
[x]-la-ak
[ ] u$_2$ Nu-ur$_2$-Eš$_{18}$-tar$_2$ nu-banda$_3$
[x] gu$_4$ u$_2$
[x] udu u$_2$
[erin$_2$] Ša-um-mi^{ki}
[x] 4 gu$_4$ u$_2$ [x] udu u$_2$
(*ending damaged*)

262: SM 1911.10.128 (Š42 xii)

obv. 33 udu e$_2$ muhaldim u$_4$ 2-kam
11 udu u$_4$ 3-kam
28 udu u$_4$ 6-kam
14 udu u$_4$ 7-kam
8 udu u$_4$ 10-la$_2$-1-kam
10 udu u$_4$ 10-kam
20 udu u$_4$ 11-kam
3 udu u$_4$ 12-kam
20 udu u$_4$ 13-kam
5 udu u$_4$ 14-kam
30 udu u$_4$ 17-kam
10 udu u$_4$ 20-la$_2$-1-kam
20 udu u$_4$ 20-kam
30 udu u$_4$ 21-kam
10 udu u$_4$ 22-kam
20 udu u$_4$ 23-kam
10 udu u$_4$ 23+[x-kam]
(*ending damaged*)
rev. (*beginning damaged*)
10 u[du u$_4$ x-kam]
30 udu [u$_4$ x-kam]
20 udu [u$_4$ x-kam]
20 udu u$_4$ [x]-kam
e$_2$ muhaldim

30 udu sa$_2$-du$_{11}$ ^{d}Gu-[la]
30 udu mu ur-ra-še$_3$
12 udu sa$_2$-du$_{11}$ gu!(AN)-ru-ru
101 udu ba-ug$_7$
====
zi-ga
Ur-ku$_3$-nun-na
iti še-KIN-ku$_5$
mu Ša-aš-ru^{ki} ba-hul
====
left 555 udu

263: SM 1911.10.133 (Š46 iii)

obv. 116 [udu]
3 gukkal
23 u$_8$
35 maš$_2$
e$_2$ muhaldim-še$_3$
5 udu ĝiri$_3$ A-hu-ni
2 udu ĝiri$_3$ Ur-^{d}Dumu-zi
1 udu ĝiri$_3$ Lu$_2$-^{d}Utu
rev. 2 udu mu-DU Ur-^{d}En-lil$_2$-la$_2$
1 udu ĝiri$_3$ Ba-ir
Ab-ba-sa$_6$-ga i$_3$-dab$_5$
2 sila$_4$ sa$_2$-du$_{11}$ Ur-^{d}Dumu-/zi-da i$_3$-dab$_5$
5 udu lu$_2$-Ma-ri$_2$^{ki}
1 udu ša$_3$ Unug^{ki}
====
šu-niĝin$_2$ [138] udu 23 u$_8$
šu-niĝin$_2$ 30+[5] maš$_2$
šu-gid$_2$ ki Na-lu$_5$-ta
mu-DU iti u$_5$-b[i$_2$-gu$_7$]
mu Ki-maš^{ki} ba-[hul]
left 196

264: SM 1911.10.135 (ŠS1 xii 28)

obv. 10 udu 23 sila$_4$

10 u$_8$ 33 ud$_5$
4 ud$_5$ maš$_2$ nu-a
mu bala ensi$_2$ Ĝir$_2$-su^{ki}-še$_3$
48 udu 52 u$_8$
12 maš$_2$ gal 27 ud$_5$
šu-gid$_2$
rev. iti ezem me-ki-ĝal$_2$
23 sila$_4$ 18 maš$_2$
mu bala ensi$_2$ Ĝir$_2$-su/^{ki}-še$_3$
25 ud$_5$ šu-gid$_2$
u$_4$ 28-kam
iti še-KIN-ku$_5$
ki Na-lu$_5$-ta
Du$_{11}$-ga i$_3$-dab$_5$
mu ^{d}Šu-^{d}EN.ZU / lugal

265: SM 1911.10.137 (-- -- --)
obv. [x] udu u$_2$
Ur-^{d}Ba-ba$_6$ dumu Tur-tur-ra
1 sila$_4$ A-da-lal$_3$
1 maš$_2$ ^{d}Šul-gi-u$_4$-su$_3$-še$_3$
1 udu Ur-lugal
4 udu Za-zi
3 udu A-la-mu
1 maš$_2$ Niĝ$_2$-du$_7$
----
1 tug$_2$ bar-dul$_5$ Lu$_2$-^{d}Utu / dumu Lugal-du$_{10}$-ur$_3$-re
1 tug$_2$ Lugal-arhuš-su$_3$
rev. 1 ^{ĝiš}na$_2$
1 ^{dug}ku-kur-du$_3$
ša$_3$ Ĝir$_2$-su^{ki}
^{d}Utu-sa$_2$-bi$_2$
1 udu Ba-ir
ša$_3$ Unug^{ki}-ga
====

266: SM 1911.10.138 (-- xii)
obv. 1 Lugal-ezem

1 Ur-pu$_2$-mun-na
0.0.4 A-hu-um
iti maš-da$_3$-gu$_7$-ta
iti še-KIN-ku$_5$-še$_3$
iti 12-kam
še-bi 6.2.0 gur
1 A-da-lal$_3$
0.0.2 Šu-Eš$_{18}$-tar$_2$
0.0.2 Gal-ušum
1 ^{d}Šul-gi-u$_4$-su$_3$-še$_3$
1 Ba-ir
1 Lu$_2$-gi-ri-da
1 Ka$_5$-a
5 26 20
rev. [1] Pi$_2$-ša-ah-DIĜIR
[1] Šeš-kal-la

1.2.2
iti ezem ^{d}Nin-a-zu-ta
iti še-KIN-ku$_5$-še$_3$
iti 8-kam
še-bi 11.2.2 gur

šu-niĝin$_2$ 17.4.2 gur
ša$_3$-bi-ta
4.2.0 Ba-ir
1.0.0 A-da-lal$_3$
0.3.0 ^{d}Šul-gi-u$_4$-su$_3$-še$_3$
2.0.0 Lugal-ezem
1.0.0 Ur-pu$_2$-mun-na
0.3.0 Lu$_2$-gi-ri-da
left a-tu$_5$-a 0.1.3 Šeš-kal-la
šu-niĝin$_2$ 11.[x.x]
mu en [ ]

267: SM 1911.10.139 (AS3 xii)

obv. 3 gu$_4$ niga A-a-mu
1 gu$_4$ niga Ar-ši-ah

kišib-bi ki Ur-šu-ga-lam-/ma i$_3$-ĝal$_2$
1 gu$_4$ niga 10 udu
A-a-kal-la
gu$_4$ Ur-sa$_6$-sa$_6$-ga / ensi$_2$-ka
1 gu$_4$ niga Ur-mes lu$_2$-ku$_6$
1 gu$_4$ niga Ur-tur sipa gu$_4$
mu en ^{d}En-lil$_2$-la$_2$-še$_3$
1 gu$_4$ niga Ur-^{d}Lamma
rev. Lu$_2$-a-a-mu
====
kišib nu-tuku
en$_3$-bi tar-re-dam
iti še-KIN-ku$_5$
iti maš-da$_3$-gu$_7$
mu ^{d}gu-za ^{d}En-lil$_2$-la$_2$ / ba-dim$_2$-ta mu us$_2$-sa-bi

268: SM 1911.10.140 (-- -- --)

obv. [ ] 37 ud$_5$
[mu]-DU u$_4$ 1-kam
[x] maš$_2$ u$_4$ 3-kam
[x] sila$_4$ 1 maš$_2$ u$_4$ 5-kam
[x] niĝ$_2$-gur$_{11}$ Saĝ-^{d}Nanna-zu
[x] u$_8$ 10 udu 3 ud$_5$ 2 maš$_2$
[ ] dumu A$_2$-bi$_2$-li$_2$-ke$_4$-ne
[x] udu ensi$_2$ Urum$_x$(UR$_2$×U$_2$)^{ki}
[x]+6 udu 2 maš$_2$ Ur-ni$_9$-[ĝar]
[xx] mu-DU didli u$_4$ [x-kam]
[ ] tum [ ]
(*ending damaged*)
rev. (*beginning damaged*)
[x] maš$_2$ ša$_3$ e$_2$ [ ]
[ ] 20 maš$_2$ Inim-^{d}[ ]
[ ] la$_2$-ia$_3$-am$_3$
[mu]-DU a$_2$-ki-ti-še$_3$
[iti] a$_2$-ki-ti
[ša$_3$] Uri$_5$^{ki}-ma
[ša$_3$] Nibru^{ki}
[ša$_3$] Tum-ma-al
[m]u-DU didli ša$_3$ kaskal

[ ] udu Na-lu$_5$

[šu-niĝin$_2$] 104 udu niga [ ]
[ ] ud$_5$
[ ]

269: SM 1911.10.141 (Š47 iv)

obv. 20 gu$_4$
15 ab$_2$
121 udu
140 u$_8$
100 maš$_2$
30 ud$_5$
eš$_3$-eš$_3$-še$_3$
==== (*erasure*)
iti u$_5$-bi$_2$-gu$_7$
30-la$_2$-1 gu$_4$
17 ab$_2$
155 udu
195 u$_8$
rev. 55 [maš$_2$]
8 [ud$_5$]
eš$_3$-eš$_3$-še$_3$
====
iti ki-siki ^{d}Nin-a-zu
bala Ur-^{d}Lamma ensi$_2$ / Ĝir$_2$-su^{ki}
====
šu-la$_2$-a
Be-li$_2$-a-zu i$_3$-dab$_5$
im gu-la-ab-tum dab$_5$-a
gi-ne$_2$-dam
mu us$_2$-sa Ki-maš^{ki} / ba-hul

270: SM 1911.10.143 (IS2 x 4)

obv. 7 u$_8$ u$_2$
19 sila$_4$ gaba
2 maš$_2$ gaba
ba-ug$_7$

u$_4$ 4-kam
ki Ur-ku$_3$-nun-na-ta
^{d}Šul-gi-iri-ĝu$_{10}$
šu ba-an-ti
rev. ĝiri$_3$ A-hu-wa-qar / šar$_2$-ra-ab-du
u$_3$ Du$_{11}$-ga ša$_3$-tam
====
iti ezem mah
mu en ^{d}Inana Unug^{ki}-/ga maš$_2$-e i$_3$-pad$_3$
left 28 udu

271: SM 1911.10.144 (AS2 iii 27)

obv. 3 [gu$_4$] dam Na-ap-la-num$_2$
mu-DU u$_4$ 7-kam
1 gu$_4$ erin$_2$ I-ku-ga-bi^{ki}
u$_4$ 10-kam
1 gu$_4$ Ur-ni$_9$-ĝar
u$_4$ 20-kam
1 gu$_4$ Lu$_2$-^{d}EN.ZU
u$_4$ 21-kam
8 gu$_4$ 1 ab$_2$
[Šu]-ru-uš-ki-i[n]
27 (*at the bottom*)
rev. [u$_4$] 26-kam
30 gu$_4$ 7 ab$_2$
ša$_3$ niĝ$_2$-mu$_{10}$-us$_2$-sa$_2$ Na-ra-am-/i$_3$-li$_2$
u$_4$ 27-kam
mu-DU lugal
4 gu$_4$ 1 ab$_2$
šu-gid$_2$ ki I-din-E$_2$-a-ta
---- (*erased*)
šu-niĝin$_2$ 48 gu$_4$
šu-niĝin$_2$ 10-la$_2$-1 ab$_2$
mu-DU ki Ab-ba-sa$_6$-ga-ta
^{d}En-lil$_2$-la$_2$ i$_3$-dab$_5$
iti [u$_5$]-bi$_2$-gu$_7$
left mu ^{d}Amar-^{d}EN.ZU / lugal-e Ur-bi$_2$-lum^{ki} / mu-hul
50+[7]

272: SM 1911.10.146 (ŠS6 viii 28)

obv. 2 udu niga 3-kam-us$_2$
2 udu aslum$_x$(A.LUM) niga 4-kam-us$_2$
1 sila$_4$
Na-we-er-DIĜIR
1 sila$_4$ A-a-kal-la ensi$_2$
1 sila$_4$ Arad$_2$-^{d}Nanna ensi$_2$
mu-DU lugal
rev. In-ta-e$_3$-a i$_3$-dab$_5$
ĝiri$_3$ ^{d}Nanna-ma-ba / dub-sar
u$_4$ 28-kam
iti ezem ^{d}Šul-gi
mu ^{d}Šu-^{d}EN.ZU / lugal Uri$_5$^{ki}-ma-ke$_4$
na-ru$_2$-a mah
^{d}En-lil$_2$ ^{d}Nin-lil$_2$-ra
mu-ne-du$_3$
left 7 udu
seal (*illegible*)

Obv. 2: Cf. AAICAB 1/4 Bod S 571, rev. ii 12' (ŠS6 viii 28).

273: SM 1911.10.148 (IS1 iii 29)

obv. 1 udu niga 4-kam-us$_2$
^{d}Ul-ma-ši-tum
1 ^{munus}aš$_2$-gar$_3$ niga sig$_5$-us$_2$
1 udu niga 3-kam-us$_2$
1 ^{munus}aš$_2$-gar$_3$ niga 4-kam-us$_2$
An-nu-ni-tum
ezem DIĜIR-ku-ku e$_3$-a / An-nu-ni-tum
rev. a$_2$-u$_4$-te-na
ĝiri$_3$ I-ṭib-ši-na-at / sagi
u$_4$ 29-kam
ša$_3$ Uri$_5$^{ki}-ma
ki ^{d}Šul-gi-i$_3$-li$_2$-ta / ba-zi
ĝiri$_3$ Šu-Eš$_{18}$-tar$_2$ šar$_2$-ra-ab-du
iti šeš-da-gu$_7$
mu ^{d}I-bi$_2$-/^{d}EN.ZU lugal
left 4 udu

274: SM 1911.10.149 (Š46 xi 9)

obv. 11 udu 1 u$_8$
8 maš$_2$ u$_4$ 5-kam
8 udu 1 u$_8$
1 maš$_2$ u$_4$ 6-kam
16 udu 4 u$_8$
10 maš$_2$ u$_4$ 7-kam
10-la$_2$-1 udu 1 u$_8$
rev. [10] maš$_2$ u$_4$ 8-kam
1 udu 1 maš$_2$
DIĜIR-dan mar-tu
6 udu
4 maš$_2$ u$_4$ 10-la$_2$-1-kam
92 (*seal*)
šu-gid$_2$ e$_2$ muhaldim
ki Na-lu$_5$-ta
Na-sa$_6$ i$_3$-dab$_5$
iti ezem Me-ki-ĝal$_2$
mu Ki-maš^{ki} ba-hul
seal [Lu$_2$-sa$_6$-ga]
dub-[sar]
dumu Gu-[za-ni kurušda]

The seal impression is reconstructed from AUCT 3 402.

275: SM 1911.10.150 (AS9 i 8)

obv. 1 sila$_4$ ^{d}Utu
^{d}En-lil$_2$-zi-ša$_3$-ĝal$_2$ / maškim
1 amar maš-da$_3$ munus
e$_2$ uz-ga
Ur-^{d}Ba-ba$_6$ muhaldim maškim
ša$_3$ mu-DU-ra-ta
rev. [u$_4$] 8-kam
[ki] Ab-ba-sa$_6$-ga-/ta
ba-zi
ĝiri$_3$ Nu-ur$_2$-^{d}EN.ZU dub-sar
iti maš-da$_3$-gu$_7$
mu us$_2$-sa en Eridu/^{ki} ba-huĝ
left 2

276: SM 1911.10.151 (Š48 xi)

obv. 8 gu$_4$ niga
1 gu$_4$ gun$_3$-a
6 gu$_4$
1 gu$_4$ ĝiš-du$_3$ gun$_3$-a
1 ab$_2$ gun$_3$-a
1 am gu$_4$
1 am gu$_4$ mu-1
1 am ab$_2$
67 udu niga
1 udu lu$_2$-ulu$_3$-um niga
rev. 10 gukkal [niga]
7 udu aslum$_x$(A.LUM) niga
1 sila$_4$ niga
1 U$_8$+HUL$_2$ niga
5 maš$_2$ gal niga
308 udu
4 udu lu$_2$-ulu$_3$-um
2 gukkal 2 gukkal ĝiš-du$_3$
1 udu aslum$_x$(A.LUM) 1 sila$_4$
1 sila$_4$ ga gukkal 1 u$_8$
71 maš$_2$ gal
mu-DU lugal
ki Na-sa$_6$-ta
left A-hu-ni i$_3$-dab$_5$
iti ezem me-ki-ĝal$_2$
mu Ha-ar-ši^{ki} / u$_3$ Ki-maš^{ki} / ba-hul

277: SM 1911.10.152 (AS1 viii 10)

obv. 1 gu$_4$ niga u$_4$ 1-kam
3 gu$_4$ niga 1 gu$_4$
u$_4$ 2-kam
3 gu$_4$ niga 6 gu$_4$
u$_4$ 3-kam
3 gu$_4$ niga u$_4$ 5-kam
36 gu$_4$ niga 137 udu
300-la$_2$-1 u$_8$ 166 maš$_2$ gal
5 sila$_4$ u$_4$ 6-kam

rev. 4 gu$_4$ niga u$_4$ 3+[x-kam]
3 gu$_4$ niga u$_4$ 10-la$_2$-1-kam
6 gu$_4$ niga u$_4$ 10-kam
(*erased line*)
====
ki Na-sa$_6$-ta
Lu$_2$-diĝir-ra i$_3$-dab$_5$
iti šu-eš$_5$-ša
mu ^{d}Amar-^{d}EN.ZU / lugal
left 673

278: SM 1911.10.153 (AS4 xi 8)

obv. 16 udu niga
[ki] Ṣe-lu-uš-^{d}/Da-gan-ta
u$_4$ 8-[kam]
Ab-ba-sa$_6$-ga
i$_3$-dab$_5$
rev. ====
iti ezem Me-ki-ĝal$_2$
mu En-mah-gal-/an-na en [^{d}Nanna] / ba-huĝ
left 16

279: SM 1911.10.154 (Š46 ii)

obv. 66 udu maš$_2$ hi-a
kišib Ur-tur
==== (*seal*)
iti šeš-da-gu$_7$
mu Ki-maš^{ki} ba-hul
rev. ==== (*seal*)
seal Ur-tur dub-sar
dumu Na-sa$_6$ kurušda

This object is an unopened envelope, but nothing is written in this regard.

280: SM 1911.10.155 (AS4)

šabra ib$_2$-dab$_5$
mu En-mah-gal-an-/na en ^{d}Nanna ba-huĝ

seal i ^{d}Amar-^{d}EN.ZU
nita$_2$ kala-ga
lugal Uri$_5$/^{ki}-ma
lugal an ub-/da limmu$_2$-ba
ii Lugal-[iti-da]
dub-[sar]
dumu Ur-[^{d}Dumu-zi-da]
arad$_2$-[zu]

This text is a duplicate of BRM 3 11.

281: SM 1911.10.156 (AS6 iv)

kurušda-e ib$_2$-dab$_5$
ki Ab-ba-sa$_6$-/ga-ta ba-zi
iti ki-siki ^{d}Nin-[a-zu]
mu Ša-aš-ru^{ki} / ba-hul

282: SM 1911.10.161 (-- -- --)

obv. (*approximately first half damaged*)
13 udu [ ]
32 maš$_2$ gal

šu-niĝin$_2$ 20 saĝ u$_8$ u$_3$ kir$_{11}$ gub
šu-niĝin$_2$ 75 udu nita$_2$ gal u$_3$ / sila$_4$ gub
šu-niĝin$_2$ 41 saĝ u$_8$ gi$_6$
šu-niĝin$_2$ 13 udu nita$_2$ gal gi$_6$
šu-niĝin$_2$ 32 maš$_2$ gal
rev. 22 ab$_2$ mah$_2$
6 ab$_2$ mu-2
2 ab$_2$ mu-1
9 ab$_2$ amar ga
11 gu$_4$ amar ga
20 gu$_4$ ĝiš
šu-niĝin$_2$ 70 gu$_4$ ab$_2$ hi-a
ki [ ]-ta
[ ]
(*ending damaged*)

283: SM 1911.10.164 (-- viii)

obv. 3 udu 2 maš$_2$
šu bala-ke-de$_3$ ša$_3$ Nibru(EN./LIL$_2$)^{ki}-še$_3$
ĝiri$_3$ Ĝiri$_3$-ni-i$_3$-sa$_6$
2 udu ĝiri$_3$ La-qi$_3$-ip
1 udu ^{d}Nin-sun$_2$
1 udu ^{d}Saĝ-šu-hal-ba
1 maš$_2$ ĝiri$_3$ La-qi$_3$-ip / [a]-ra$_2$ 2-kam
rev. 1 maš$_2$ ša$_3$ Ĝir$_2$-su^{ki}
ĝiri$_3$ Lu-tu-gal-du
1 udu aslum$_x$(A.LUM) ba-uš$_2$
1 udu ^{d}Ba-ba$_6$-tug$_2$-šu-/kur-bi$_2$
====
šu-niĝin$_2$ 13 udu maš$_2$ hi-a
ki ^{d}Šu-^{d}EN.ZU-ba-ni-/ta
ba-zi
iti šu-eš$_5$-ša

284: SM 1911.10.165 (ŠS8 ix)

obv. 1 [ ]
2 gu$_4$ niga
ki I-zu-sa-[bar]-/ta
Nu-ur$_2$-i$_3$-li$_2$
i$_3$-dab$_5$
rev. iti ezem ^{d}Šu-^{d}EN.ZU
==== (*seal*)
mu ^{d}Šu-^{d}EN.ZU / lugal Uri$_5$^{ki}-ma-ke$_4$ / ma$_2$-gur$_8$ mah ^{d}En-[lil$_2$] / ^{d}Nin-[lil$_2$] [mu-ne$_2$-dim$_2$]
seal Nu-ur$_2$-i$_3$-li$_2$
dumu SI.A-a

285: SM 1911.10.167 (ŠS7 viii 24)

obv. [2] gu$_4$ niga 4-kam-us$_2$
2 udu niga 3-kam-us$_2$
7 udu niga
6 udu 8 maš$_2$ [gal]
[kaš]-de$_2$-a Lugal-a$_2$-zi-/da šabra
[a$_2$]-ĝi$_6$-ba-a

rev. e$_2$ diĝir-e-ne-ke$_4$ ba-ab-dab$_5$
u$_4$ 24-kam mu-DU
In-ta-e$_3$-a i$_3$-dab$_5$
ĝiri$_3$ Lugal-amar-ku$_3$ / dub-sar
iti ezem ^{d}Šul-gi
mu ^{d}Šu-[^{d}EN.ZU] / lugal Uri$_5$[^{ki}-ma-ke$_4$] / ma-da Za-a[b-ša-li^{ki}] / mu-[hul]
left 2 gu$_4$ 23 udu

286: SM 1911.10.169 (ŠS6 iv --)

obv. 1 sila$_4$
Arad$_2$-ĝu$_{10}$
mu-DU lugal
In-ta-e$_3$-a
i$_3$-dab$_5$
ĝiri$_3$ Nu-ur$_2$-^{d}EN.ZU / dub-sar
rev. u$_4$ [x]-kam
iti u$_5$-bi$_2$-gu$_7$
mu us$_2$-sa ^{d}Šu-^{d}EN.ZU / lugal Uri$_5$^{ki}-ma-ke$_4$ / bad$_3$ mar-tu Mu-ri-/iq-Ti-id-ni-im / mu-du$_3$-a mu-us$_2$-sa-/bi
left 1
seal i [^{d}Šu-^{d}EN.ZU]
lugal kala-ga
lugal Uri$_5$^{ki}-[ma]
lugal an ub-/da limmu$_2$-ba
ii Nu-[ur$_2$-^{d}EN.ZU]
dub-sar
dumu I-di$_3$-Er$_3$-r[a]
arad$_2$-zu

287: SM 1911.10.170 (Š48 xii)

obv. [10] dusu$_2$ nita$_2$
12 anše libir nita$_2$ šu-gid$_2$
3 anše libir nita$_2$ mu-1
10 anše libir munus
8 anše libir munus šu-gid$_2$
3 anše libir munus mu-2

3 anše libir munus mu-1
mu-DU lugal
rev. ki Na-sa$_{6}$-ta
Šu-^{d}Idim i$_{3}$-dab$_{5}$
====
iti še-KIN-ku$_{5}$
mu Ha-ar-ši^{ki} / u$_{3}$ Ki-maš^{ki} ba-hul
====
left 50-la$_{2}$-1

288: SM 1911.10.173 (AS9 xii 29)

obv. 1 gu$_{4}$ niga ki ^{d}EN.ZU
1 gu$_{4}$ ^{d}En-lil$_{2}$
1 gu$_{4}$ ^{d}Nin-lil$_{2}$
gu$_{4}$ ĝi$_{6}$-kam
A-tu sagi maškim
iti u$_{4}$ 30-la$_{2}$-1 ba-zal
rev. bala ensi$_{2}$ Ĝir$_{2}$-[su^{ki}]
ki Lu$_{2}$-sa$_{6}$-ga-[ta]
ba-zi
==== (*seal*)
iti še-KIN-ku$_{5}$
mu en ^{d}Nanna Kar-/zi-da ba-huĝ
seal ^{d}Amar-^{d}EN.ZU
lugal kala-ga
lugal Uri$_{5}$^{ki}-ma
lugal an ub-da limmu$_{2}$-ba
Ur-^{d}Šul-pa-e$_{3}$
dub-sar
dumu Ur-^{d}Ha-ia$_{3}$
arad$_{2}$-zu

289: SM 1911.10.174 (-- ix)

obv. (*beginning damaged*)
[ ] šu-a [ ]
[x g]u$_{4}$ 20-la$_{2}$-1 ab$_{2}$
A$_{2}$-na-na

[iti šu]-eš$_5$-ša
[x] gu$_4$ 3 ab$_2$
[iti eze]m mah
[x] gu$_4$ 2 ab$_2$
[za]bar-dab$_5$
(*ending damaged*)
rev. (*beginning damaged*)
====
[šu-niĝin$_2$ x]+120+10-la$_2$-1 [gu$_4$]
[šu-niĝin$_2$ x]+10+2 ab$_2$
[ ]-ba
[ ] ^{d}En-lil$_2$-la$_2$
[mu ^{d}E]N.ZU lugal
(*ending damaged*)

290: SM 1911.10.177 (AS1 xi 18)

obv. 1 sila$_4$
1 maš$_2$ zabar-dab$_5$
1 sila$_4$ A$_2$-zi-da
1 maš$_2$ Zi-ir-ki-lum / aga$_3$-us$_2$
1 sila$_4$ ensi$_2$ Nibru^{ki}
1 sila$_4$ Lu$_2$-^{d}Nanna
rev. u$_4$ 18-kam
====
mu-DU Ab-ba-sa$_6$-/ga i$_3$-dab$_5$
iti ezem Me-ki-ĝal$_2$
mu ^{d}Amar-^{d}EN.ZU / lugal
left 6

291: SM 1911.10.178 (ŠS3 xid 16)

obv. 3 udu aslum$_x$(A.LUM) niga 3-kam-/us$_2$
1 sila$_4$
Lu$_2$-^{d}Nanna dumu Du-u[k]-ra
1 sila$_4$ ^{d}Šul-gi-zi-/mu
1 sila$_4$ Ba-a-a nu-banda$_3$
1 sila$_4$ Tu-ra-am-/^{d}Da-gan
rev. ==== (*seal*)
u$_4$ 16-kam mu-DU

In-ta-e$_3$-a i$_3$-dab$_5$
ĝiri$_3$ Nu-ur$_2$-^{d}EN.ZU / dub-sar
iti diri ezem Me-ki-ĝal$_2$ us$_2$-/sa
mu Si-ma-num$_2$^{ki} ba-/hul
left 7
seal Nu-ur$_2$-^{d}EN.ZU
dub-sar
[dumu I-di$_3$-Er$_3$-ra]

292: SM 1911.10.179 (-- v)

obv. 190 kir$_{11}$
25 udu
170-la$_2$-1 ^{munus}aš$_2$-gar$_3$
85 maš$_2$
ki Na-sa$_6$-ta
Šu-^{d}Idim
rev. i$_3$-dab$_5$
iti ezem ^{d}Nin-/a-zu
[mu] EN [ ]
left 470-la$_2$-1

293: SM 1911.10.180 (ŠS4 i)

obv. 11 sila$_4$
e$_2$ siskur$_2$-še$_3$
ki Lugal-amar-ku$_3$-ta
Lugal-me-lam$_2$ i$_3$-dab$_5$
rev. iti še-KIN-ku$_5$
====
mu us$_2$-sa Si-ma-/num$_2$^{ki} ba-hul
seal Lugal-[me-lam$_2$]
dub-[sar]
dumu [^{d}En-lil$_2$-la$_2$]

294: SM 1911.10.181 (-- vi 24)

obv. 1 udu niga 4-kam-us$_2$
gul-pa-e$_3$ du$_6$-ku$_3$-ga

	ĝiri$_3$ Ur-^{d}Gibil$_6$ / sagi
	^{d}En-lil$_2$-zi-ša$_3$-ĝal$_2$ / maškim
	ša$_3$ Nibru^{ki}
rev.	a$_2$-u$_4$-te-na
	[iti] u$_4$ 24 ba-zal
	[ki Ib]-ni-^{d}EN.ZU-ta ba-zi
	[ĝiri$_3$ Ur]-^{d}Gilgames$_x$(BIL$_4$.MES.GA) / [šar$_2$-r]a-ab-du
	[iti a$_2$-ki]-ti
	[mu ^{d}Šu-^{d}E]N.ZU / [ ]^{ki} / [mu]-hul
left	1 udu
seal	Ur-^{d}Gilgames$_x$(BIL$_4$.[MES.GA])
	dub-[sar]

Obv. 3: For this PN, see BIN 3 567 (ŠS4 iv 21).

295: SM 1911.10.183 (IS1 x)

obv.	2 maš$_2$ ĝiri$_3$ DIĜIR-/lu$_2$-sa$_6$
	2 maš$_2$ ĝiri$_3$ Hu-nu-nu-/ur
	ki A-al-la-mu-/ta ba-zi
rev.	==== (*seal*)
	iti ezem mah
	mu ^{d}I-bi$_2$-/^{d}EN.ZU lugal
seal	Du$_{11}$-ga dub-sar
	dumu Lu$_2$-^{d}Nin-ĝir$_2$-su
	sipa na-gab$_2$-tum

296: SM 1911.10.184 (AS8 i)

obv.	3.0.0 še gur lugal
	sa$_2$-du$_{11}$-še$_3$
	ki Šu-Eš$_{18}$-tar$_2$-ta
	Bi$_2$-du$_{11}$-i$_3$-sa$_6$
rev.	šu ba-ti
	====
	iti maš-da$_3$-gu$_7$
	mu us$_2$-sa Hu-uh$_2$-/nu-ri^{ki} ba-hul
seal	Bi$_2$-du$_{11}$-[i$_3$-sa$_6$]
	dumu Zu-[ ]

297: SM 1911.10.186 (IS1 xii)

obv. 2 udu
1 maš$_2$
šu-gid$_2$
ki In-ta-e$_3$-/a-ta
Ur-ku$_3$-nun-na
rev. i$_3$-dab$_5$
====
iti ezem Me-ki-gal$_2$
mu ^{d}I-bi$_2$-/^{d}EN.ZU lugal
seal Du$_{11}$-ga dub-[sar]
dumu Lu$_2$-[^{d}Nin-ĝir$_2$-su]
sipa [na-gab$_2$]-tum

298: SM 1911.10.187 (AS6 iv 4)

obv. 3 gu$_4$
491 udu
10 sila$_4$
95 sila$_4$ gub
1283 u$_8$
47 kir$_{11}$ gub
47 maš$_2$
rev. 46 maš$_2$ gub
532 ud$_5$
44 ^{munus}aš$_2$-gar$_3$ gub
šu-gid$_2$ u$_4$ 4-kam
ki Ab-ba-sa$_6$-ga-ta
In-ta-e$_3$-a i$_3$-dab$_5$
iti ki-siki ^{d}Nin-a-zu
mu Ša-aš-ru^{ki} ba-hul
left 3 gu$_4$ 2595 udu

299: SM 1911.10.190 (Š48 xi 22)

obv. 1 udu niga LU$_2$.SU
^{d}En-lil$_2$
1 maš$_2$-gal niga LU$_2$.SU
^{d}Nin-lil$_2$

zabar-dab$_5$ maškim
1 sila$_4$ e$_2$ uz-ga
Ur-^{d}Ba-ba$_6$ maškim
mu-DU Ṣe-lu-uš-/^{d}Da-gan
rev. 45 udu 15 maš$_2$-gal
šu-gid$_2$ e$_2$ muhaldim-še$_3$
u$_4$ 22-kam
====
ki Na-sa$_6$-ta ba-zi
iti ezem Me-ki-ĝal$_2$
mu Ha-ar-ši^{ki} / u$_3$ Ki-maš^{ki} ba-hul

300: SM 1911.10.192 (AS3 viii)

obv. 1 sila$_4$
ki Ab-ba-sa$_6$-ga-/[ta]
MU [ ]
rev. (*beginning damaged*)
====
iti šu-eš$_5$-ša
mu ^{d}gu-za ^{d}/En-lil$_2$-la$_2$ ba-dim$_2$
seal [ ]
dub-sar
dumu [ ]

301: SM 1911.10.194 (AS1 viii 7)

obv. 4 gu$_4$ 3 ab$_2$
7 udu 3 u$_8$
šu-gid$_2$
e$_2$ muhaldim-še$_3$
u$_4$ 7-kam
ki Na-sa$_6$-ta / ba-zi
rev. iti šu-eš$_5$-ša
mu ^{d}Amar-^{d}EN.ZU / lugal
====

302: SM 1911.10.197 (ŠS9 ix 25)

obv. [2] ab$_2$ u$_2$
1 gu$_4$ mu-3
10 u$_8$ u$_2$
15 ud$_5$ u$_2$
šu-gid$_2$ e$_2$ muhaldim
mu aga$_3$-us$_2$ u$_3$ lu$_2$ / [šuku-r]a-ke$_4$-ne-še$_3$
rev. Arad$_2$-ĝu$_{10}$ maškim
[u$_4$] 25-kam
ki Ur-ku$_3$-nun-na-ta
ba-zi
ĝiri$_3$ ^{d}Nanna-ma-ba
u$_3$ Lu$_2$-ša-lim
iti ezem ^{d}Šu-^{d}EN.ZU
mu ^{d}Šu-^{d}EN.ZU / lugal Uri$_5$^{ki}-ma-ke$_4$ / e$_2$ ^{d}Šara$_2$ Umma^{ki}-/ka mu-du$_3$
left [3 gu$_4$] 25 udu
seal ^{d}Šu-^{d}EN.ZU
[lugal kala]-ga
[lugal ŠE]Š.A[B]/^{ki}-ma
[lu]gal an ub-/da [limmu$_2$-b]a
[^{d}Nanna-ma-ba]
[dub-sar]
du[mu U$_2$-na-ab-/[še-en$_6$]
ara[d$_2$ zu]

Cf. Fs Levine 132-38, v 20 (ŠS9 ix 25).

303: SM 1911.10.199 (Š48 xi 27)

obv. 1 sila$_4$ ^{d}En-lil$_2$
1 sila$_4$ ^{d}Nin-lil$_2$
mu-DU Nu-i$_3$-da
zabar-dab$_5$ maškim
2 gu$_4$ 18 udu
Na-ap-la-nu-um mar-tu
1 gu$_4$ 10 udu
[Nu-uk-r]a-[nu-u]m
rev. [100 udu 20 maš$_2$]
[e$_2$ muhaldim]

Arad$_2$-ĝu$_{10}$ maš[kim]
u$_4$ 27-kam
====
ki Na-sa$_6$-ta ba-zi
iti ezem Me-ki-ĝal$_2$
mu Ha-ar-ši^{ki} u$_3$ / Ki-maš^{ki} ba-hul

Obv. 8-rev. 10: For the reconstruction of three lines, see BCT 1 74, rev. 13-16 (Š48 xi 27).

304: SM 1911.10.200 (Š45 ix)

obv. 3 ab$_2$
7 gu$_4$
5 dusu$_2$ hi-a
158 udu / maš$_2$ hi-a
gu$_4$ udu su-ga
rev. ki Wa-ta$_2$-ru-um / saĝĝa Mar$_2$-da^{ki}-ta
mu-DU
^{d}Nanše-kam i$_3$-dab$_5$
iti ezem mah
mu Ur-bi$_2$-lum/^{ki} ba-hul

305: SM 1911.10.202 (-- -- 10)

obv. (*beginning damaged*)
[^{d}]En-ki
[ša$_3$] Eridu^{ki}
2 gu$_4$ niga ^{d}Nin-sun$_2$
1 gu$_4$ niga ^{d}Asar-lu$_2$-hi
1 gu$_4$ niga ^{d}Šul-gi
ša$_3$ Kuara^{ki}
zabar-dab$_5$ maškim
rev. 2 amar az
e$_2$ uz-ga
mu-DU Šu-^{d}EN.ZU
Ur-^{d}Ba-ba$_6$ maškim
u$_4$ 10-kam

[ki Ab-ba-sa$_6$-g]a-ta

[ba-zi]
[iti]
[mu]
left [x]+5

306: SM 1911.10.207 (AS7 xii 1+)

obv. 2 udu
U-bar-tum a-zu
2 udu
Ur-dam u$_4$-da-tuš
DIĜIR-dan sukkal maškim
ša$_3$ mu-DU-ra-[ta]
rev. u$_4$ 1+[x-kam]
ki Ab-ba-[sa$_6$-ga]-/ta ba-[zi]
iti še-KIN-ku$_5$
mu Hu-uh$_2$-nu-ri/^{ki} ba-hul
left 4

307: SM 1911.10.208 (IS1 xii 3)

obv. 1 sila$_4$
lugal-e in-šum
U-bi-^{d}EN.ZU-a-bu
šu ba-ti
u$_4$ 3-kam
rev. ki In-ta-e$_3$-/a-ta ba-zi
ĝiri$_3$ Nu-ur$_2$-^{d}EN.ZU / dub-sar
iti ezem ^{d}Me-ki-ĝal$_2$
mu ^{d}I-bi$_2$-/^{d}EN.ZU lugal
left 1
seal i [^{d}Šu-^{d}EN.ZU]
lugal kala-ga
lugal Uri$_5$/^{ki}-ma
lugal an ub-/da limmu$_2$-ba
ii [Nu-ur$_2$-^{d}EN.ZU]
dub-sar
dumu I-[di$_3$]-/E[r$_3$-ra]
arad$_2$-zu

308: SM 1911.10.209 (AS4 ix)

obv.	0.4.0 še lugal
	a$_2$ lu$_2$-huĝ-ĝa$_2$ al-/ak ^{ĝiš}kiri$_6$ gu$_2$-še$_3$
	ki Šu-^{d}Iš-ha-ra-/t[a]
rev.	Šu-^{d}IŠKUR
	šu ba-ti
	====
	iti ezem mah
	mu En-mah-gal-/an-na en ^{d}Nanna / ba-huĝ
seal	(*illegible*)

309: SM 1911.10.211 (Š39 ii)

obv.	5 gin$_2$ siki saĝ / lugal
	a-tu$_5$-a / e$_2$-u$_4$-7
	ša$_3$ na-ga-tum-/ma-ka
rev.	ki Lugal-dub-la$_2$-ta
	ba-zi
	ĝiri$_3$ Lu$_2$-^{d}Inana
	E$_2$-saĝ-da-na
	Nibru^{ki}-ka
	iti šah$_2$-ku$_3$-gu$_7$
	mu e$_2$ PU$_3$.ŠA-iš-/$^{[d]}$Da-gan ba-du$_3$

310: SM 1911.10.212 (AS4 xii 5)

obv.	10 gu$_4$ niga ab$_2$ 2-/ta ki-ba ĝa$_2$-ĝa$_2$
	100 udu mu u$_8$-še$_3$
	u$_4$ 5-kam
	šu-la$_2$-a
	ki Ab-ba-sa$_6$-ga-/ta
rev.	Be-li$_2$-a-zu
	i$_3$-dab$_5$
	====
	iti še-KIN-ku$_5$
	mu [En-mah]-gal-an-/[na en ^{d}Nan]na [ba]-huĝ
left	10 gu$_4$ 100 udu

311: SM 1911.10.213 (ŠS1 iv 2)

obv. 4 udu niga
^{d}En-ki
ša$_3$ Eridu^{ki}-ga
ĝiri$_3$ ^{d}Nanna-palil / sagi
rev. iti u$_4$ 2 ba-zal
ki Na-lu$_5$-ta
ba-zi
ša$_3$ Uri$_5$^{ki}-ma
[iti] ki-siki ^{d}Nin-a-zu
mu ^{d}Šu-^{d}EN.ZU / lugal

312: SM 1911.10.215 (AS6 iv 4)

obv. 177 udu
543 u$_8$
70 maš$_2$-gal
110 ud$_5$
ki Ur-ku$_3$-nun-na-ta
rev. Unug^{ki}-še$_3$
Ur-^{d}Nanše i$_3$-dab$_5$
====
iti ki-siki ^{d}Nin-a-zu / u$_4$ 4-kam
mu Ša-aš-ru^{ki} / ba-hul
left 900

313: SM 1911.10.217 (AS8 i 16)

obv. 2 amar maš-da$_3$ nita$_2$
^{d}En-lil$_2$
2 amar maš-da$_3$ nita$_2$
^{d}Nin-lil$_2$
A-tu sagi / maškim
rev. iti u$_4$ 16 ba-zal
ki Lu$_2$-diĝir-ra-ta
ba-zi
iti maš-da$_3$-gu$_7$
mu en Eridu^{ki} / ba-huĝ
seal Ur-^{d}Nin-ĝiš-zi-da
dub-sar
dumu I$_3$-kal-la

314: SM 1911.10.218 (AS9 iii)

obv. 1 sila$_4$
ki Ab-ba-sa$_6$-/ga-ta
I-ri-bu-um / i$_3$-dab$_5$
rev. iti u$_5$-bi$_2$-[gu$_7$]
==== (*seal*)
mu en ^{d}Nanna Kar-/zi-da ba-huĝ
seal I-ri-ib
dumu SI.A-a
arad$_2$ lugal

315: SM 1911.10.219 (IS1 viii 4)

obv. 1 gu$_4$ u$_2$
šu-gid$_2$ e$_2$ muhaldim
mu lu$_2$ šuku-ra-ke$_4$-/ne-še$_3$
Šu-E$_2$-a sukkal maškim
u$_4$ 4-kam
rev. ki Ur-[ku$_3$-nun-na-ta]
ba-[zi]
[ĝiri$_3$] ^{d}[Nanna-ma-ba dub-sar]
iti ezem ^{d}Š[ul-gi]
mu ^{d}I-[bi$_2$]-/^{d}EN.ZU [lugal]
left 1 gu$_4$
seal i ^{d}Šu-^{d}EN.ZU
lugal kala-ga
lugal Uri$_5$/^{ki}-ma
lugal an ub-/da limmu$_2$-ba
ii ^{d}Nanna-ma-ba
dub-sar
dumu U$_2$-na-ab-[še-en$_6$]
[arad$_2$-zu]

316: SM 1911.10.220 (-- xi)

obv. (*beginning damaged*)
kišib ensi$_2$ Umma^{ki}
iti ezem mah
40-la$_2$-1 udu 1 sila$_4$
70 maš$_2$-gal 70+[x] maš$_2$

kišib ensi$_2$ Šuruppag^{ki}
iti ezem An-na
rev. 50 udu 100-la$_2$-1 sila$_4$
25 maš$_2$
kišib Ar-ši-ah
iti ezem Me-ki-ĝal$_2$
====
šu-niĝin$_2$ 591 udu
šu-niĝin$_2$ 82+[x] u$_8$
(*ending damaged*)
left [x]+57

317: SM 1911.10.221 (AS1 i)

obv. 3 [ ]
si-i$_3$-tum
ki Na-sa$_6$-[ta]
Kal-la i$_3$-dab$_5$
rev. iti maš-da$_3$-gu$_7$
mu ^{d}Amar-^{d}EN.ZU / lugal
====

318: SM 1911.10.222 (IS1 vi)

obv. 2 si[la$_4$]
ki A-ba-^{d}En-[lil$_2$-gin$_7$-ta]
gaba-ri
kišib Ab-ba-kal-la
ĝiri$_3$ Ur-^{d}Nin-mu$_2$
rev. ====
iti ezem ^{d}Nin-a-zu
mu ^{d}I-bi$_2$-/^{d}EN.ZU lu[gal]

319: SM 1911.10.223 (AS2 vii 20)

obv. 2 lulim nita$_2$
13 maš$_2$-gal a-dara$_4$
1 az
u$_4$ 20-kam

ki Ab-ba-sa$_6$-ga-/ta
rev. Lu$_2$-diĝir-ra i$_3$-dab$_5$
iti ezem ^{d}Šul-gi
mu ^{d}Amar-^{d}EN.ZU / lugal-e Ur-bi$_2$-/lum^{ki} mu-hul
====
left 16

Cf. P235687 (AS2 vii 20).

320: SM 1911.10.224 (AS8 viii 13)

obv. 114 udu
98 maš$_2$
u$_4$ 13-kam
ki Ab-ba-[sa$_6$]-ga-/[ta]
rev. Du$_{11}$-ga
i$_3$-dab$_5$
====
iti šu-eš$_5$-ša
mu en Eridu/^{ki} [ba-huĝ]
left 212

321: SM 1911.10.227 (AS7 vii 15)

obv. 1 amar maš-da$_3$ nita$_2$
e$_2$ uz-ga
mu-DU Lu$_2$-^{d}Nanna
Ur-^{d}Ba-ba$_6$ maškim
u$_4$ 15-kam
ki Ab-ba-sa$_6$-ga-ta
rev. ba-zi
====
iti ezem ^{d}Šul-gi
mu Hu-uh$_2$-nu-/ri^{ki} ba-hul
left 1

322: SM 1911.10.228 (Š48 viii)

obv. 4 ha-bu-um

mu-DU lugal
ki Na-ra-am-/i$_{3}$-li$_{2}$-ta
Ṣe-lu-uš-^{d}Da-/gan i$_{3}$-dab$_{5}$
rev. iti šu-eš-ša
====
mu Ha-ar-ši^{ki} / Ki-maš^{ki} Hu-ur$_{5}$-ti^{ki} / u$_{3}$ ma-da-bi u$_{4}$ 1-a ba-hul

This text is a duplicate of Tavolette 365 (Š48 viii).
Obv. 1: These animals may be identical with 4 ha-bu-um in ARRIM 8 53, 6 3 (Š48 viii 13).

323: SM 1911.10.230 (AS2 v)

obv. 80 še gur lugal
ki Šu-^{d}Iš-ha-ra-ta
Nu-ur$_{2}$-i$_{3}$-li$_{2}$
šu ba-ti
ša$_{3}$ Ha-am-ša-um-ma
rev. ====
iti ezem ^{d}Nin-a-zu
mu ^{d}Amar-^{d}EN.ZU lugal-/ke$_{4}$ Ur-bi$_{2}$-lum/^{ki} mu-hul

Obv. 5: The geographical name Ha-am-ša-um-ma is attested only in this text.

324: SM 1911.10.231 (Š47 ii)

obv. 2 u$_{8}$
siskur$_{2}$ ša$_{3}$ kaskal-la
u$_{4}$ ^{ĝiš}tukul ba-sig$_{3}$-a$_{2}$
ĝiri$_{3}$ Lu$_{2}$-^{d}Nanna / sagi
rev. zi-ga
ki Be-li$_{2}$-a-zu
iti šeš-da-/gu$_{7}$
mu us$_{2}$-sa / Ki-maš^{ki} ba-hul

For this text, cf. BPOA 7 2488 (Š47 ii).

325: SM 1911.10.232 (AS6 ix 17)

obv. 10 gu$_4$ niga
4 gu$_4$
4 udu
1 maš$_2$-gal
u$_4$ 17-kam
rev. ki Ab-ba-sa$_6$-ga-/ta
Šu-Ma-ma i$_3$-dab$_5$
====
iti ezem mah
mu Ša-aš-ru^{ki} / ba-hul
left 14 gu$_4$ 5 udu

This is the original record for SACT 1 187, vi 6'-10' (AS6 ix 17).

326: SM 1911.10.233 (AS9 iii 2)

obv. 132 udu
a-ra$_2$ 1-kam
16 maš$_2$-[gal]
a-ra$_2$ 2-[kam]
6 udu LU$_2$.SU
6 maš$_2$-gal LU$_2$.SU
rev. a-ra$_2$ 3-kam
160
u$_4$ 2-kam
Na-lu$_5$ i$_3$-[dab$_5$]
iti u$_5$-bi$_2$-gu$_7$
mu en ^{d}Nanna / [Kar]-zi-da ba-huĝ

327: SM 1911.10.235 (Š43 i)

obv. 1.0.0 še-gur lugal
še gi$_4$-gi$_4$-dam
ki Ur-^{d}Ba-ba$_6$-/ta
rev. U$_2$-u$_2$-mu
šu ba-ti
iti maš-ku$_3$-gu$_7$
mu en ^{d}/Nanna maš-e / i$_3$-pad$_3$

328: SM 1911.10.236 (AS4 ix)

obv. 5 še gur lugal
dub-ta sar-ra
ki Lu$_2$-ša-lim-ta
Šu-Eš$_{18}$-tar$_2$
šu ba-ti
rev. iti ezem mah
====
mu en ^{d}Nanna ba-/huĝ

Cf. PDT 1 367 (AS4 ix).

329: SM 1911.10.237 (AS2 ix 19)

obv. 4 udu
3 gukkal
6 ud$_5$
šu-gid$_2$ e$_2$ muhaldim-še$_3$
u$_4$ 20-la$_2$-1-kam
rev. ki Ab-ba-sa$_6$-/ga-ta ba-zi
iti ezem mah
mu ^{d}Amar-^{d}EN.ZU / lugal-e Ur-bi$_2$-/lum^{ki} mu-hul
left 13

This is the original record for SAT 2 724, vi 7 (AS2 ix 19).

330: SM 1911.10.238 (-- -- 24)

obv. 2 u$_8$ 1 maš$_2$
u$_4$ 24-kam
Nibru^{ki}
gub-ba
kišib Kaš$_4$
rev. ==== (*seal*)
seal Kaš$_4$
dub-sar
dumu Na-s[a$_6$] / kurušda

331: SM 1911.10.239 (ŠS1 xi)

obv. [ ]
la$_2$-ia$_3$ niĝ$_2$-ka$_9$-a[k]
ki Eš$_{18}$-tar$_2$-al-[šu-ta]
kišib ^{d}Nan[na]-/kam
rev. ĝiri$_3$ I-din-[ ]
u$_3$ ^{d}Šu-^{d}EN.[ZU]-/ha-ma-[ti]
iti ezem me-ki-[ĝal$_2$]
mu ^{d}Šu-^{d}EN.ZU / lugal

Rev. 6: Cf. MVN 13 123; MVN 3 258.

332: SM 1911.10.240 (AS4 viii 16)

obv. 1 udu ša$_3$ mu-DU-/ra-ta
1 maš$_2$ Da-da-ga / nu-banda$_3$
u$_4$ 16-kam
mu-DU ^{d}Šul-gi-/ra
rev. Ab-ba-sa$_6$-ga
i$_3$-dab$_5$
====
iti šu-eš$_5$-ša
mu En-mah-gal-an-na / en ^{d}Nanna ba-huĝ
left 2

This is the original record for RA 10 210 (= Nisaba 8 37), i 19-21 (AS4 viii 16).

333: SM 1911.10.241 (AS7 viii 17)

obv. 6 sila$_4$
u$_4$ 17-kam
ki Ab-ba-sa$_6$-/ga-ta
rev. In-ta-e$_3$(UD./DU)-a
i$_3$-dab$_5$
iti šu-eš$_5$-ša
mu Hu-uh$_2$-nu-/ri^{ki} ba-hul
left 6

334: SM 1911.10.242 (AS9 ii 27)

obv. 8 udu
1 maš$_2$-gal
u$_4$ 27-kam
ki Ab-ba-sa$_6$-ga-/ta
rev. Zu-ba-ga
i$_3$-dab$_5$
====
iti šeš-da-gu$_7$
mu en ^{d}Nanna / Kar-zi-da ba-huĝ
left 10-la$_2$-1

335: SM 1911.10.243 (AS6 vi 9)

obv. 4 sila$_4$
4 maš$_2$
u$_4$ 10-la$_2$-1-kam
ki Ab-ba-sa$_6$-ga-/ta
rev. In-ta-e$_3$-a
i$_3$-dab$_5$
====
iti a$_2$-ki-ti
mu Ša-aš-ru^{ki} / ba-hul
left 8

336: SM 1911.10.244 (AS9 i)

obv. (*beginning damaged*)
1' [ ] UM
rev. i$_3$-dab$_5$
====
iti maš-da$_3$-gu$_7$
mu us$_2$-sa en Eridu^{ki} ba-huĝ

337: SM 1911.10.245 (AS8 ii 2)

obv. 1 amar maš-[da$_3$]
e$_2$ uz-[ga]

mu-DU Ur-^{d}Nin-/gublaga nar
Ur-^{d}Ba-ba$_{6}$ muhaldim / maškim
rev. u$_{4}$ 2-kam
ki Lugal-amar-ku$_{3}$-ta
ba-zi
====
iti šeš-da-gu$_{7}$
mu En-nun-e-^{d}/Amar-^{d}EN.ZU-ra-ki-aĝ$_{2}$ / en Eridu^{ki} [ba-huĝ]
left 1

338: SM 1911.10.247 (Š45 xii)

obv. 7 gu$_{2}$ siki gi
10 gu$_{2}$ siki gir$_{2}$ gul
ki Kalam-he$_{2}$-na-gi-/ta
e$_{2}$-gal-la ba-an-ku$_{x}$(KWU147)
rev. I-šar-ti-gal$_{2}$-/la-šu-um maškim
====
iti še-KIN-ku$_{5}$
mu Ur-bi$_{2}$-lum^{ki} / Lu-lu-bu^{ki} Si-mu-ru-um^{ki} u$_{3}$ / Kar$_{2}$-har^{ki} aš-še$_{3}$ sag-/bi šu-bur$_{2}$-a bi$_{2}$-ra-a

339: SM 1911.10.248 (AS8 i 13)

obv. 1 amar maš-da$_{3}$ nita$_{2}$
u$_{4}$ 13-kam
ki Ab-ba-sa$_{6}$-ga-/ta
Lu$_{2}$-diĝir-ra i$_{3}$-dab$_{5}$
rev. ====
iti maš-da$_{3}$-gu$_{7}$
mu en Eridu^{ki} / ba-huĝ
left 1

340: SM 1911.10.249 (-- i 22)

obv. 1 sila$_{4}$ Lu$_{2}$-ša-lim
1 Nu-ur$_{2}$-^{d}IŠKUR
1 He$_{2}$-na-lah$_{5}$
1 ĝiri$_{3}$ Lugal-/u$_{2}$-šim-e

rev. la$_2$-i$_3$-am$_3$
2 udu 12 sila$_4$
7 maš$_2$
ki siskur$_2$-ra
3 sila$_3$ ša$_3$ 4
Ka$_5$-a i$_3$-dab$_5$
ša$_3$ PU$_3$.ŠA-^{d}/Da-gan
left iti maš-da$_3$-gu$_7$ / u$_4$ 22 ba-zal

341: SM 1911.10.250 (AS4 i 18)

obv. 1 sila$_4$ 1 maš$_2$
Ama-bara$_2$ šu im-/mi-us$_2$
2 amar maš-da$_3$
Igi-an-na-ke$_4$-zu / šu im-mi-[us$_2$]
rev. u$_4$ 18-kam
mu-DU
Ab-ba-sa$_6$-ga
i$_3$-dab$_5$
iti maš-da$_3$-gu$_7$
mu us$_2$-sa gu-za / ^{d}En-lil$_2$-la$_2$ ba-dim$_2$
left 4

Obv. 3-4: Cf. AUCT 1 724 (AS4 i 18).

342: SM 1911.10.251 (AS7 iii 25)

obv. 2 udu niga
u$_4$ 25-kam
ki Ab-ba-sa$_6$-/ga-ta
A-hu-We-er
rev. i$_3$-dab$_5$
====
iti u$_5$-bi$_2$-gu$_7$
mu Hu-uh$_2$-nu-ri/^{ki} ba-hul
left 2

343: SM 1911.10.253 (Š46 ii)

obv. 7 gu$_4$
3 ab$_2$
ša$_3$ la$_2$-ia$_3$ su-ga
U$_2$-u$_2$-mu-ka
ugu$_2$ ^{d}En-lil$_2$-la$_2$-/ka-ka
rev. ba-a-ĝa$_2$-ar
iti šeš-da-gu$_7$
mu Ki-maš^{ki} / ba-hul
====

344: SM 1911.10.254 (AS1 iii)

obv. 4 dusu$_2$ nita$_2$
3 dusu$_2$ munus
====
ki Ku-li-ta
Kal-la
rev. i$_3$-dab$_5$
iti u$_5$-bi$_2$-gu$_7$
mu Amar-^{d}EN.ZU / lugal
====

345: SM 1911.10.255 (AS4 iii 28)

obv. 20 maš$_2$-gal
[u$_4$] 28-kam
ki Ab-ba-sa$_6$-/ga-ta
Na-lu$_5$ i$_3$-dab$_5$
rev. ====
iti u$_5$-bi$_2$-gu$_7$
mu us$_2$-sa ^{d}/gu-za ^{d}En-lil$_2$-la$_2$ / ba-dim$_2$
left 20

346: SM 1911.10.256 (AS4 vii 20)

obv. 10 sila$_4$
u$_4$ 20-kam
ki Ab-ba-sa$_6$-/ga-ta

In-ta-e$_3$-/a
rev. i$_3$-dab$_5$
iti ezem ^{d}/Šul-gi
mu en ^{d}Nanna / ba-huĝ
left 10

347: SM 1911.10.257 (Š47 ix)

obv. 20 ad$_6$ gu$_4$
ki Na-ra-am-i$_3$-/li$_2$-ta
Ur-ni$_9$-ĝar
rev. šu ba-ti
====
iti ezem mah
mu us$_2$-sa Ki-maš/^{ki} ba-hul

348: SM 1911.10.258 (AS8 i 8)

obv. 2 amar maš-da$_3$ munus
u$_4$ 8-kam
ki Ab-ba-sa$_6$-ga-/ta
Lu$_2$-diĝir-ra
i$_3$-dab$_5$
rev. ====
iti maš-da$_3$-gu$_7$
mu en Eridu/^{ki} ba-huĝ
left 2

Obv. 1: For these animals, see OIP 121 105 (AS8 i 8).

349: SM 1911.10.260 (AS6 x 9)

obv. 13 sila$_4$
u$_4$ 10-la$_2$-1-kam
ki Ab-ba-sa$_6$-ga-/ta
In-ta-e$_3$-a
rev. i$_3$-dab$_5$
====

iti ezem An-na
mu Ša-aš-ru^{ki} / ba-hul
left 13

350: SM 1911.10.261 (IS1 viii)

obv. 36 maš$_2$-gal
sa$_2$-du$_{11}$ An-nu-ni-/tum Unug^{ki}-še$_3$
ki In-ta-e$_3$-a-/ta
rev. Ur-^{d}IŠKUR / šabra i$_3$-dab$_5$
iti ezem ^{d}Šul-/gi
mu ^{d}I-bi$_2$-/^{d}EN.ZU lugal

351: SM 1911.10.262 (AS6 vii 22)

obv. 2 az
u$_4$ 22-kam
ki Ab-ba-sa$_6$-ga-/ta
Lu$_2$-diĝir-ra
rev. i$_3$-dab$_5$
====
iti ezem ^{d}Šul-gi
mu Ša-aš-ru^{ki} ba-/hul
left 2

352: SM 1911.10.263 (AS2 x 25)

obv. 1 amar šeg$_9$-bar munus
1 maš$_2$-gal a-dara$_4$
1 ud$_5$ a-dara$_4$
1 maš$_2$ ga a-dara$_4$
1 ^{munus}aš$_2$-gar$_3$ a-dara$_4$
1 maš-da$_3$
1 az
ba-ug$_7$ u$_4$ 25-kam
rev. ki Lu$_2$-diĝir-ra-ta
Ur-ni$_9$-ĝar
šu ba-ti
iti ezem An-na
mu ^{d}Amar-^{d}EN.ZU / lugal-e Ur-bi$_2$-/lum^{ki} mu-hul

353: SM 1911.10.265 (AS3 xii 27)

obv. 1 udu
5 u$_8$
1 maš$_2$-gal
1 kir$_{11}$
5 sila$_4$ ga
ba-ug$_7$ u$_4$ 27-kam
rev. ki A-hu-We-er-ta
^{d}Šul-gi-iri-ĝu$_{10}$
šu ba-ti
iti še-KIN-ku$_5$
mu ^{d}gu-za ^{d}En-/lil$_2$-la$_2$ ba-dim$_2$
left 13

354: SM 1911.10.266 (AS8 xi 14)

obv. 4 udu
1 maš$_2$-gal
u$_4$ 14-kam
ki Ab-ba-sa$_6$-/ga-ta
rev. Na-lu$_5$ i$_3$-dab$_5$
iti ezem Me-ki-ĝal$_2$
mu en Eridu/^{ki} ba-huĝ
left 5

355: SM 1911.10.267 (AS3 i)

obv. 2 gu$_4$
ugu$_2$ Ur-šu-ga-/lam-ma ba-a-ĝar
ki ^{d}En-lil$_2$-la$_2$-ta
ba-zi
rev. iti maš-da$_3$-gu$_7$
mu ^{d}gu-za / ^{d}En-lil$_2$-la$_2$ ba-dim$_2$
====
left 2

356: SM 1911.10.268 (AS8 i 12)

obv. 1 amar maš-da$_3$ nita$_2$
ba-uš$_2$ e$_2$ kišib-ba-še$_3$
^{d}Šul-gi-iri-ĝu$_{10}$ / šu ba-ti
u$_4$ 12-kam
rev. ki Ab-ba-sa$_6$-/ga-ta ba-zi
====
iti maš-da$_3$-gu$_7$
mu en Eridu^{ki} / ba-huĝ
left 1

357: SM 1911.10.269 (Š37 viii)

obv. 47 tug$_2$ guz-za du
11 tug$_2$ sag uš-bar
mu-DU
A$_2$-na-na
rev. I-di$_3$-Er$_3$-r[a]
šu ba-ti
iti šu-eš-ša
mu bad$_3$ ma-da / ba-du$_3$

358: SM 1911.10.270 (AS8 i 2)

obv. 17 udu šu-gid$_2$
u$_4$ 2-kam
ki Ab-ba-sa$_6$-ga-ta
Du$_{11}$-ga
i$_3$-dab$_5$
rev. ====
iti maš-da$_3$-gu$_7$
mu us$_2$-sa Hu-uh$_2$-/nu-ri^{ki} ba-hul
left 17

359: SM 1911.10.271 (AS1 x 28)

obv. 4 gu$_4$
1 sila$_4$ gukkal
u$_4$ 28-kam
ki Ab-ba-sa$_6$-/ga-ta

A-hu-ni
rev. i$_3$-dab$_5$
====
iti ezem An-na
mu ^{d}Amar-^{d}EN./ZU lugal
left 5

Obv. 1: Cf. CST 217 (AS1 x 28).

360: SM 1911.10.272 (AS7 vii 17)

obv. 3 udu niga
u$_4$ 17-kam
ki Ab-ba-sa$_6$-/ga-ta
Šu-Ma-ma i$_3$-dab$_5$
rev. ====
iti ezem ^{d}Šul-gi
mu Hu-uh$_2$-/nu-ri^{ki} ba-hul
left 3

361: SM 1911.10.273 (AS4 iv 13)

obv. 8 udu niga
3 udu 1 sila$_4$
u$_4$ 13-kam
ki Ab-ba-sa$_6$-ga-/ta
rev. Na-lu$_5$
i$_3$-dab$_5$
iti ki-siki ^{d}Nin-a-zu
mu En-mah-gal-an-na / en ^{d}Nanna ba-huĝ
left 12

362: SM 1911.10.274 (AS9 ix 29)

obv. 4 udu
1 u$_8$
1 u$_8$ gukkal
ba-ug$_7$ u$_4$ 30-la$_2$-1-kam
rev. ki Igi-^{d}En-lil$_2$-še$_3$-ta

^{d}Šul-gi-iri-ĝu$_{10}$
šu ba-ti
iti ezem mah
mu en ^{d}Nanna Kar-/zi-da ba-huĝ
left 6 udu

363: SM 1911.10.275 (AS5 i 11)

obv. 1 dara$_4$ nita$_2$
1 dara$_4$ munus
3 udu
ba-ug$_7$
u$_4$ 11-kam
rev. ki Na-lu$_5$-ta
^{d}Šul-gi-iri-ĝu$_{10}$
šu ba-ti
iti maš-da$_3$-gu$_7$
mu us$_2$-sa en ^{d}/Nanna ba-huĝ

364: SM 1911.10.276 (AS1 xii 17)

obv. 2 udu
u$_4$ 17-kam
ki Ab-ba-sa$_6$-ga-/ta
^{d}Šul-gi-a-a-ĝu$_{10}$
rev. i$_3$-dab$_5$
iti še-KIN-ku$_5$
mu ^{d}Amar-^{d}EN./ZU lugal
left 2

This text is a duplicate of Hirose 106 (AS1 xii 17).

365: SM 1911.10.277 (AS3 vii 28)

obv. 22 udu
134 u$_8$
106 u$_8$ gi$_6$
ša$_3$ nam-ra-ak
u$_4$ 20-kam

7 [u$_{8}$]
3 sila$_{4}$ 1 [ud$_{5}$]
[niĝ$_{2}$-gur$_{11}$ Lu$_{2}$-ša-lim]
[u$_{4}$ 28-kam]
rev. a-[gu$_{3}$ Ur-ku$_{3}$-nun-na-ka ba-a-ĝa$_{2}$-ar]
kišib-bi nu-[um-tum$_{2}$]
tukum-bi i[m-ma-tum$_{2}$]
zi-re-dam
iti ezem ^{d}Šul-gi
mu ^{d}gu-za ^{d}En-lil$_{2}$-la$_{2}$ / ba-dim$_{2}$
left 273

This text is reconstructed from its duplicated text, AUCT 1 28.

366: SM 1911.10.279 (AS4 i)

obv. 1 še gur lugal
ki ^{d}Nanna-ki-aĝ$_{2}$-ta
A-da-lal$_{3}$ šabra
šu ba-ti
rev. ==== (*seal*)
iti maš-da$_{3}$-gu$_{7}$
mu us$_{2}$-sa gu-za / ^{d}En-lil$_{2}$-la$_{2}$ ba-dim$_{2}$
seal Nam-nin-gal-he$_{2}$-du$_{7}$
dumu-munus lugal
A-da-lal$_{3}$
sukkal arad$_{2}$-zu

367: SM 1911.10.280 (ŠS8 x)

obv. [x] ma-na [x] gin$_{2}$ [ ]
mu ^{uruda}si-im-da ^{ĝiš}[gu]-/za-še$_{3}$
ki Ur-ni$_{9}$-ĝar-ta
Lugal-igi-huš
rev. šu ba-ti
====
iti ezem mah

mu ^{d}Šu-^{d}EN.ZU / lugal Uri$_5$^{ki}-ma-/ke$_4$ / [ma$_2$]-gur$_8$ mah [^{d}En-lil$_2$ ^{d}Nin-lil$_2$-ra mu-ne$_2$-dim$_2$]

368: SM 1911.10.282 (-- -- --)

obv. 6 gu$_4$ niga
ki Uš-gi-na / A-bi$_2$-si$_2$-im-/ti-ta
A-hu-We-er i$_3$-dab$_5$
rev. (*all damaged*)

369: SM 1911.10.283 (-- ix 6)

obv. 10 guruš huĝ-ĝa$_2$ u$_4$ 1-še$_3$
^{ĝiš}dih$_3$ ku$_5$!-ta 20 sar-ta
a$_2$ 6 sila$_3$-ta
a-ša$_3$-bi 3 gan$_2$
še-bi 0.1.0
ugula Ur-^{d}Bil$_3$
5 guruš huĝ-ĝa$_2$ u$_4$ 1-še$_3$
al 5 sar-ta
a-ša$_3$-bi 25 sar
rev. še-bi 0.0.3
gan$_2$ I-di$_3$-Er$_3$-ra
6 guruš ša$_3$-gu$_4$
al 2 sar-ta
gan$_2$ I-di$_3$-Er$_3$-ra
iti-ta u$_4$ 6 ba-ra-zal
iti ezem mah
====

370: SM 1911.10.286 (AS9 xiid 17)

obv. 2 udu niga 4-kam-us$_2$
^{d}Ištaran siskur$_2$ ša$_3$ e$_2$-gal
mu dumu-munus Ur-^{d}En-lil$_2$-la$_2$-še$_3$
2 udu niga gu$_4$-e us$_2$-sa
2 maš$_2$ gal niga gu$_4$-e us$_2$-sa
e$_2$ muhaldim

mu A-da-lal$_{3}$ šagina / u$_{3}$ dam-a-ni-še$_{3}$
^{d}Šul-gi-iri-<ĝu$_{10}$> sukkal maškim
1 udu niga
1 udu niga gu$_{4}$-e us$_{2}$-sa
Ha-bu-ri-tum
mu Ku$_{8}$-ba-tum-še$_{3}$
rev. 4 udu niga e$_{2}$ muahldim
mu dumu-munus Ur-^{d}En-lil$_{2}$-la$_{2}$-še$_{3}$
Arad$_{2}$-ĝu$_{10}$ maškim
1 udu niga
1 sila$_{4}$ niga
KA-izi-še$_{3}$
A-a-kal-la muhaldim maškim
3 udu niga ^{d}IŠKUR
siskur$_{2}$ ša$_{3}$ e$_{2}$-gal
A-tu sagi maškim
zi-ga u$_{4}$ 17-kam
ki En-diĝir-ĝu$_{10}$-ta
ba-zi
iti diri še-KIN-ku$_{5}$
mu en ^{d}Nanna Kar-/zi-da ba-huĝ
left 17 udu
seal i ^{d}Amar-^{d}EN.ZU
lugal kala-ga
lugal Uri$_{5}$^{ki}-ma
lugal an ub-da limmu$_{2}$-ba
ii Ur-^{d}Šul-pa-e$_{3}$
dub-sar
dumu-Ur-^{d}Ha-ia$_{3}$
arad$_{2}$-zu

371: SM 1911.10.287 (-- -- --)
obv. 2 udu niga
tak$_{4}$-e dah-he-/dam
rev. ====

372: SM 1911.10.288 (ŠS1 v 4)

obv. 2 maš-da$_3$ ^{d}En-lil$_2$
1 maš-da$_3$ ^{d}Nin-lil$_2$
lugal ku$_x$(KWU147)-ra
8 udu šu-gid$_2$
1 gu$_4$ ba-uš$_2$
e$_2$ muhaldim
rev. mu aga$_3$-us$_2$-e-[ne-še$_3$]
u$_4$ 4-[kam]
====
ki Du$_{11}$-ga-ta ba-zi
iti ezem ^{d}Nin-a-zu
mu ^{d}Šu-^{d}EN.ZU / lugal
seal ^{d}Šu-^{d}EN.ZU
lugal kala-ga
lugal Uri$_5$^{ki}-ma
lugal an ub-da limmu$_2$-ba
Ur-^{d}Šul-pa-e$_3$
dub-sar
dumu Ur-^{d}Ha-ia$_3$
arad$_2$-zu

373: SM 1911.10.289 (ŠS9 xi 21)

obv. 3 gu$_4$ šu-gid$_2$
18 udu šu-gid$_2$
6 udu 2 sila$_4$ ba-ug$_7$
e$_2$ muhaldim
mu aga$_3$-us$_2$ u$_3$ / lu$_2$ šuku-ra-ke$_4$-ne-še$_3$
u$_4$ 21-kam
rev. ki Ur-ku$_3$-nun-na-ta
ba-zi
==== (*seal*)
iti ezem An-na
mu ^{d}Šu-^{d}EN.ZU / lugal Uri$_5$^{ki}-ma-ke$_4$ / e$_2$ ^{d}Šara$_2$ Umma^{ki}-/ka mu-du$_3$
seal i ^{d}Šu-^{d}EN.ZU
lugal kala-ga
lugal Uri$_5$/^{ki}-ma

lugal an ub-/da limmu$_2$-ba
ii Ur-^{d}Šul-pa-/e$_3$
dub-sar
dumu Ur-^{d}Ha-ia$_3$
arad$_2$-zu

374: SM 1911.10.291 (IS1 v/vi --)

obv. 1 sila$_4$ Ur-mes ensi$_2$
1 sila$_4$ Šu-Eš$_{18}$-tar$_2$ dumu / Eš$_{18}$-tar$_2$-al-šu
1 sila$_4$ Ša$_3$-ku$_3$-ge
mu-DU lugal
In-ta-e$_3$-a
rev. i$_3$-dab$_5$
ĝiri$_3$ [Nu]-ur$_2$-^{d}EN.ZU / [dub]-sar
u$_4$ [x]-kam
iti [^{d}Ni]n-a-zu
mu ^{d}[I]-bi$_2$-/^{d}EN.ZU lugal
left 3
seal i ^{d}Šu-^{d}EN.ZU
lugal kala-ga
lugal Uri$_5$/^{ki}-ma
lugal an ub-/da limmu$_2$-ba
ii Nu-ur$_2$-[^{d}EN.ZU]
dub-sar
dumu I-di$_3$-/Er$_3$-[ra]
arad$_2$-[zu]

375: SM 1911.10.292 (IS1 xii)

obv. 11 udu kišib Šu-za-kam
2 udu u$_2$
kišib Ur-^{d}Nin-a-zu
2 udu u$_2$
1 maš$_2$ gal
kišib Ur-^{d}Nin-a-zu
1 udu kišib Ib-ni-DIĜIR
rev. ki Lu$_2$-^{d}EN.ZU-ta
Lu$_2$-^{d}Nin-ĝir$_2$-su

šu ba-ti
==== (*seal*)
iti ezem ^{d}Me-ki-ĝal$_{2}$
mu ^{d}I-bi$_{2}$-^{d}EN./ZU lugal
seal Lu$_{2}$-^{d}Nin-[ĝir$_{2}$-su]
dub-sar
dumu Ur-sa$_{6}$-ga
sipa gu$_{4}$ niga

376: SM 1911.10.295 (ŠS5 ix 15)

obv. [2 udu] en ^{d}Inana
1 gu$_{4}$ u$_{2}$
A-zu lu$_{2}$ Ra-bi$_{2}$^{ki}
mu-DU lugal
In-ta-e$_{3}$-a
i$_{3}$-dab$_{5}$
rev. ĝiri$_{3}$ Nu-ur$_{2}$-^{d}EN.ZU / dub-sar
u$_{4}$ 15-kam
iti ezem ^{d}Šu-^{d}EN.ZU
mu us$_{2}$-sa ^{d}Šu-^{d}EN.ZU / lugal Uri$_{5}$^{ki}-ma-ke$_{4}$
bad$_{3}$ mar-tu Mu-ri-iq-/Ti-id-ni-im / mu-du$_{3}$
left 1 gu$_{4}$ 2 udu
seal i [^{d}Šu-^{d}EN.ZU]
lugal kala-ga
lugal Uri$_{5}$/^{ki}-ma
lugal an ub-/da limmu$_{2}$-ba
ii [Nu-ur$_{2}$-^{d}EN.ZU]
dub-[sar]
dumu I-di$_{3}$-/[Er$_{3}$-ra]
arad$_{2}$-[zu]

377: SM 1911.10.296 (ŠS4 vi)

obv. 20.0.4 zu$_{2}$-lum / gur
2.1.4 2 sila$_{3}$ u$_{4}$-hi-in!(LUM) gur
kab$_{2}$-du$_{11}$-ga ^{ĝiš}kiri$_{6}$
Lu$_{2}$-^{d}Nin-šubur / šandana
ĝiri$_{3}$ Ur-sa$_{6}$-ga dub-sar

====
iti ezem ^{d}Nin-a-zu
mu us$_2$-sa Si-ma-/num$_2$^{ki} ba-hul

378: SM 1911.10.298 (ŠS8 v)

obv. 15 udu niga
ki A-ba-^{d}En-lil$_2$-/gin$_7$-ta
PU$_3$.ŠA-^{d}En-lil$_2$
i$_3$-dab$_5$
rev. ==== (*seal*)
iti ki-siki ^{d}Nin-a-zu
mu ma$_2$-gur$_8$ mah / ba-dim$_2$
seal Lu$_2$-^{d}EN.ZU
dumu Ur-sa$_6$-ga
sipa gu$_4$ [niga]

379: SM 1911.10.301 (AS9 v)

obv. 0.0.3 dabin lugal
zi$_3$ ninda-ka-še$_3$
ki Šu-Eš$_{18}$-tar$_2$-ta
PU$_3$.ŠA-a-bi / su-si-ig
rev. šu ba-ti
==== (*seal*)
iti a$_2$-ki-ti
mu en ^{d}Nanna / Kar-zi-da ba-huĝ
seal PU$_3$.ŠA-a-bi$_2$
lu$_2$ arad$_2$ Nin-kal-la

380: SM 1911.10.306 (ŠS3 i 6)

obv. 3 sila$_4$
2 amar maš-da$_3$ nita$_2$
1 amar maš-da$_3$ munus
u$_4$ 6-[kam]
rev. ki In-ta-e$_3$-/a-ta
Du$_{11}$-ga i$_3$-dab$_5$
iti maš-da$_3$-gu$_7$

mu us$_2$-sa ma$_2$-dara$_3$ / abzu ba-ab-du$_8$
seal Ur-mes
dumu La-na kurušda

381: SM 1911.10.307 (ŠS - i)

obv. (*beginning damaged*)
[ ] saĝ šum$_2$-[sikil]
80 sa šum$_2$-sikil
0.4.2 numun šum$_2$-sikil
0.4.0 gu$_2$-gal-gal
1.4.0 še-lu$_2$ gur
mu-DU
rev. a-ša$_3$ I-šum$_2$-ma
====
iti maš-da$_3$-gu$_7$
mu ^{d}Šu-^{d}EN.ZU / lugal Uri$_5$^{ki}-ma-ke$_4$ [ ]

382: SM 1911.10.309 (AS2 xii)

obv. 2 [ ] babbar$_2$
1 [ ] gun$_3$-a
3 [ ] ĝiš-du$_3$ gun$_3$-a
1 [ ] ĝiš-du$_3$
3 gu$_4$
1 gu$_4$ amar ga gun$_3$-a
6 ab$_2$ babbar$_2$
3 ab$_2$ gun$_3$-a
rev. 6 ab$_2$
1 ab$_2$ amar ga
šu-niĝin$_2$ 27 gu$_4$ ab$_2$ hi-a
gu$_4$ mar-tu
mu-DU lugal
ki Na-ra-am-i$_3$-li$_2$-ta
Lu$_2$-^{d}Nanna šabra i$_3$-dab$_5$
iti še-KIN-ku$_5$
mu ^{d}Amar-^{d}EN.ZU lugal / mu us$_2$-sa-bi

383: SM 1911.10.311 (AS8 --)

obv. 6 ša$_{3}$-tuku$_{5}$ na$_{2}$ / lugal BAD
ki A-mur-DIĜIR-ta
Lugal-ku$_{3}$-zu
šu ba-ti
rev. ====
iti ezem [ ]
mu En-[^{d}Nanna]-/^{d}Amar-^{d}EN.[ZU-ra]-/ki-aĝ$_{2}$ An-na / ba-huĝ
left 6

384: SM 1911.10.315 (ŠS2 x 11)

obv. 1 udu niga 3-kam-[us$_{2}$]
1 sila$_{4}$ niga ^{d}Nanna
ša$_{3}$ Ga-eš^{ki}
2 udu niga sig$_{5}$-us$_{2}$
kišib A-ši-bu
u$_{4}$ 11-kam
ki In-ta-e$_{3}$-a-/ta
rev. ba-zi
====
iti ezem An-na
mu ma$_{2}$ ^{d}En-ki-ka / ba-ab-[du$_{8}$]
seal [^{d}Šu-^{d}EN.ZU]
lugal kala-[ga]
lugal Uri$_{5}$[^{ki}-ma]
lugal an ub-[da limmu$_{2}$-ba]
Ur-^{d}Šul-[pa-e$_{3}$]
dub-[sar]
dumu Ur-[^{d}Ha-ia$_{3}$]
[arad$_{2}$-zu]

385: SM 1911.10.316 (ŠS1 xiid 17)

obv. 15 udu
mu kaš$_{4}$-e-ne-še$_{3}$
5 udu 1 amar maš-da$_{3}$ nita$_{2}$
ba-ug$_{7}$ e$_{2}$ muhaldim
mu aga$_{3}$-us$_{2}$-e-ne-še$_{3}$

u$_4$ 17-kam
rev. ki Du$_{11}$-ga-ta
ba-zi
==== (*seal*)
iti diri še-KIN-ku$_5$
mu ^{d}Šu-^{d}EN./ZU lugal
seal ^{d}Amar-^{d}EN.ZU
lugal kala-ga
lugal Uri$_5$[^{ki}-ma]
lugal an ub-d[a limmu$_2$-ba]
[Ur-^{d}Šu]l-pa-e$_3$
[dub-sar]
[dumu Ur-^{d}Ha-ia$_3$]
[arad$_2$-zu]

For this seal impression reconstruction, see PPAC 4 191 and PDT 1 244.

386: SM 1911.10.317 (ŠS2 iv)

obv. 1 še$_3$-tuku$_5$ siki / [ud$_5$-ta]
ki A-mur-DIĜIR-ta
Lugal-ku$_3$-zu
šu ba-ti
rev. ša$_3$ PU$_3$.ŠA-iš-/^{d}Da-gan
iti ki-siki ^{d}Nin-a-zu
mu ^{d}Šu-^{d}EN.ZU / lugal-e ma$_2$ ^{d}En-ki-/ka in-dim$_2$

387: SM 1911.10.318 (IS2 vi)

obv. 60.0.0 in-n[u gur]
e$_2$ Lugal-ma$_2$-[gur$_8$]-/re-še$_3$
ĝiri$_3$ U$_2$-ṣi-/na-wi-ir ra$_2$-gaba
rev. ki ^{d}Nanna-ku$_3$-/zu sipa gu$_4$ niga
==== (*seal*)
iti ezem ^{d}[Nin]-/a-zu
mu en ^{d}Inana [Unug^{ki}-ga] / maš$_2$-e i$_3$-pad$_3$
seal i ^{d}I-bi$_2$-/^{d}EN.ZU
lugal kala-ga
lugal Uri$_5$/^{ki}-ma

lugal an ub-/da limmu$_2$-ba
ii Nu-ur$_2$-^{d}EN.[ZU]
dub-sar
dumu I-di$_3$-/Er$_3$-[ra]
arad$_2$-zu

388: SM 1911.10.319 (ŠS3 vi 20)

obv. 2 udu niga
^{d}Inana Unug^{ki}-ga
A-hu-ni sagi / maškim
iti u$_4$ 20 ba-zal
rev. ki Ur-^{d}Nanna-ta
ba-zi
==== (*seal*)
iti a$_2$-ki-ti
mu Si-ma-num$_2$^{ki} / ba-hul
seal (*illegible*)

389: SM 1911.10.320 (Š44 x)

obv. 26 gu$_4$ niga
33 gu$_4$
3 ab$_2$
505 udu
162 maš$_2$
mu-DU lugal
rev. ki Na-ra-am-i$_3$-li$_2$-/ta
bala-a zi-ga
A-hu-a ensi$_2$ Šuruppag^{ki}
i$_3$-dab$_5$
iti ezem An-na
mu Si-mu-ru-um^{ki} / u$_3$ Lu-lu-bu^{ki} / a-ra$_2$ 10-la$_2$-1-kam-aš ba-hul

390: SM 1911.10.321 (ŠS1 xii 19)

obv. 2 gu$_4$
10 udu
šu-gid$_2$

2 udu ba-ug$_7$
e$_2$ muhaldim
mu aga$_3$-us$_2$-e-ne-/še$_3$
rev. Arad$_2$-ĝu$_{10}$ maškim
u$_4$ 20-la$_2$-1-kam
ki Du$_{11}$-ga-ta / ba-zi
iti še-KIN-ku$_5$
mu ^{d}Šu-^{d}EN.ZU / lugal
seal [^{d}Amar]-^{d}EN.ZU
lugal kala-ga
lugal Uri$_5$^{ki}-ma
lugal an ub-da limmu$_2$-ba
Ur-^{d}Šul-pa-e$_3$
dub-sar
dumu Ur-^{d}Ha-ia$_3$
arad$_2$-zu

391: SM 1911.10.323 (ŠS2 ix)
obv. 2 sila$_4$
ki In-ta-e$_3$-/a-ta
Du$_{11}$-ga i$_3$-dab$_5$
====
rev. iti ezem mah
==== (*seal*)
mu ma$_2$-dara$_3$ abzu / ba-ab-du$_8$
seal Ur-mes
dumu La-na kurušda

392: SM 1911.10.324 (ŠS2 xii)
obv. 3 gu$_4$ niga 3-kam-us$_2$
3 gu$_4$ niga 4-kam-us$_2$
4 gu$_4$ niga
iti šu-eš$_5$-ša
7 udu niga
1 maš$_2$-gal niga
1 maš$_2$-gal niga gu$_4$-e-us$_2$-sa
1 udu

rev. [1] maš$_2$-gal
iti ezem mah
1 gu$_4$ niga 3-kam-us$_2$
2 gu$_4$ niga 4-kam-us$_2$
iti še-KIN-ku$_5$
ki Ta$_2$-hi-iš-a-tal-ta
Kur-bi-la-ak i$_3$-dab$_5$
mu ma$_2$-dara$_3$ abzu / ^{d}En-ki-ka ba-ab-du$_8$
left 13 gu$_4$ 11 udu

393: SM 1911.10.325 (IS3 iii)

obv. 1 še gur
ki Si-ru-ta
Šu-ad-mu
šu ba-ti
rev. ĝiri$_3$ Ur-ni$_9$-[ĝar]
==== (*seal*)
iti šeš-da-gu$_7$
mu ^{d}I-bi$_2$-^{d}EN.ZU / lugal Uri$_5$^{ki}-ma/-ke$_4$ Si-mu-ru-um^{ki} / mu-hul
seal Šu-ad-mu
lu$_2$-[x]
dumu DU$_{10}$-i$_3$-li$_2$

394: SM 1911.10.326 (ŠS7 vii 19)

obv. 10 [ ]
mu [ ]-e-/ne-še$_3$
5 u$_8$ u$_2$ mu kaš$_4$-ke$_4$-ne-še$_3$
šu-gid$_2$ e$_2$ muhaldim
Arad$_2$-ĝu$_{10}$ maškim
u$_4$ 19-kam
rev. ki Ur-ku$_3$-nun-na-ta
ba-zi
ĝiri$_3$ Lu$_2$-ša-lim dub-sar
iti a$_2$-ki-ti
mu ^{d}Šu-^{d}EN.ZU / lugal Uri$_5$^{ki}-ma-ke$_4$ / ma-da Za-ab-ša-li^{ki} / mu-hul
left 15 udu
seal (*illegible*)

395: SM 1911.10.327 (-- -- --)

obv. 2 gu$_4$ niga 8 udu
kaš-de$_2$-a Da-da / gala
6 udu kaš-de$_2$-a / Arad$_2$-ĝu$_{10}$
a$_2$-ĝi$_6$-ba-a
e$_2$ diĝir-e-ne-ke$_4$ / ba-ab-dab$_5$
rev. (*all damaged*)

396: SM 1911.10.328 (AS8 i 7)

obv. 1 sila$_4$ niga
KA-izi-še$_3$
Ur-^{d}Ba-ba$_6$
i$_3$-dab$_5$
rev. u$_4$ 7-[kam]
====
iti maš-da$_3$-gu$_7$
mu us$_2$-sa Hu-/uh$_2$-nu-ri^{ki} / ba-hul
seal Ma-an-gi$_4$
dumu Ur-sa$_6$-[ga]
muhaldim lugal

397: SM 1911.10.329 (IS2 vi 23)

obv. 1 gu$_4$ u$_2$
šu-gid$_2$ e$_2$ muhaldim
mu lu$_2$ šuku-ra-/ke$_4$-ne-še$_3$
Arad$_2$-ĝu$_{10}$ maškim
u$_4$ 23-kam
[ki] Ur-ku$_3$-nun-na-ta
rev. ba-zi
ĝiri$_3$ ^{d}Nanna-ma-ba / [dub-sar]
iti ezem ^{d}Nin-a-zu
mu en ^{d}Inana / Unug^{ki}-ga maš$_2$-e / i$_3$-pad$_3$
left 1 gu$_4$
seal i [^{d}Šu-^{d}EN.ZU]
lugal kala-ga
lugal Uri$_5$/^{ki}-ma
[lugal a]n ub-da / [limmu$_2$-ba]

ii $^{[d]}$Nanna-ma-ba
dub-sar
dumu U$_2$-na-ab-/še-[en$_6$]
[arad$_2$-zu]

398: SM 1911.10.330 (ŠS9)

obv. 6 ma-na siki / gi
bar udu 60-kam
ki Ur-^{d}En-lil$_2$-la$_2$-/ta
Ur-ku$_3$-nun-na
rev. šu ba-ti
==== (*seal*)
mu e$_2$ ^{d}Šara$_2$ / ba-du$_3$
seal i ^{d}Šu-^{d}EN.ZU
lugal kala-ga
lugal Uri$_5$/^{ki}-ma
lugal an ub-/da limmu$_2$-ba
ii Ur-ku$_3$-nun-na
dub-sar
[dumu Lu$_2$-^{d}Nin-ĝir$_2$-su] kurušda
[arad$_2$-zu]

399: SM 1911.10.333 (IS2 xi 6)

obv. (*all damaged*)
rev. u$_4$ 6-kam
ĝiri$_3$ Du$_{11}$-ga / dub-sar
iti ezem An-na
mu en ^{d}Inana / Unug^{ki}-ga maš$_2$-e / i$_3$-pad$_3$

400: SM 1911.10.336 (AS8 iii 27)

obv. 2 udu niga
^{d}Nanna-igi-du$_8$-a
A-tu sagi maškim
2 udu niga sig$_5$
mu-du-lum-še$_3$
^{d}Šul-gi-iri-ĝu$_{10}$ maškim

5 udu šu-gid$_2$ e$_2$ muhaldim
mu gar$_3$-du-e-ne-še$_3$
rev. 1 udu niga La-qi$_3$-pu-[um] / lu$_2$ Ma-ri$_2$^{ki}
ĝiri$_3$ Šu-ab-ba sukkal
Arad$_2$-ĝu$_{10}$ maškim
iti u$_4$ 27 ba-zal
ki Šu-Ma-ma-ta ba-zi
iti u$_5$-bi$_2$-gu$_7$
mu en Eridu^{ki} ba-huĝ
left 10-la$_2$-1 udu
seal BU-la
dub-sar
arad$_2$ ^{d}Nin-[ ]

401: SM 1911.10.338 (IS2 xi 17)

obv. 1 sila$_4$
lugal-e in-šum
u$_4$ 17-kam
ki In-ta-e$_3$-a-ta
ba-zi
rev. ĝiri$_3$ Nu-ur$_2$-^{d}EN.ZU / dub-sar
iti ezem An-na
mu en ^{d}Inana Unug^{ki}-/ga maš$_2$-e i$_3$-pad$_3$
left 1 udu
seal i ^{d}Šu-^{d}EN.ZU
lugal kala-ga
lugal Uri$_5$/^{ki}-ma
lugal an ub-/da limmu$_2$-ba
ii Nu-ur$_2$-^{d}EN.ZU
dub-sar
dumu I-di$_3$-Er$_3$-r[a]
arad$_2$-zu

402: SM 1911.10.340 (AS4 vi 11)

obv. 7 udu kun-gid$_2$
40 u$_8$ kun-gid$_2$
u$_4$ 11-kam
ĝiri$_3$ Ib-ni-DIĜIR sukkal

ki Nu-i_3-da-ta
mu-DU
Ab-ba-sa_6-ga
rev. i_3-dab_5
====
iti a_2-ki-ti
mu En-mah-gal / en ^{d}Nanna ba-/huĝ
left 47

403: SM 1911.10.342 (Š47 iii)

obv. 1/2 $sila_3$ i_3-ĝiš
ki Ur-^{d}Lamma-ta
Ur-^{d}Nanše
šu ba-ti
rev. iti u_5-bi_2-gu_7
==== (*seal*)
mu us_2-sa Ki-maš^{ki} / ba-hul
seal Ur-^{d}Nanše
dumu Gu-[za-ni kurušda]

404: SM 1911.10.343 (-- -- --)

obv. 1 ^{munus}$aš_2$-gar_3 2 udu
e_2-$še_3$
1 $sila_4$ Lu_2-an-na
$ša_3$ Eridu^{ki} ki-be_2 gi_4-a
1 $maš_2$ babbar ma_2-a gub-ba
Uri_5!(DAH.AB)^{ki}-ta
2 $sila_4$ ma_2-a gub-ba
$ĝiri_3$ Ur-^{d}Ba-ba_6
rev. (*all damaged*)
left 2 $sila_4$ mu-DU en ^{d}Nanna i_3-dab_5
1 $sila_4$ Ur-^{d}Nin-$ĝir_2$-su

405: SM 1911.10.345 (AS9 iv 16)

obv. 10-la_2-1 udu
1 $maš_2$-gal

u_4 16-kam
ki Ab-ba-sa_6-ga-/ta
rev. Na-lu_5
i_3-dab_5
====
iti ki-siki ^{d}Nin-a-zu
mu en ^{d}Nanna / Kar-zi-da ba-huĝ
left 10 udu

406: SM 1911.10.346 (ŠS1 iii)

obv. 0.3.0 $imgaga_3$ lugal
sa_2-du_{11}-$še_3$
ki Lu_2-ša-lim-ta
Lu_2-du_{10}-ga
šu ba-ti
rev. $ĝiri_3$ Lu_2-^{d}Nanna
====
iti u_5-bi_2-gu_7
mu ^{d}Šu-^{d}EN.ZU / lugal

407: SM 1911.10.347 = SM 1911.10.635 (-- -- --)

obv. 0.2.0 dabin DUB [ ]
pisan-dub-ba
$ša_3$ e_2 PU_3.[ŠA-iš]-/^{d}Da-[gan^{ki}]
ki Ur-^{d}Iš[taran-ta]
ba-[zi]
rev.* 28 ^{anše}$kunga_2$
$niĝ_2$-gur_{11} Šu-^{d}EN.ZU
1 ^{anše}$kunga_2$
$niĝ_2$-gur_{11} ^{d}Šul-[gi]-/kalam-ma-[me-te-bi]
(*ending damaged*)

This tablet is an artificial mixture of different obverses and reverses. The reverse (SM 1911.10.635) is not the reverse of this tablet (SM 1911.10.347) but the reverse of another unknown tablet, which was lost artificially at some time (either ancient or modern).

408: SM 1911.10.349 (ŠS7 i 20)

obv. 1 gu$_4$ u$_2$ šu-gid$_2$
mu ur-mah-še$_3$
Arad$_2$-ĝu$_{10}$ maškim
u$_4$ 20-kam
ki Ur-ku$_3$-nun-na-ta / ba-zi
rev. ĝiri$_3$ ^{d}Nanna-ma-ba / dub-sar
iti še-KIN-ku$_5$
mu ^{d}Šu-^{d}EN.ZU / lugal Uri$_5$^{ki}-ma / ma-da Za-ab-ša-/li^{ki} mu-hul
left 1 gu$_4$
seal i [^{d}Šu-^{d}EN.]ZU
lugal kala-ga
lugal Uri$_5$/^{ki}-ma
lugal an ub-/da limmu$_2$-ba
ii ^{d}Nanna-[ma-ba]
dub-[sar]
dumu [U$_2$-na-ab-še-en$_6$]
arad$_2$-[zu]

409: SM 1911.10.351 (-- x)

obv. 4 gu$_4$ niga
dal-ba-na-še$_3$
6 gu$_4$ niga
e$_2$-u$_4$-15-še$_3$
10 gu$_4$ niga
e$_2$-u$_4$-sakar-še$_3$
1 gu$_4$ niga
rev. [ki ^{d}E]N.ZU-še$_3$
====
[šu-niĝin$_2$] 21 gu$_4$ niga
ki A-hu-ni-ta
^{d}En-lil$_2$-la$_2$
i$_3$-dab$_5$
iti ezem An-na

410: SM 1911.10.352 (AS7 viii)

obv. 4.2.3 še-gur / lugal
ša$_3$-gal ^{anše}kunga$_2$

dah-hu iti 3-kam
ki DI.KU$_5$-i$_3$-li$_2$-ta
Ur-^{d}Dumu-zi-da
rev. šu ba-ti
iti a$_2$-ki-ti-ta
iti šu-eš$_5$-ša-še$_3$
====
mu Hu-uh$_2$-nu-ri^{ki} / ba-hul

411: SM 1911.10.353 (Š41 viii)

obv. 2 [ ]
Geme$_2$-^{d}Nin-lil$_2$-la$_2$
^{d}EN.ZU-ILLAT-su / maškim
rev. ki E$_2$-a-DIĜIR-ta
ba-zi
iti šu-eš$_5$-ša
mu us$_2$-sa PU$_3$.ŠA-/iš-^{d}Da-gan ba-du$_3$ / mu-us$_2$-sa-bi

Cf. Nisaba 8 386 (Š41 vii-ix).

412: SM 1911.10.354 (AS2 vi)

obv. [7] har ku$_3$-babbar 20 gin$_2$-/ta
ša$_3$-ni-[x]
Nam-ha-ni [maškim]
PU$_3$.ŠA-Er$_3$-ra
rev. (*beginning damaged*)
ša$_3$ PU$_3$.ŠA-iš-/^{d}Da-gan
iti a$_2$-ki-ti
mu ^{d}Amar-^{d}[EN].ZU / lugal-e Ur-bi$_2$-/lum^{ki} mu-hul
====
left 7

This text is published in BPOA 10, pl. 22 SM 1911.10.354 (AS2 vi).

413: SM 1911.10.355 (AS7 vi 5)

obv. 1 sila$_4$ Bur-Ma-ma / dam-gar$_3$
1 sila$_4$ Lu$_2$-^{d}Inana / dam-gar$_3$

1 sila$_4$ Da-da-ni
u$_4$ 5-kam
rev. mu-DU
Ab-ba-sa$_6$-ga <i$_3$-dab$_5$>
====
iti a$_2$-ki-ti
mu Hu-uh$_2$-nu-/ri^{ki} ba-hul
left 3

Obv. 1-3: For three lambs, see SACT 1 46 (AS7 vi 5).

414: SM 1911.10.356 (AS4 xi)

obv. 1 uruda [ ]
ki-la$_2$-bi [ ]
ne-saĝ-[ ] / ki-ba [ ]
ki Šeš-[ ]
a-ša$_3$ [ ]
rev. Ur-[ ] / dumu [ ]
šu ba-[ti]
====
iti ezem Me-ki-[ĝal$_2$]
mu En-mah-[gal]-/an-na en ^{d}[Nanna] / [ba]-huĝ

415: SM 1911.10.357 (AS9 xii 12)

obv. 1 sila$_4$ ga
e$_2$-u$_4$-15-ka / e$_2$-gal-la ba-an-ku$_x$(KWU147)
ME-^{d}Ištaran
ĝiri$_3$ Na-lu$_5$ / kurušda
rev. iti u$_4$ 12 ba-zal
ki Na-lu$_5$-ta
ba-zi
ša$_3$ Nibru^{ki}
ĝiri$_3$ Ur-^{d}En-lil$_2$-la$_2$ dub-sar
iti še-KIN-ku$_5$
mu en ^{d}Nanna Kar-/zi-da ba-huĝ
left 1

416: SM 1911.10.358 (ŠS4 vi)

obv. 3 udu niga
sa$_2$-du$_{11}$ Geme$_2$-^{d}En-lil$_2$-la$_2$
dumu-munus en-na
iti 1-kam
ki Na-lu$_5$-[ta]
rev. ba-z[i]
ša$_3$ Nibru^{ki}
iti ezem ^{d}Nin-a-zu
mu us$_2$-sa Si-ma-/num$_2$^{ki} ba-hul

417: SM 1911.10.359 (ŠS2 xi)

obv. 20 [ ]
(*ending damaged*)
rev. gig Lu$_2$-^{d}En-/lil$_2$-la$_2$ dam-gar$_3$
====
iti ezem Me-ki-ĝal$_2$
mu ma$_2$-dara$_3$ Abzu / ^{d}En-ki-ka ba-ab-du$_8$

418: SM 1911.10.361 (AS6 v)

obv. [ ] i$_3$-/ĝiš
[ki Lugal]-he$_2$-ĝal$_2$-/ta
Lu$_2$-^{d}Nin-šubur
šu ba-ti
ša$_3$ Ba-ba-az^{ki}
rev. ====
iti ezem ^{d}Nin-a-zu
mu ^{d}Amar-^{d}EN.ZU / lugal-e Ša-aš-ru^{ki} / mu-hul

Obv. 5: The geographical name is also attested in OrSP 47-49 134.

419: SM 1911.10.362 (-- -- --)

obv. 10 udu
10 maš$_2$ gal
Ur-tur i$_3$-dab$_5$
ki A-al-la-/mu-ta

rev. ba-zi
==== (*seal*)
seal i ^{d}Šu-^{d}EN.ZU
lugal kala-ga
lugal Uri$_5$/^{ki}-ma
lugal an ub-/da limmu$_2$-ba
ii Ur-ku$_3$-nun-na
dub-sar
dumu Lu$_2$-^{d}Nin-/ĝir$_2$-su
arad$_2$-zu

420: SM 1911.10.363 (ŠS9 i)

obv. 47 udu ma[š$_2$ hi-a]
ki Za-zi-ta
104 sila$_4$ si
ki Lugal-ezem-ta
[120]+56 udu maš$_2$ hi-a
rev. zi-ga ša$_3$ Unug^{ki} / Uri$_5$^{ki} u$_3$ [ ]
ki Ur-mes-ta
kišib Ab-ba-kal-[la]
==== (*seal*)
iti še-KIN-ku$_5$
mu e$_2$ ^{d}Šara$_2$ ba-du$_3$
left 326+[1 x]
seal Ab-ba-kal-la
dub-sar
dumu Lu$_2$-[^{d}Nin-ĝir$_2$-su]

421: SM 1911.10.365 (ŠS3 vi)

obv. 29 ma-na / siki gi
bar-udu mu-DU-ra
mu-DU
Nu-ur$_2$-^{d}EN.ZU
rev. šu ba-ti
ĝiri$_3$ Nu-ur$_2$-^{d}IŠKUR / dub-sar
iti a$_2$-ki-ti
mu Si-ma-num$_2$^{ki} / ba-hul

seal [Nu-ur$_2$-^{d}IŠKUR]
dumu [Šu-^{d}IŠKUR]
kuš$_7$ lugal

The seal impression is reconstructed from TLB 3 32.

422: SM 1911.10.366 (AS6 iii 4)

obv. 1 si[la$_4$]
[ ]
1 [ ]
1 sila$_4$ [ ]
u$_4$ 4-kam
rev. [ ]
zi-[ga]
[ki] En-[ ]
iti u$_5$-bi$_2$-gu$_7$
[m]u Ša-aš-ru$^{[ki]}$ / ba-hul

423: SM 1911.10.367 (ŠS1 iv 19)

obv. 2 udu niga
ki-a-naĝ ^{d}Šul-gi
2 udu niga
ki-a-naĝ ^{d}Amar-^{d}EN.ZU
ki u$_4$ 3-še$_3$
ezem A-bu-um-ma
rev. ĝiri$_3$ Šu-^{d}Nin-šubur
Lugal-ku$_3$-zu maškim
iti u$_4$ 20-la$_2$-1 ba-zal
ki Na-lu$_5$-ta ba-zi
ša$_3$ Uri$_5$^{ki}-ma
iti ki-siki ^{d}Nin-a-zu
mu ^{d}Šu-^{d}EN.ZU lugal
left 4

Cf. JCS 46 124 EM 2 (ŠS1 iv 23).

424: SM 1911.10.368 (-- -- --)

obv. [ ] 12 [x]
[x]+21 udu
5 u$_8$
200 maš$_2$
105 ud$_5$
mu-DU lugal
rev. ====
Ab-[ba-sa$_6$-ga i$_3$-dab$_5$]
(*ending damaged*)

425: SM 1911.10.370 (AS2 iii)

obv. 1/3 {ša} ku$_3$-[babbar]
ma-ša-lum-še$_3$
Nam-ha-ni
ki PU$_3$.ŠA-Er$_3$-/ra-ta
ba-zi
rev. ša$_3$ PU$_3$.ŠA-iš-/^{d}Da-gan
iti u$_5$-bi$_2$^{mušen}-gu$_7$
mu ^{d}Amar-^{d}EN.ZU / lugal-e Ur-bi$_5$-⟨lum^{ki}⟩ / mu-hul
left 1/3 {ša}

426: SM 1911.10.372 (AS8 viii 25)

obv. 2 gu$_4$ niga
14 udu
1 sila$_4$
5 maš$_2$
bala ensi$_2$ Umma^{ki}
u$_4$ 25-kam
rev. ki Ab-ba-sa$_6$-/ga-ta
Lu$_2$-sa$_6$-ga
i$_3$-dab$_5$
----
iti šu-eš$_5$-ša
mu en Eridu^{ki} / ba-huĝ
left 2 gu$_4$ 20 udu

427: SM 1911.10.373 (Š40 vii)

obv. 5 sila$_3$ ninda
Bu$_3$-ša-num$_2$
2 sila$_3$ U-bar ugula uš-/bar
2 sila$_3$ Lu$_2$-^{d}Inana
4 sila$_3$ Ur-li
rev. ====
e$_2$ kišib-ba-ta
====
iti ezem ^{d}Šul-gi
mu us$_2$-sa e$_2$ / PU$_3$.ŠA-iš-^{d}Da-/gan ba-du$_3$

428: SM 1911.10.374 (Š38 vii)

obv. 1 še gur lugal
sa$_2$-du$_{11}$ Geme$_2$-^{d}Nin-/lil$_2$-la$_2$-ka-še$_3$
ki Ki-tuš-lu$_2$-ta
Ur-^{d}Ig-alim
rev. šu ba-ti
====
iti ezem ^{d}Šul-gi
mu us$_2$-sa bad$_3$ / ma-da ba-du$_3$

429: SM 1911.10.375 (AS8 x 4)

obv. 1 gu$_4$
u$_4$ 4-kam
ki Ab-ba-sa$_6$-ga-/ta
Ur-šu-ga-lam-ma
rev. i$_3$-dab$_5$
====
iti ezem An-na
mu en Eridu^{ki} / ba-huĝ
left 1

430: SM 1911.10.376 (ŠS4 vii 19)

obv. 1 udu u$_2$ ba-uš$_2$
e$_2$ muhaldim

mu lu$_2$ šuku-ra-/ke$_4$-ne-še$_3$
iti u$_4$ 19 ba-zal
rev. 5 ki Ur-ku$_3$-nun-na-/ta ba-zi
ĝiri$_3$ Hu-la-al / dub-sar
iti a$_2$-ki-ti
mu us$_2$-sa Si-ma-/num$_2^{ki}$ ba-hul
left 1 udu

431: SM 1911.10.377 (AS - ix 18)

obv. (*beginning damaged*)
1' [u$_4$] 18-kam
ki Ab-ba-sa$_6$-ga-/ta
In-ta-e$_3$-a
rev. 1 i$_3$-dab$_5$
====
[iti ezem] mah
[mu]

432: SM 1911.10.378 (ŠS1 ix)

obv. 1 2 ab$_2$
ba-ug$_7$
mu-DU
e$_2$-gal-še$_3$
5 ki Du$_{11}$-ga-ta
rev. ====
iti ezem mah
mu ^{d}Šu-^{d}EN.ZU / lugal

433: SM 1911.10.379 (AS8 viii 10+)

obv. 1 60 udu
40 maš$_2$-gal
u$_4$ 10+[x]-kam
ki A[b-ba-s]a$_6$-/[ga-ta]
rev. 5 Na-lu$_5$
i$_3$-dab$_5$
====

iti šu-eš-ša
mu en Eridu^{ki} / ba-hul
left 100 udu

434: SM 1911.10.381 (Š36 v)

obv. 2 gu$_4$
la$_2$-ia$_3$ su-ga SI.A
A-ab-ba-bi
i$_3$-dab$_5$
rev. iti ezem ^{d}Nin-a-zu
mu ^{d}Nanna Kar-/zi-da a-ra$_2$ 2-kam-aš / e$_2$-a-na ba-an-ku$_4$
====

435: SM 1911.10.382 (IS1 iv)

obv. 1 gu$_4$ šu-gid$_2$
ĝiri$_3$ PU$_3$.ŠA-/u$_3$-gur ra$_2$-gaba
ki Nu-ur$_2$-zu-ta
gaba-ri
kišib Ab-ba-kal-la
rev. ====
iti u$_3$-bi$_2$-gu$_7$
mu ^{d}I-bi$_2$-/^{d}EN.ZU lugal

436: SM 1911.10.383 (AS7 i 10)

obv. 1 sila$_4$ Ur-ni$_9$-[ĝar]
1 sila$_4$
Da-da-u$_3$
u$_4$ 10-kam
mu-DU
Ab-ba-sa$_6$-ga
rev. i$_3$-dab$_5$
====
iti maš-da$_3$-gu$_7$
mu Hu-uh$_2$-/nu-ri^{ki} ba-hul
left 2

437: SM 1911.10.384 (ŠS7 vii 6)

obv.	2 udu u$_2$
	1 u$_8$ u$_2$
	ba-ug$_7$ u$_4$ 6-kam
	ki Ur-ku$_3$-nun-na-ta
	$^{[d]}$Šul-gi-iri-ĝu$_{10}$
	šu ba-ti
rev.	ĝiri$_3$ I-din-Er$_3$-/ra
	iti a$_2$-ki-ti
	mu ^{d}Šu-^{d}EN.ZU / lugal Uri$_5$^{ki}/-ma
	ma-da Za-ab-ša/-li^{ki} mu-hul
left	3 udu
seal	[ ]
	dub-sar
	dumu [x]-ne-ne

438: SM 1911.10.385 (AS6 v 7)

obv.	2 sila$_4$
	u$_4$ 7-kam
	ki Ab-ba-sa$_6$-/ga-ta
	In-ta-e$_3$-a
rev.	i$_3$-dab$_5$
	====
	iti ezem ^{d}Nin-/a-zu
	mu Ša-aš-ru^{ki} / ba-hul

This text is a duplicate of OIP 121 329 (AS6 v 7). For these animals, see PDT 2 1187 (AS6 v 7).

439: SM 1911.10.386 (AS5 i 30)

obv.	1 uz-tur
	1 ir$_7$^{mušen}
	5 tu-gur$_4$^{mušen}
	[ ]
rev.	u$_4$ 30-kam
	zi-ga
	[ki] ^{d}Šul-gi-/^{d}Lamma-mu-ta

iti maš-da$_3$-gu$_7$
mu en ^{d}Inana / [ba-huĝ]

440: SM 1911.10.387 (-- vi)

obv. 17 u$_8$
8 maš$_2$
ki DU$_{10}$-i$_3$-li$_2$-/ta
rev. Ur-^{d}Nanše
i$_3$-dab$_5$
iti a$_2$-ki-/ti

Cf. AUCT 1 671 (AS5).

441: SM 1911.10.388 (AS5 x)

obv. 1 še lugal
ki Ur-šu-ga-lam-ma-/ta
Geme$_2$-ra-maš-ri$_2$-si dam
E$_2$-an-na
rev. šu ba-ti
====
iti ezem An-na
mu En-unu$_6$-/gal ^{d}Inana ba-huĝ

442: SM 1911.10.389 (Š45 iii)

obv. 1 udu
ba-uš$_2$
ki Kalam-he$_2$-na-/gi-ta
e$_2$-gal-la [ba-an]-ku$_x$(KWU147)
rev. ====
iti u$_5$-bi$_2$-gu$_7$
mu us$_2$-sa Si-mu-ru-um/^{ki} Lu-lu-bu^{ki} / a-ra$_2$ 10-la$_2$-1-kam-aš / ba-hul

443: SM 1911.10.390 (Š45 i 3)

obv. 1 maš$_2$-gal a-dara$_4$
3 maš-da$_3$

5 amar maš-da$_3$
ba-ug$_7$
u$_4$ 3-kam
rev. ki A-hu-ni-ta
Ur-ni$_9$-ĝar
šu ba-ti
iti maš-da$_3$-gu$_7$
mu us$_2$-sa Si-mu-ru-um^{ki} / Lu-lu-bu^{ki} a-ra$_2$ / 10-la$_2$-1-kam-aš ba-hul

444: SM 1911.10.391 (ŠS1 xii 23)

obv. 2 udu
1 maš$_2$ gal
ba-ug$_7$ u$_4$ 23-kam
ki Ur-^{d}Ig-alim-<ta>
rev. ^{d}Šul-gi-iri-/ĝu$_{10}$
šu ba-ti
iti še-KIN-ku$_5$
mu ^{d}Šu-^{d}EN.ZU / lugal

445: SM 1911.10.392 (ŠS1 v 13)

obv. 2 udu niga
2 udu
ba-ug$_7$ u$_4$ 13-kam
ki Be-li$_2$-i$_3$-li$_2$-/ta
rev. ^{d}Šul-gi-iri-/ĝu$_{10}$
šu ba-ti
iti ezem ^{d}Nin-a-zu
mu ^{d}Šu-^{d}EN.ZU / lugal
left 4 udu

446: SM 1911.10.393 (AS2 vii 16)

obv. 1 gu$_4$
u$_4$ 16-kam
ki Ab-ba-sa$_6$-/ga-ta
^{d}Šul-gi-/a-a-ĝu$_{10}$
rev. i$_3$-dab$_5$

----
iti ezem ^{d}Šul-/gi
mu ^{d}Amar-^{d}EN.ZU / lugal-e Ur-[bi$_{2}$]-/lum^{ki} mu-[hul]
left 1

447: SM 1911.10.394 (AS4 x 6)

obv. 5 udu niga
1 sila$_{4}$ niga
u$_{4}$ 6-kam
ki Ab-ba-sa$_{6}$-ga-/ta
rev. Na-lu$_{5}$ i$_{3}$-dab$_{5}$
----
iti ezem An-na
mu En-mah-gal-/an-na en ^{d}Nanna / ba-huĝ
left 6

448: SM 1911.10.395 (ŠS8 v 18)

obv. 3 ^{munus}aš$_{2}$-gar$_{3}$ niga gu$_{4}$-e us$_{2}$-sa
1 ^{munus}aš$_{2}$-gar$_{3}$ niga
^{d}Inana
siskur$_{2}$ ša$_{3}$ e$_{2}$-gal
ĝiri$_{3}$ A-bi$_{2}$-si$_{2}$-/im-ti
^{d}EN.ZU-a-bu-šu sagi maškim
rev. ša$_{3}$ PU$_{3}$.ŠA-iš-[^{d}Da-gan]
a$_{2}$-ĝi$_{6}$-ba-[a]
u$_{4}$ 18-[kam]
ki PU$_{3}$.ŠA-^{d}En-lil$_{2}$-ta / ba-zi
iti ki-siki ^{d}Nin-a-zu
mu ^{d}Šu-^{d}EN.ZU / lugal Uri$_{5}$^{ki}-ma-ke$_{4}$ / ma$_{2}$-gur$_{8}$ mah ^{d}En-lil$_{2}$ / ^{d}Nin-lil$_{2}$-ra mu-ne-/dim$_{2}$
left 4
seal i ^{d}Šu-^{d}EN.ZU
lugal kala-ga
lugal Uri$_{5}$^{ki}-ma
lugal an ub-da [limmu$_{2}$-ba]
ii [Ur]-^{d}Šul-pa-e$_{3}$
dub-sar

du[mu U]r-^{d}[Ha-ia$_3$]
[arad$_2$-zu]

449: SM 1911.10.398 (ŠS1 i 8)

obv. 3 udu niga
2 maš$_2$-gal niga
e$_2$ muhaldim
mu kaš$_4$-e-ne-še$_3$
5 udu niga gu$_4$-e-us$_2$-sa
5 maš$_2$ gal niga gu$_4$-e-us$_2$-sa
Me-nu-tum
e$_2$-gi$_4$-a Šu-ru-uš-ki-/in
ĝiri$_3$ ^{d}Nanna-kam sukkal
Arad$_2$-ĝu$_{10}$ maškim
2 udu
rev. 3 maš$_2$ niga
Ba-ba-ti KAM.ME lugal
Tu-ra-am-^{d}Da-gan / ra$_2$-gaba maškim
iti u$_4$ 8 ba-zal
ki Na-lu$_5$-ta
ba-zi
ša$_3$ Nibru^{ki}
ĝiri$_3$ Ur-^{d}En-lil$_2$-la$_2$ dub-sar
iti maš-da$_3$-gu$_7$
mu ^{d}Šu-^{d}EN.ZU / lugal
left 20
seal Ur-^{d}[En-lil$_2$-la$_2$]
dub-sar
dumu Lugal-[ur$_2$]-ra-ni

450: SM 1911.10.399 (ŠS3 xi 5)

obv. 2 udu niga 3-kam us$_2$
2 udu [niga] 4-kam us$_2$
^{d}Nin-lil$_2$
eš$_3$-eš$_3$ e$_2$-u$_4$-7
lugal ku$_4$-ra
1 udu niga 4-kam us$_2$

1 ^{munus}aš$_2$-gar$_3$ niga 3-kam us$_2$
^{d}Inana
rev. [ ] 4-kam us$_2$
$^{[d]}$Utu
siskur$_2$ ša$_3$ e$_2$-gal
====
iti u$_4$ 5 ba-zal
ki ^{d}En-lil$_2$-zi-ša$_3$-ĝal$_2$-ta
ba-zi
iti ezem Me-ki-ĝal$_2$
mu ^{d}Šu-^{d}EN.ZU lugal-e / Si-ma-num$_2$^{ki} mu-hul
seal ^{d}Šu-^{d}EN.ZU
lugal kala-ga
lugal Uri$_5$^{ki}-ma
lugal an ub-da limmu$_2$-ba
Ur-^{d}Šul-pa-e$_3$
dub-sar
dumu Ur-^{d}Ha-ia$_3$
arad$_2$-zu

451: SM 1911.10.402 (Š42 xi)

obv. 0.1.0 še lugal
a-ra$_2$ 1-kam
0.1.0 a-ra$_2$ 2-kam
0.1.0 a-ra$_2$ 3-kam
e$_2$-še$_3$ ME-^{d}En-[lil$_2$]
ugula PU$_3$.ŠA-Er$_3$-ra ma$_2$-lah$_5$
0.0.1 Šu-^{d}IŠKUR
0.0.1 A$_2$-bi$_2$-li$_2$
ša$_3$-bi-[t]a
0.0.2 sa$_{10}$ gi Har-ra-[an]-/^{ĝiš}gigir
5 sila$_3$ sa$_{10}$ gi
Lugal-bad$_3$
1.0.2 ša$_3$-gal kin-na-še$_3$
rev. An-da-ga
0.0.2 še ^{anše}kunga$_2$ U$_3$-ma-/ni kuš$_7$
5 sila$_3$ sa$_{10}$ gi A$_2$-nin-ĝa$_2$-ta
0.0.1 sa$_{10}$ gi Ur-^{d}Gilgames$_x$(BIL$_3$./GA.MES)

0.1.0 Na-ap-li$_2$-is ma$_2$-lah$_5$
====
šu-niĝin$_2$ 2.0.4 gur
zi-ga še U$_3$-ṣa-ru-um-a-/ur$_2$-ra^{ki} e$_2$-da-ba-ta
iti ezem Me-ki-ĝal$_2$
mu Ša-aš-ru-um^{ki} ba-hul

Obv. 10: For this PN, cf. ITT 3 6546.

452: SM 1911.10.404 (AS9 vii 27)

obv. 1 udu niga ^{ĝiš}gu-za / ^{d}Šul-gi
1 udu niga ^{ĝiš}gu-za ^{d}Amar-^{d}EN.ZU
Ur-^{d}Šul-pa-e$_3$ muhaldim / maškim
2 udu niga sig$_5$-us$_2$
2 udu niga 3-kam-us$_2$
2 maš$_2$ gal niga 3-kam-us$_2$
2 udu niga 4-kam-us$_2$
A-bi$_2$-si$_2$-im-ti
rev. Unug^{ki}-še$_3$ ma$_2$-a ba-na-/a-gub
ĝiri$_3$ Šar-ru-um-i$_3$-li$_2$ sagi
iti u$_4$ 27 ba-zal
ki Igi-^{d}En-lil$_2$-še$_3$-ta
ba-zi
ĝiri$_3$ [Ma-num$_2$]-ki-^{d}Šul-/gi dub-sar
iti [ezem ^{d}Šul]-gi
mu [^{d}Nanna Ka]r-zi-/[da ba-huĝ]
left 10 udu

453: SM 1911.10.409 (Š35 xi)

obv. 185 gu$_4$ niga
201 gu$_4$ u$_2$
480 udu gal
3600+147 udu
240 sila$_4$ ga
2400+287 maš$_2$
111 maš$_2$ ga
mu-DU lugal

ki Na-ra-am-i$_3$-li$_2$-/ta
rev. (*beginning damaged*)
[iti -^{d}Nin-a]-zu-ta
[iti ezem Me]-ki-ĝal$_2$-še$_3$
[iti x]-kam
mu us$_2$-sa An-/ša-an^{ki} ba-hul
iti diri 1-am$_3$ Unug^{ki} ša$_3$-ba / i$_3$-ĝal$_2$

454: SM 1911.10.411 (Š35)
left 1 eme$_6$ šu-gi$_4$
6 dur$_3$ šu-gi$_4$
ki Lu$_2$-banda$_3$^{da} ensi$_2$-ta
Lugal-ur$_2$-ra-ni / sipa-ur i$_3$-dab$_5$
rev. mu us$_2$-sa An-ša-an^{ki} ba-hul
seal i ^{d}Šul-gi
nita kala-ga
lugal Uri$_5$/^{ki}-ma
ii Lugal-ur$_2$-[ra-ni]
sipa ur
arad$_2$-zu

Note that this text is an envelope.

455: SM 1911.10.412 (AS7 xi)
obv. 66 udu
18 sila$_4$
120 u$_8$
32 maš$_2$ gal
5 maš$_2$
5 ud$_5$ mu-DU lugal
6 sila$_4$ gu-gu-tum-ma
180 udu
20 u$_8$
5 maš$_2$-gal 150-la$_2$-1 maš$_2$
7 ^{munus}aš$_2$-gar$_3$
rev. šu-gid$_2$ ĝiri$_3$ sipa-e-ne

šu-niĝin$_2$ 270 udu

šu-niĝin$_2$ [120]+20 u$_8$
šu-niĝin$_2$ [180]+11 maš$_2$
šu-niĝin$_2$ 12 ud$_5$
ki In-ta-e$_3$-a-ta
Ur-ku$_3$-nun-na i$_3$-dab$_5$
iti e[zem M]e-ki-ĝal$_2$
mu Hu-uh$_2$-nu-ri^{ki} / ba-hul
left 613

For the content, cf. PDT 1 575 (AS7 xi).

456: SM 1911.10.413 (AS6 xi)

obv. 4 gu$_4$
iti šeš-da-gu$_7$
2 gu$_4$ niga 3 gu$_4$
60 udu
iti ezem Me-ki-ĝal$_2$
ki ^{d}Šul-gi-a-a-/ĝu$_{10}$-ta
mu Ta$_2$-din-Eš$_{18}$-tar$_2$-še$_3$
rev. Ur-[^{d}En-l]il$_2$-la$_2$ i$_3$-dab$_5$
dub ^{d}Lamma-[igi-d]u
ba-an-bala
====
mu Ša-aš-ru^{ki} / ba-hul

Rev. 9-10: For the term dub-bi ... bala "to go over the account," see J. A. Halloran, *Sumerian Lexicon: A Dictionary Guide to the Ancient Sumerian Language*, Los Angeles: Logogram Publishing, 2006, p. 47.

457: SM 1911.10.414 (-- -- --)

obv. 4 ab$_2$
17 udu u$_2$
4 ^{munus}aš$_2$-gar$_3$
kišib Šu-i$_3$-li$_2$
56 udu u$_2$
kišib-bi 3-am$_3$
rev. kišib Ur-ku$_3$-nun-na

3 [x]
kišib Ur-[ ]
====
gaba-ri kišib [x]
====

458: SM 1911.10.415 (ŠS4 viii 6)

obv. 2 gu$_4$ niga
6 udu u$_2$
2 sila$_4$
8 maš$_2$
kaš-de$_2$-a
Nir-i$_3$-da-ĝal$_2$
rev. a$_2$-ĝi$_6$-ba-a
2 gu$_4$ niga
8 udu u$_2$ 4 maš$_2$
kaš-de$_2$-a Lugal-a$_2$-zi-/da šabra
a$_2$-u$_4$-te-na
e$_2$ diĝir-e-ne-še$_3$ ba-ab-dab$_5$
ĝiri$_3$ Lugal-amar-ku$_3$ dub-sar
u$_4$ 6-kam
mu-DU In-ta-e$_3$-a i$_3$-dab$_5$
iti ezem ^{d}Šul-gi
mu bad$_3$ Mu-ri-[iq]-Ti-id-/ni-i[m ba-d]u$_3$
left 4 gu$_4$ 28 udu
seal Lugal-[amar-ku$_3$]
dub-sar
dumu Na-sa$_6$

Cf. No. 285; BPOA 6 87; AAICAB 1/4 Bod S 574.

459: SM 1911.10.416 (ŠS9 x 16)

obv. 1 gu$_4$ niga 3-kam us$_2$
kaš-de$_2$-a
^{d}Inana ^{ĝiš}tukul
ša$_3$ e$_2$-gal
lugal ku$_4$-ra

u$_4$ 16-kam
[ki] PU$_3$.ŠA-^{d}En-lil$_2$-/ta
rev. ba-zi
ša$_3$ Uri$_5$^{ki}-ma
====
iti ezem mah
mu ^{d}Šu-^{d}EN.ZU / lugal Uri$_5$^{ki}-ma-ke$_4$ / [e$_2$] ^{d}Šara$_2$ Umma^{ki}-/[k]a mu-du$_3$
seal i ^{d}Šu-^{d}EN.ZU
lugal kala-ga
lugal Uri$_5$/^{ki}-ma
lugal an ub-/da limmu$_2$-ba
ii Ur-^{d}Šul-pa-e$_3$
dub-sar
dumu Ur-^{d}Ha-ia$_3$
arad$_2$-zu

460: SM 1911.10.417 (ŠS4 vii 2)

obv. 1 gu$_4$ mu-3
1 gu$_4$ amar ga
4 udu u$_2$
ba-ug$_7$ e$_2$ muhaldim
mu lu$_2$ šuku-ra-/ke$_4$-ne-še$_3$
rev. [u$_4$] 2-kam
[ki] Ur-ku$_3$-nun-na-/ta ba-zi
====
iti a$_2$-ki-ti
mu us$_2$-sa Si-ma-/num$_2$^{ki} ba-hul
seal ^{d}Šu-^{d}EN.ZU
lugal kala-ga
lugal Uri$_5$^{ki}-ma
lugal an ub-da limmu$_2$-ba
Ur-[^{d}Šul-pa-e$_3$]
dub-[sar]
dumu Ur-^{d}[Ha-ia$_3$]
[arad$_2$-zu]

461: SM 1911.10.418 (AS9 v)

obv. 5 maš$_2$
ki Lugal-iti-da-ta
Ur-^{d}Amar-^{d}EN.ZU
i$_3$-dab$_5$
rev. kišib Lu$_2$-^{d}Da-/mu
==== (*seal*)
iti ezem ^{d}Nin-a-zu
mu en ^{d}Nanna / Kar-zi-da ba-huĝ
seal Lu$_2$-^{d}[Da-mu]
dub-[sar]
dumu [ ]

462: SM 1911.10.420 (Š33 ix)

obv. 12 maš-da$_3$ ba-ug$_7$
iti a$_2$-ki-ti
====
2 maš-da$_3$ ba-ug$_7$ iti ezem mah
Šu-ku$_8$-bu-um-e šu [ba]-ti
rev. mu us$_2$-sa a-ra$_2$ / 3-kam-aš Si-mu-ru-um/^{ki} ba-hul
====
seal i Geme$_2$-^{d}EN.ZU
dam Šul-gi
lugal Uri$_5$/^{ki}-ma
ii Šu-ku-bu-um
ra$_2$-[gaba]
arad$_2$-[zu]

463: SM 1911.10.421 (-- -- --)

obv. [ ]
[ ]
[ ]
ĝiri$_3$ [ ]-sa$_6$
3 maš-da$_3$ nita$_2$ 3 maš-da$_3$ munus
1 amar maš-da$_3$ nita$_2$ 3 amar maš-da$_3$ munus
ĝiri$_3$ Ur-ĝar
[ki] In-ta-e$_3$-a-ta

[ ] 40-la$_2$-1 udu ĝiri$_3$ Du$_{11}$-ga
[ ] maš$_2$ ĝiri$_3$ Ur-ĝar
rev. [ ] ensi$_2$ Adab^{ki}
[ki ^{d}]EN.ZU-ta
[ ]-mu i$_3$-dab$_5$
[ ] u$_8$ 2 sila$_4$ ga
[ ] maš$_2$ gal
[ ]-ta
[ ] Nu-ur$_2$-^{d}EN.ZU-ta
[ ] i$_3$-dab$_5$
[ ] la
[L]u$_2$-me-lam$_2$ i$_3$-dab$_5$
[ ] IM DA ZU
[ ] la
3 sila$_4$ ^{d}EN.ZU-ba-ni u$_4$ 10-la$_2$-1-kam
3 sila$_4$ ša$_3$ 6 u$_4$ 14-kam
left [ ] 25 udu 52 az
ki A-hu-We-[er-ta]

464: SM 1911.10.422 (ŠS7 vii)

obv. [ ] še lugal
[ ] ni-iš / [x] Šu-^{d}Nin-šubur
[ ] dah-hu-am$_3$
bala Ur-e$_2$-an-na / ensi$_2$
rev. [iti] a$_2$-ki-ti
[mu] ^{d}Šu-^{d}EN.ZU / lugal Uri$_5$^{ki}-ma-/ke$_4$
ma-da Za-ab-ša-/li^{ki}
mu-hul
left [ ]

465: SM 1911.10.423 (IS1 iv)

obv. 15 udu u$_2$
15 maš$_2$ gal u$_2$
ba-ug$_7$ sa$_2$-du$_{11}$ ur-gi$_7$-ra
PU$_3$.ŠA-^{d}En-lil$_2$ / sipa ur-gi$_7$-ra-ke$_4$
šu ba-ti
rev. ugula Šu-^{d}Ma-mi-tum

ki Ur-ku$_3$-nun-na-ta
ba-zi
ĝiri$_3$ Nu-ur$_2$-^{d}EN.ZU / dub-sar
iti u$_5$-bi$_2$^{mušen}-gu$_7$
mu ^{d}I-bi$_2$-^{d}EN.ZU / lugal
left 30 udu
seal i ^{d}Šu-^{d}EN.ZU
lugal kala-ga
lugal Uri$_5$/^{ki}-ma
lugal an ub-/da limmu$_2$-ba
ii Nu-ur$_2$-^{d}EN.ZU
dub-sar
dumu I-di$_3$-Er$_3$-ra
arad$_2$-zu

466: SM 1911.10.425 (ŠS6 iii 6)
obv. 1 sila$_4$ Ur-mes ensi$_2$
1 sila$_4$ ^{d}Šul-gi-/na-da
mu-DU lugal
In-ta-e$_3$-a
[i$_3$]-dab$_5$
obv. [ĝiri$_3$] ^{d}Nanna-ma-ba / dub-sar
[u$_4$] 6-kam
iti šeš-da-gu$_7$
mu us$_2$-sa ^{d}Šu-^{d}EN.ZU / lugal Uri$_5$^{ki}-ma-ke$_4$ / bad$_3$ mar-tu Mu-ri-iq-/
Ti-id-ni-im mu-du$_3$ / mu us$_2$-sa-bi
left 2 u[du]
seal i ^{d}Šu-^{d}EN.ZU
lugal kala-ga
lugal Uri$_5$/^{ki}-ma
lugal an ub-/da limmu$_2$-ba
ii ^{d}[Nanna-ma-ba]
dub-sar
dumu U$_2$-na-ab-/še-en$_6$
[arad$_2$-zu]

467: SM 1911.10.426 (ŠS3 i 29)

obv. 20-la$_2$-1 udu
[x] sila$_4$
u$_4$ 27-kam
1 [udu] 1 sila$_4$ 1 maš$_2$
5 amar maš-da$_3$
u$_4$ [30]-la$_2$-1-kam
rev. [ki In]-ta-e$_3$-a-ta
[Du$_{11}$]-ga i$_3$-dab$_5$
==== (*seal*)
iti maš-da$_3$-gu$_7$
mu us$_2$-sa ma$_2$ ^{d}En-ki-/ka ba-ab-du$_8$
seal Ur-[mes]
dumu La-[na kurušda]

468: SM 1911.10.427 (-- iii 24)

obv. 2 udu niga gu$_4$-e us$_2$-sa
mu šagina-ne-še$_3$
4 udu niga gu$_4$-e-us$_2$-sa
mu aga$_3$-us$_2$-e-ne-še$_3$
e$_2$ muahldim-še$_3$
3 udu niga
rev. 2 maš$_2$-gal niga
Da-da gala
[ ]
iti u$_4$ 24 ba-zal
ki Na-lu$_5$-ta
ba-zi
ša$_3$ Nibru^{ki}
ĝiri$_3$ Ur-^{d}En-lil$_2$-la$_2$
iti u$_5$-bi$_2$-gu$_7$
left 11
seal (*illegible*)

469: SM 1911.10.428 (ŠS9 iv)

obv. 6 0.0.4 še lugal
[x] ša$_3$ [x] še gur / [P]U$_3$.ŠA-[ ]
rev. ĝiri$_3$ Da-mu
====
iti u$_5$-bi$_2$-gu$_7$
mu e$_2$ ^{d}Šara$_2$ / ba-du$_3$
seal PU$_3$.ŠA-[ ]
dumu Nu-hi-DIĜIR

470: SM 1911.10.429 (AS - ii)

obv. 0.0.2 3 sila$_3$ ^{ĝiš}hašhur had$_2$
0.0.3 3 sila$_3$ ĝi$_6$-par$_4$
0.0.1 1 sila$_3$ ĝeštin had$_2$
0.0.1 1 sila$_3$ ga ar$_3$
0.0.1 1 sila$_3$ [ ]
5 sila$_3$ [ ]
6 [ ]
rev. [ ]
20 ma-sa$_2$-ab [ ]
30 ba-ti-um
ma$_2$ su-a
ša$_3$ Unug^{ki}-ga
====
iti šeš-da-gu$_7$
[mu] gu-za / [ ]

471: SM 1911.10.430 (ŠS5 xi 28)

obv. 10 udu u$_2$ šu-gid$_2$
e$_2$ muhaldim
mu [lu$_2$ šu]ku-ra-/ke$_4$-ne-še$_3$
Ur-^{d}Šu-^{d}EN.ZU / sukkal maškim
rev. u$_4$ 28-kam
ki Ur-ku$_3$-nun-na-[ta] / ba-zi
ĝiri$_3$ Hu-la-al dub-sar
iti ezem An-na
mu us$_2$-sa ^{d}Šu-^{d}EN.ZU / lugal Uri$_5$^{ki}-ma-ke$_4$ / bad$_3$ mar-tu Mu-ri-iq-/Ti-id-ni-im / mu-du$_3$

left 10 udu
seal (*illegible*)

472: SM 1911.10.431 (IS2 x 1)

obv. 1 udu u$_2$
1 sila$_4$
zag-u en ^{d}Inana
u$_4$ 1-kam
ki In-ta-e$_3$-a-/ta ba-zi
rev. ĝiri$_3$ ^{d}Nanna-ma-ba / dub-sar
iti ezem mah
mu en ^{d}Inana / Unug^{ki}-ga / maš$_2$-e i$_3$-pad$_3$
left 2 udu
seal ^{d}Šu-^{d}EN.ZU
lugal kala-ga
lugal Uri$_5$/^{ki}-ma
lugal an ub-/da limmu$_2$-ba
^{d}Nanna-ma-ba
dub-sar
dumu [U$_2$-na-ab-še-en$_6$]
arad$_2$-[zu]

473: SM 1911.10.433 (ŠS1 xi 23)

obv. 8 udu
3 sila$_3$ ^{d}En-lil$_2$
8 udu
3 sila$_3$ ^{d}Nin-lil$_2$
siskur$_2$ alan-na
^{d}En-lil$_2$-zi-ša$_3$-ĝal$_2$ / maškim
u$_4$ 23-kam
rev. ki Du$_{11}$-ga-ta
ba-zi
====
iti ezem Me-ki-ĝal$_2$
mu [^{d}Šu]-^{d}EN.ZU / lugal
seal (*illegible*)

474: SM 1911.10.435 (ŠS4 ix 12)

obv.	1 gu$_4$ niga 3-kam-us$_2$
	^{d}En-lil$_2$
	1 udu niga sig$_5$
	1 u$_8$ niga sig$_5$
	1 udu niga 3-kam-us$_2$
	2 udu niga 4-kam-us$_2$
	^{d}Nin-lil$_2$
	1 udu niga 4-kam us$_2$ ^{d}Nin-hur-saĝ
rev.	2 udu niga sig$_5$ du$_6$-[ku$_3$]
	1 udu niga ^{d}Ba-ba$_6$
	1 udu niga ^{d}EN.ZU
	eš$_3$-eš$_3$ e$_2$-u$_4$-15
	a$_2$-ĝi$_6$-ba-a
	lugal ku$_4$-ra
	iti u$_4$ 12 ba-zal
	ki ^{d}En-lil$_2$-zi-ša$_3$-ĝal$_2$-[ta]
	ba-zi
	ĝiri$_3$ I-zu-sa-bar [dub-sar]
	iti ezem ^{d}Šu-^{d}E[N.ZU]
	mu bad$_3$ mar-tu [ba-du$_3$]
left	1 gu$_4$ 10 udu
seal	I-zu-sa-bar
	dub-[sar]
	arad$_2$ ^{d}[ ]

475: SM 1911.10.436 (AS9 iv)

obv.	1.3.3 še gur / lugal
	si-i$_3$-tum niĝ$_2$-ka$_9$-ak
	ša$_3$ 62.0.0 še gur
	Lugal-ma$_2$-gur$_8$-re
	in-da-ĝal$_2$
rev.	====
	iti ki-siki ^{d}Nin-a-zu
	mu en ^{d}Nanna / Kar-zi-da ba-huĝ

476: SM 1911.10.437 (ŠS4 ix)

obv. 1 udu [ ]
3 maš$_2$ gal gub
2 ^{munus}aš$_2$-gar$_3$ [ ]
1 maš$_2$ gal a-dara$_4$
niĝ$_2$-ka$_9$-a-še$_3$
libir-a-ni
rev. A-hu-We-er
i$_3$-dab$_5$
====
iti ezem ^{d}Šu-^{d}[EN.ZU]
mu bad$_3$ mar-tu / ba-du$_3$
left gur$_{11}$-gur$_{11}$-ra-a ba-a-ĝar

Cf. AAICAB 1/1 pl. 78 1924-2162 (ŠS4 ix).

477: SM 1911.10.438 (Š41 xiid)

obv. 12 gu$_4$ u$_2$
4 ab$_2$
10 udu u$_2$ 8 udu u$_2$ gi$_6$
2 u$_8$ gi$_6$
187 ud$_5$
42 maš$_2$-gal
mu-DU
rev. ensi$_2$ Šušin^{ki}
ki Ku-li kurušda-ta
Ur-^{d}Ig-alim šabra / i$_3$-dab$_5$
ĝiri$_3$ Lu$_2$-kal-la
iti diri še-KIN-ku$_5$
mu us$_2$-sa e$_2$ PU$_3$./ŠA-iš-^{d}Da-gan ba-du$_3$-a / mu-us$_2$-sa-bi

478: SM 1911.10.439 (AS9 xi)

obv. 60.0.0 še gur lugal
še-ba-še$_3$
še Šeš-kal-la
ki ^{d}Nisaba-an-/dul$_3$-ta
Lu$_2$-^{d}Nin-šubur

rev. šu ba-ti
ša$_3$ PU$_3$.ŠA-iš-/^{d}Da-gan
====
iti ezem Me-ki-ĝal$_2$
mu ^{d}Nanna Kar-/zi-da ba-huĝ

479: SM 1911.10.440 (AS3 ix 25)

obv. 2 udu niga ^{d}En-lil$_2$
1 maš$_2$ gal niga ^{d}gu-za
1 maš$_2$ gal niga hur-saĝ-ga-/lam-ma
2 udu niga ^{d}Nin-lil$_2$
1 udu niga ^{d}Nin-tin-ug$_5$-ga
^{d}Nanše-ul$_4$-gal maškim
4 udu niga siskur$_2$ alan
ša$_3$ e$_2$-gal
rev. Maš-tur sagi maškim
1 udu niga 1 maš$_2$ gal niga
um-me-da ^{d}Nin-lil$_2$-/e-ma-<ki>-aĝ$_2$
Arad$_2$-ĝu$_{10}$ maškim
iti u$_4$ 25 ba-zal
ki Na-lu$_5$-ta ba-zi
ša$_3$ Nibru^{ki}
iti ezem mah
mu ^{d}gu-za ^{d}En-lil$_2$-/la$_2$ ba-dim$_2$
left 13

480: SM 1911.10.441 (ŠS1 i 15)

obv. 1 gu$_4$ niga 3-kam us$_2$
e$_2$ muhaldim
mu kaš$_4$-ke$_4$-ne-še$_3$
Arad$_2$-ĝu$_{10}$ maškim
iti u$_4$ 15 ba-zal
rev. ki Be-li$_2$-i$_3$-li$_2$-ta
ba-zi
====
iti maš-da$_3$-gu$_7$
mu ^{d}Šu-^{d}EN.ZU / lugal
seal ^{d}Amar-^{d}EN.ZU

lugal kala-ga
lugal Uri$_{5}^{ki}$-ma
lugal an ub-da limmu$_2$-ba
Ur-^{d}Šul-pa-e$_3$
dub-sar
dumu Ur-^{d}Ha-ia$_3$
arad$_2$-zu

481: SM 1911.10.444 (ŠS4 vii 22)

obv. 1 gu$_4$ niga 4-kam-us$_2$
ezem ma$_2$ An-na
ša$_3$ e$_2$-gal
ša$_3$ Nibru^{ki}
a$_2$-ĝi$_6$-ba-a
iti u$_4$ 22 ba-zal
rev. ki Ib-ni-^{d}EN.ZU-ta
ba-zi
ĝiri$_3$ Ur-^{d}Šul-gi-/ra šar$_2$-ra-ab-du
iti a$_2$-ki-ti
mu ^{d}Šu-^{d}EN.ZU lugal-e / bad$_3$ Mu-ri-iq-Ti-/id-ni-im mu-du$_3$
left 1 gu$_4$
seal (*illegible*)

482: SM 1911.10.445 (ŠS8 ix 1)

obv. 8 udu ba-ug$_7$
e$_2$ muhaldim
mu lu$_2$ šuku-ra-ke$_4$/-ne-še$_3$
u$_4$ 1-kam
ki Ur-ku$_3$-nun-na-ta
rev. ba-zi
====
iti ezem ^{d}Šu-^{d}EN.ZU
mu ^{d}Šu-^{d}EN.ZU / lugal Uri$_{5}^{ki}$-ma-ke$_4$ / ma$_2$-gur$_8$ ^{d}En-lil$_2$ / ^{d}Nin-lil$_2$-ra mu-/du$_3$
seal ^{d}Šu-^{d}EN.ZU
lugal kala-ga
[lu]gal [Uri$_{5}^{ki}$-ma]

lugal an ub-da limmu$_2$-ba
Ur-^{d}Šul-pa-[e$_3$]
dub-sar
dumu Ur-^{d}Ha-ia$_3$
arad$_2$-zu

483: SM 1911.10.446 (ŠS9 xii 13)

obv. 1 gukkal niga 3-kam-us$_2$
2 udu aslum$_x$(A.LUM) niga 3-kam-us$_2$
A-mur-DIĜIR
PU$_3$.ŠA-Eš$_{18}$-tar$_2$ maškim
u$_4$ 13-kam
ki In-ta-e$_3$-a-ta
rev. ba-zi
ĝiri$_3$ Nu-ur$_2$-^{d}EN.ZU dub-/sar
iti ezem Me-ki-ĝal$_2$
[mu] ^{d}Šu-^{d}EN.ZU / lugal Uri$_5$^{ki}-ma-ke$_4$ / e$_2$ ^{d}Šara$_2$ Umma^{ki}-ka / mu-du$_3$
left 5 [ud]u
seal i ^{d}Šu-^{d}EN.ZU
lugal kala-ga
lugal Uri$_5$/^{ki}-ma
lugal an ub-/da limmu$_2$-ba
ii Nu-ur$_2$-[^{d}EN.ZU]
dub-sar
dumu I-[di$_3$]-/Er$_3$-[ra]
arad$_2$-[zu]

484: SM 1911.10.449 (IS2 ii)

obv. 1 amar maš-da$_3$ nita$_2$
1 amar maš-da$_3$ munus
^{d}En-lil$_2$
1 amar maš-da$_3$ munus
(*ending damaged*)
rev. (*beginning damaged*)
ba-[zi]
ĝiri$_3$ Ib-ni-^{d}[IŠKUR] / šar$_2$-ra-ab-du

ĝiri$_3$ ^{d}Nanna-ma-ba ša$_3$-tam / u$_3$ Pu$_5$-um-wa-qar dub-sar
iti maš-da$_3$-gu$_7$
mu en ^{d}Inana / Unug^{ki}-ga maš$_2$-e / i$_3$-pad$_3$
left 3 maš-da$_3$

485: SM 1911.10.450 (AS9 xii 22)

obv. 1 sila$_4$ a-udu hur-saĝ
1 maš$_2$ a-dara$_4$
^{d}En-lil$_2$
1 sila$_4$ a-udu hur-saĝ
1 ^{munus}aš$_2$-gar$_3$ a-dara$_4$
^{d}Nin-lil$_2$
ša$_3$-ge guru$_7$-a
rev. ^{d}Nanna-igi-du sagi / maškim
iti u$_4$ 22 ba-zal
ki Ta$_2$-hi-iš-a-tal-ta
ba-zi
ĝiri$_3$ ^{d}Šul-gi-i$_3$-li$_2$ / dub-sar
iti še-KIN-ku$_5$
mu en ^{d}Nanna Kar-/zi-da ba-huĝ
left 4
seal (*illegible*)

486: SM 1911.10.451 (AS6 x 4)

obv. 8 maš$_2$
mu-DU ^{d}Šul-/gi-ra
ki Ur-sa$_6$-ga kuš$_7$-/ta
u$_4$ 4-kam
mu-DU
rev. Ab-ba-sa$_6$-ga
i$_3$-dab$_5$
ša$_3$ Uri$_5$^{ki}-ma
====
iti ezem An-na
mu Ša-aš-ru^{ki} ba-/hul
left 8

487: SM 1911.10.452 (ŠS2 ii 24)

obv. 4 udu Hu-li-bar / [ensi$_2$] Du$_8$-du$_8$-li$_2$^{ki}
ĝiri$_3$ Ur-^{d}Ha-ia$_3$ sukkal
2 udu 5 u$_8$
[ ]
[ ]
2 udu ba-ug$_7$ e$_2$ muhaldim
rev. mu aga$_3$-us$_2$-e-ne-še$_3$
Arad$_2$-ĝu$_{10}$ maškim
u$_4$ 24-kam
ki Du$_{11}$-ga-ta ba-zi
ĝiri$_3$ Nu-ur$_2$-^{d}IŠKUR / dub-sar
iti šeš-da-gu$_7$
mu ma$_2$-dara$_3$ abzu / ^{d}En-ki-ka ba-ab-[du$_8$]
left 13
seal [Nu-ur$_2$-^{d}IŠKUR]
[dumu Šu-^{d}IŠKUR]
[kuš$_7$ lugal]

The seal impression is reconstructed from AUCT 3 441, BIN 3 215, and BPOA 6 877.

488: SM 1911.10.453 (ŠS3 i 8)

obv. 2 udu aslum$_x$(A.LUM)
2 sila$_4$
ME-^{d}Ištaran
niĝ$_2$-dab$_5$ e$_2$-u$_4$-15-ka-na
ki-ba ba-na-a-ĝa$_2$-ar
[ša$_3$] mu-DU-ra-ta
rev. [u$_4$] 8-kam
[ki] In-ta-e$_3$-a-ta
ba-zi
ĝiri$_3$ ^{d}Nanna-ma-[ba] / dub-[sar]
iti maš-da$_3$-gu$_7$
mu us$_2$-sa ma$_2$ ^{d}En-ki-/ka ba-ab-du$_8$
left 4
seal ^{d}Nanna-ma-ba
dub-[sar]
dumu U$_2$-na-a[b-š]e-/en$_6$

489: SM 1911.10.454 (-- iii)

obv. [x] gu$_2$ 15 ma-na / siki SAR-ka
en-nu-ta
MAR [x] TU kaš$_4$
rev. gaba-ri kišib Lu$_2$-/diĝir-ra
ĝiri$_3$ Šu-^{d}Nin-šubur
====
iti u$_5$-bi$_2$-/gu$_7$

490: SM 1911.10.455 (AS8 iii 6)

obv. 3 udu
12 u$_8$
5 maš$_2$ gal
mu kaš$_4$-ke$_4$-ne-še$_3$
10 u$_8$ mu gar$_3$-du-/e-ne-še$_3$
šu-gid$_2$ e$_2$ muhaldim
rev. Arad$_2$-ĝu$_{10}$ maškim
u$_4$ 6-kam
ki Du$_{11}$-ga-ta
ba-zi
iti u$_5$-bi$_2$-gu$_7$
mu en Eridu^{ki} / ba-huĝ
left 30
seal i ^{d}Amar-^{d}EN./ZU
nita$_2$ kala-ga
lugal Uri$_5$/^{ki}-ma
[lugal an ub-da limmu$_2$-ba]
ii [ ]
dub-[sar]
dumu [ ]
arad$_2$-[zu]

491: SM 1911.10.456 (IS2 vi 12)

obv. 1 udu niga ^{d}En-lil$_2$
1 udu niga ^{d}Nin-lil$_2$
lugal ku$_x$(KWU147)-ra
ša$_3$ a$_2$-ki-ti-še$_3$

u$_4$ 12-kam
[ki] In-ta-e$_3$-a-/[ta]
[ba]-zi
rev. ĝiri$_3$ Nu-ur$_2$-[^{d}EN.ZU dub-sar]
iti ezem ^{d}N[in-a-zu]
mu en [^{d}Inana] / Unug^{ki}-[ga maš$_2$-e i$_3$-pad$_3$]
left 2 udu
seal ^{d}Šu-^{d}EN.ZU
[lugal kala]-ga
[lugal Uri$_5$^{ki}-ma]
[lugal an ub-da limmu$_2$-ba]
[Nu-ur$_2$-^{d}EN.ZU]
[dub-sar]
[dumu I-di$_3$-Er$_3$-ra]
[arad$_2$-zu]

492: SM 1911.10.458 (AS2 i 9)

obv. 2 amar maš-da$_3$
e$_2$ uz-ga
mu-DU U$_3$-ku
Ur-^{d}Ba-ba$_6$ maškim
11 gu$_4$
110 udu
rev. 75 maš$_2$
e$_2$ muhaldim-še$_3$
ĝišbun$_2$ ša$_3$ e$_2$-gal
Arad$_2$-ĝu$_{10}$ maškim
u$_4$ 10-la$_2$-1-kam
ki Ab-ba-sa$_6$-ga-ta
ba-zi
iti maš-da$_3$-gu$_7$
mu Ur-bi$_2$-lum/^{ki} ba-hul
left 198

493: SM 1911.10.461 (ŠS5 ii 12)

obv. 1 sila$_4$ Arad$_2$-ĝu$_{10}$
1 dara$_3$ nita$_2$ ga

1 dara$_3$ munus ga
Nir-i$_3$-da-ĝal$_2$
1 maš-da$_3$ nita$_2$ 1 maš-da$_3$ munus
Šeš-sa$_6$-ga
1 sila$_4$ ^{d}UTU-ba-ni
1 sila$_4$ Lugal-a$_2$-zi-d[a]
2 udu aslum$_x$(A.LUM) niga 3-kam-us$_2$ 1 s[ila$_4$]
Da-da ensi$_2$
1 sila$_4$ 1 amar maš-da$_3$ munus
Lu$_2$-kala-ga
1 sila$_4$ Lu$_2$-^{d}Nanna
1 sila$_4$ A-da-gal
14
mu-DU lugal

šu-niĝin$_2$ 2 udu aslum$_x$(A.LUM) niga 3-kam-[us$_2$]
šu-niĝin$_2$ 7 [sila$_4$]
rev. šu-niĝin$_2$ 1 dara$_3$ [nita$_2$ ga]
šu-niĝin$_2$ 1 dara$_3$ [munus ga]
šu-niĝin$_2$ 1 maš-da$_3$ [nita$_2$]
šu-niĝin$_2$ 1 maš-da$_3$ [munus]
šu-niĝin$_2$ 1 amar maš-da$_3$ [munus]
14
ša$_3$-bi-[ta]
1 [sila$_4$]
1
Ur-ku$_3$-nun-na i$_3$-[dab$_5$]
1 dara$_3$ munus ga
I-ku-un-pi$_4$-^{d}En-lil$_2$
2 udu aslum$_x$(A.LUM) niga 3-kam-us$_2$
udu-bi Be-li$_2$-i$_3$-li$_2$ ki-ba [ĝa$_2$]-/ĝa$_2$
6 sila$_4$
1 dara$_3$ nita$_2$ ga
1 maš-da$_3$ nita$_2$ 1 maš-da$_3$ munus
1 amar maš-da$_3$ munus
ME-^{d}Ištaran
niĝ$_2$-dab$_5$ e$_2$-u$_4$ 15-ka-ni
ša$_3$ mu-DU-ra-ta
13$^{!}$(14)

zi-ga lugal
[ki-be$_2$ gi$_4$]-a In-ta-e$_3$-a
iti [maš]-da$_3$-gu$_7$
mu us$_2$-sa ^{d}Šu-^{d}EN.ZU lugal Uri$_5$/^{ki}-ma-ke$_4$ bad$_3$ mar-tu Mu-ri-iq-/
Ti-id-[ni]-im mu-du$_3$
left u$_4$ 12-kam

Cf. AAICAB 1/4 J.-C. Faye 1 (ŠS5 ii 12).

494: SM 1911.10.463 (Š43 iii)

obv. 2 ab$_2$ 5 u$_8$
kišib Lu$_2$-bala-sa$_6$-ga dumu / Lu$_2$-Ma$_2$-gan-na
iti ezem An-na
mu 2-kam us$_2$ e$_2$ ba-du$_3$
2 ab$_2$ kišib Ĝiri$_3$-ni-i$_3$-sa$_6$ dumu Ur-/^{ĝiš}gigir
4 ab$_2$ kišib ^{d}Šul-gi-ur-saĝ
4 ab$_2$ kišib 2-kam
kišib Ur-sa$_6$-ga-mu pisan-dub-ba / ^{d}En-ki
4 ab$_2$ kišib Ur-^{d}En-ki / kurušda Ur-^{d}EN.ZU
iti ezem ^{d}Nin-a-zu
2 ab$_2$ kišib Ĝiri$_3$-ni-i$_3$-sa$_6$ / mu Ur-^{d}Nin-sun$_2$-še$_3$
8 ab$_2$ kišib I$_3$-la-la / mu Lu$_2$-du$_{10}$-ga kuš$_7$-še$_3$
10 ab$_2$ kišib Bu$_3$-u$_2$-du
1 ab$_2$ kišib Šu-^{d}Nin-šubur / mu Na-di dumu lugal-še$_3$
7 ab$_2$ 20 u$_8$
kišib-bi 2-am$_3$
kišib Al-la-mu
2 ab$_2$ kišib A-ab-ba sipa gu$_4$
iti ezem mah
mu Ša-aš-ru^{ki} ba-hul
rev. ====
šu-niĝin$_2$ 46 ab$_2$
šu-niĝin$_2$ 25 u$_8$
⟨gu$_4$⟩ udu sila-a sig$_7$-a
e$_3$-e$_3$-de$_3$
ki Na-sa$_6$-ta
Ur-sa$_6$-ga šu ba-ti
iti u$_5$-bi$_2$-gu$_7$

mu en ^{d}Nanna maš-e i$_{3}$-pad$_{3}$
====

Rev. 23-24: For the phrase sila-a sig$_{7}$-a e$_{3}$-e$_{3}$-de$_{3}$ "on the street to be sent out," see M. Sigirst, *Drehem*, Bethesda, MD: CDL Press, 1992, p. 112; and M. Molina and M. Such-Gutiérrez, "On Terms for Cutting Plants and Noses in Ancient Sumer," *JNES* 63 (2004), p. 5.

495: SM 1911.10.465 (ŠS8 ix 22)

obv. 37 udu gub-ba-am$_{3}$
iti ezem ^{d}Šul-gi u$_{4}$ 18 ba-zal
406 udu mu-DU ša$_{3}$ Tum-ma-al
14 udu ki Nu-ur$_{2}$-zu-ta
7 udu ki ^{d}Nanna-ma-ba-ta
4 udu ki Lugal-ur$_{2}$-ra-ni-ta
12 udu ki A$_{2}$-saga$_{10}$-ta
2 udu ki U$_{4}$-lam-ma-ta
----
7 udu ki Nu-ur$_{2}$-^{d}IŠKUR-ta
11 udu ki Nu-ur$_{2}$-^{d}IŠKUR min-ta
2 udu ki Arad$_{2}$-ĝu$_{10}$-ta
410-la$_{2}$-1 udu mu-DU ša$_{3}$ Nibru$^{k[i]}$
73 udu ki Lugal-ezem-t[a]
26 udu ki Šu-i$_{3}$-li$_{2}$-ta
1014 udu
ša$_{3}$-bi-ta
rev. 202 udu kišib [ ]
(*some lines damaged*)
zi-ga-am$_{3}$
592 udu gub-ba
----
niĝ$_{2}$-ka$_{9}$-ak Za-zi
iti ezem ^{d}Šu-^{d}EN.ZU u$_{4}$ 22 ba-zal
mu ma$_{2}$-gur$_{8}$ mah ba-dim$_{2}$

496: SM 1911.10.466 (-- -- --)

obv. (*beginning damaged*)
[x] A-ab-ba-[ ]
[x] Lugal-si-ĝar
[x] Ur-^{d}Nin-da
1 In-za-mu
4 Ur-^{d}Šara$_2$
5 A-ga
52 A-tu
8 Ur-^{d}Ba-ba$_6$
6 An-bu-a
50-la$_2$-1 Kal-la
15 Ur-ĝar
[x] I-ku-nu-um
2 Ur-lu$_2$-lal$_3$
1 Ur-^{d}Lamma
2 G[u]-du
2 ^{d}[U]tu-me-lam$_2$
[x] ^{d}Nanna-i$_3$-sa$_6$
[x] Lugal-dur$_2$
1 Ur-^{d}EN.ZU
2 Lugal-me-lam$_2$
2 Ur-^{d}Ba-ba$_6$
[x]+5 gu$_4$ A$_2$-na-na
rev. 3 anše ki Lu$_2$-bi-mu-ta
274
ki Unug$_3$-e-ne-ta
3 gu$_4$ Ur-^{d}Nirah
3 gu$_4$ Lugal-he$_2$-ĝal$_2$
ki ^{d}En-lil$_2$-la$_2$-ta
1 gu$_4$ ki ^{d}En-lil$_2$-la$_2$-i$_3$-sa$_6$-ta
158 gu$_4$ 2 dusu$_2$
ki Ab-ba-sa$_6$-ga-ta
ša$_3$-bi-ta
8 gu$_4$ ba-ug$_7$ ša$_3$ kišib ^{d}Šara$_2$-kam / lu$_2$ mar-sa in-su
----
šu-niĝin$_2$ 441 gu$_4$
(*ending damaged*)

Cf. MVN 8 146 (Š42 i-xii).

497: SM 1911.10.467 (Š45 iv)

obv. 44 gu$_4$ hi-a
33 udu maš$_2$ hi-a
si-i$_3$-tum niĝ$_2$-ka$_9$-ak
kišib Na-sa$_6$
mu e$_2$ PU$_3$.ŠA-iš-^{d}Da-gan ba-du$_3$
67 udu maš$_2$ hi-a
kišib-bi 2-am$_3$
ša$_3$ Uri$_5$^{ki}-ma
iti ezem mah
mu An-ša-an^{ki} ba-hul

šu-niĝin$_2$ 44 gu$_4$ 100 udu
ki U$_3$-sa$_6$-a-ta
Na-sa$_6$ i$_3$-dab$_5$
saĝ niĝ$_2$-gur$_{11}$-ra-kam ša$_3$-bi-ta
44 gu$_4$ kar-ru kišib didli u$_3$ sila-ta
2 gu$_4$ niga udu-da la$_2$-a ša$_3$ / mu en ^{d}Nanna maš$_2$-e i$_3$-pad$_3$ / bar-ta ĝal$_2$-la
rev. ki ^{d}En-lil$_2$-la$_2$-ta
63 udu maš$_2$ hi-a
kišib didli-bi 5-am$_3$
kišib Ur-^{d}Ha-ia$_3$
15 udu kišib U$_3$-sa$_6$-a
ša$_3$ kišib-ba
libir-am$_3$
10 udu gu$_4$-da la$_2$-a ša$_3$ Tum-al
ĝiri$_3$ ^{d}En-lil$_2$-la$_2$ mu en ^{d}Nanna maš-e i$_3$-pad$_3$ / bar-ta ĝal$_2$-la
----
šu-niĝin$_2$ 46 gu$_4$ 88 udu
Du$_{11}$-ga-gi-na A$_2$-la-la-kam
1 udu kišib Ur-^{d}Ha-ia$_3$ DUL$_3$-la GAN$_2$-bi / gudu$_x$(HI×NUN)-e ba-ab-du$_{11}$
1 gu$_4$ ki ^{d}En-lil$_2$-la$_2$-ta
10 udu e$_2$ udu Nin$_9$-kal-la Na-lu$_5$-/ta
ĝiri$_3$ Zu-u$_2$-zu
bar-ta ĝal$_2$-la gur$_{11}$-ra diĝir-da-am$_3$ / A$_2$-la-la-kam
niĝ$_2$-ka$_9$-ak gu$_4$ udu U$_3$-sa$_6$-a-ka
iti ki-siki ^{d}Nin-a-zu 2-kam
mu Ur-bi$_2$-lum^{ki} ba-hul

Rev. 27: The phrase Du$_{11}$-ga-gi-na A$_{2}$-la-la-kam means "Duga-gina of Alala." The PN Du$_{11}$-ga-gi-na is also attested in JCS 35 200 1 (ŠS 6 vi). For the term A$_{2}$-la-la-kam, see BE 3/1 1 (ŠS 5 xii).

498: SM 1911.10.468 (AS8 iv)

obv. 77 u$_{8}$ 20+[3 udu]
bar-ĝ[al$_{2}$]
4 u$_{8}$ 6 udu bar-s[u]
ša$_{3}$ kišib-ba ĝiri$_{3}$ Za-z[i]
4 udu bar-ĝal$_{2}$ 2 u$_{8}$ bar-ĝal$_{2}$
ki sipa Maš-kan$_{2}$-du-du^{ki}-[ta]

šu-niĝin$_{2}$ 27 udu bar-ĝal$_{2}$
šu-niĝin$_{2}$ 80-la$_{2}$-1 u$_{8}$ bar-ĝal$_{2}$
šu-niĝin$_{2}$ 6 udu bar-su 4 u$_{8}$ bar-su
116
ša$_{3}$-bi-ta
24 udu bar-ĝal$_{2}$
rev. 6 udu bar-su-ga
57 u$_{8}$ bar-ĝal$_{2}$ 4 u$_{8}$ bar-su-ga
91
sipa Maš-kan$_{2}$-du-du^{ki} i$_{3}$-dab$_{5}$
3 udu bar-ĝal$_{2}$ 22 u$_{8}$ bar-ĝal$_{2}$
25
DIĜIR-ba-ni i$_{3}$-dab$_{5}$
====
niĝ$_{2}$-ka$_{9}$-ak Hu-ru-[ ]
iti ki-siki ^{d}Nin-a-[zu]
mu en Eridu[^{ki} ba-huĝ]

499: SM 1911.10.469 (AS3 viii)

obv. 6 gu$_{4}$
1000 udu
618 maš$_{2}$
ib$_{2}$-tak$_{4}$ kišib dab-ba didli
10-la$_{2}$-1 maš-da$_{3}$
a$_{2}$-ĝi$_{6}$-il$_{2}$-la Ur-mes / ensi$_{2}$ Iri-saĝ-rig$_{7}$^{ki}

2 gu$_4$ ĝiri$_3$ ensi$_2$ Ĝir$_2$-su^{ki}
4 gu$_4$ niga ĝiri$_3$ ^{d}En-lil$_2$-la$_2$
2 gu$_4$ niga ĝiri$_3$ In-ta-e$_3$-a
45 gu$_4$ 34 ab$_2$
rev. ĝiri$_3$ Ab-ba-sa$_6$-ga

šu-niĝin$_2$ 6 gu$_4$ niga
šu-niĝin$_2$ 53 gu$_4$ 34 ab$_2$
šu-niĝin$_2$ 1000 udu
šu-niĝin$_2$ 618 maš$_2$ 10-la$_2$-1 maš-da$_3$
93 gu$_4$ / 1618 udu 10-la$_2$-1 maš-/da$_3$
šu-šum$_2$-ma ki Ab-ba-sa$_6$-ga-ta
In-ta-e$_3$-a i$_3$-dab$_5$
iti šu-eš$_5$-ša ba-zal
mu gu-za ^{d}En-lil$_2$-la$_2$ / ba-dim$_2$

500: SM 1911.10.470 (Š41 ix --)

obv. 1 sila$_4$ u$_4$ 2-kam
2 sila$_4$ u$_4$ 5-kam
13 udu u$_4$ 7-kam
5 udu KU.KU u$_4$ 8-kam
80 udu u$_4$ 10-kam
60 udu u$_4$ 11-kam
30-la$_2$-3 udu u$_4$ 12-kam
90 udu u$_4$ 14-kam
90 udu u$_4$ 16-kam
40 udu u$_4$ 17-kam
40 udu u$_4$ 20-la$_2$-1-kam
68 udu u$_4$ 21-kam
420 udu u$_4$ 22-kam
90 udu u$_4$ 23-kam
30 udu u$_4$ 24-kam
40 udu u$_4$ 25-kam
rev. 30 udu u$_4$ 20+[x-kam]
240-la$_2$-1 udu u$_4$ [x-kam]
e$_2$ muhaldim [ ]
11 udu e$_2$ ki[šib-ba]
30 udu sa$_2$-du$_{11}$ [ ]

30 udu ba-ug$_7$ DIĜIR-[ba-ni šu b]a-ti
852 udu zi-ga lugal
30-la$_2$-1 udu zi-ga Ta$_2$-di$_3$-Eš$_{18}$-tar$_2$ / kišib E$_2$-a-ni-ša
bala ensi$_2$ Ĝir$_2$-su^{ki} ba-zi
====
zi-ga iti ezem mah
mu us$_2$-sa e$_2$ ba-du$_3$-a / mu us$_2$-sa-bi
left šu-niĝin$_2$ 2317 udu maš$_2$ hi-a

Obv. 4: The sign KU.KU may be read eh$_3$ "cripple," although the term udu eh$_3$ "crippled sheep" is never attested in any Ur III texts.

501: SM 1911.10.471 (ŠS8 x 26)

obv. 210 udu [ ]
5 udu la$_2$-ia$_3$ [su-ga]
iti ezem ^{d}Šul-gi u$_4$ 8 ba-zal
50 udu Sa-bu-um^{ki}
ki In-ta-e$_3$-a-ta
36 udu mu-DU
ki Du$_{11}$-ga-ta
ša$_3$ kišib-ba
15 udu ki A-la-mu-ta
8 udu ki Šu-i$_3$-li$_2$-ta
ša$_3$ udu Uri$_5$^{ki}-še$_3$ er-ra
324
ša$_3$-bi-ta
73 udu a-ra$_2$ 1-kam
90 udu a-ra$_2$ 2-kam
kišib Za-zi
rev. 27 udu ĝiri$_3$ A-a-diĝir
37 udu e$_2$ muhaldim-še$_3$
kišib Du$_{11}$-ga
2 udu kišib ^{d}EN.ZU-ba-ni
11 udu kišib sipa ur-ra
70 udu kišib A-a-diĝir
kišib dab-ba didli
5 udu ĝiri$_3$ Lu$_2$-diĝir-ra
Ur-ku$_3$-nun-na i$_3$-dab$_5$

bar-[ta] ĝal$_2$-la
315
zi-ga-am$_3$
10-la$_2$-1 udu la$_2$-ia$_3$-am$_3$
niĝ$_2$-ka$_9$-ak Lugal-ezem
iti ezem mah u$_4$ 26 ba-zal
mu ma$_2$-gur$_8$ mah ba-[dim$_2$]

Obv. 11: Cf. AAICAB 1/2 pl. 106 1937-072, BIN 3 249: ša$_3$-gal udu Uri$_5$^{ki}-še$_3$ er-ra.

502: SM 1911.10.472 (AS8 iv)

obv. 12 udu
^{d}IŠKUR-ILLAT na-gada i$_3$-dab$_5$
8 u$_8$
3 kir$_{11}$ ga
5 sila$_4$ ga
Li-lum na-gada i$_3$-dab$_5$
21 u$_8$
3 kir$_{11}$ ga
5 sila$_4$ ga
Ma-at-i$_3$-li$_2$ na-gada i$_3$-dab$_5$
17 ud$_5$
8 ^{munus}aš$_2$-gar$_3$ ga
1 maš$_2$-gal
rev. 6 maš$_2$ ga
DIĜIR-su$_2$-ba-ni na-gada i$_3$-dab$_5$
ki Ab-ba-sa$_6$-ga-ta
sipa nam-en-na-ke$_4$
ib$_2$-dab$_5$
ugula A-hu-ni kuš$_7$
====
iti ki-siki ^{d}Nin-a-zu
mu En-nun-e-^{d}Amar-^{d}EN.ZU-/ra-ki-aĝ$_2$ en Eridu^{ki} / ba-huĝ
left 90-la$_2$-1

503: SM 1911.10.473 (AS2 viii 14)

obv. [2]+6 lulim nita$_2$ niga
126 lulim nita$_2$

120-la$_2$-1 lulim munus
27 šeg$_9$-bar nita$_2$
40 šeg$_9$-bar munus
3 ^{anše}si$_2$-si$_2$ nita$_2$
4 ^{anše}si$_2$-si$_2$ munus
1 amar ^{anše}si$_2$-si$_2$ munus
1 anše ^{d}Šul-gi-ra / sum-ma munus
13 udu hur-saĝ
1 u$_8$ hur-saĝ
rev. šu-gid$_2$
60-la$_2$-1 az
u$_4$ 14-ka[m]
ki Ab-ba-sa$_6$-ga-ta
Lu$_2$-diĝir-ra i$_3$-dab$_5$
====
iti šu-eš$_5$-ša
mu ^{d}Amar-^{d}EN.ZU / lugal-e Ur-bi$_2$-/lum^{ki} mu-hul
left 402

Obv. 9: Cf. AUCT 2 191.

504: SM 1911.10.474 (AS4 ix 1)

obv. 4 gu$_4$ 15 udu 15 maš$_2$ / gal
^{d}En-lil$_2$ ^{d}Nin-lil$_2$
^{d}Nanše-ul$_4$-gal maškim
3 udu udu a-da-min-še$_3$
Nam-ha-ni kuš$_7$ maškim
1 udu 1 maš$_2$ gal
^{d}gu-za ^{d}Šul-gi-ra
Ša$_3$-ta-ku$_3$-zu ra$_2$-gaba maškim
10 gu$_4$ 30 udu 30 maš$_2$ gal
A-bu-ni
A-bu-um-DIĜIR ra$_2$-gaba maškim
rev. 20 udu Lugal-a$_2$-zi-da
Lugal-kaš$_4$-e du-[x]-/ku-ni 10-am$_3$ in-TAG-/a-se$_3$
ĝiri$_3$ A-hu-ni sukkal
Tah-ša-tal ra$_2$-gaba maškim
ša$_3$ mu-DU Ṣe-lu-uš-^{d}/Da-gan
u$_4$ 1-kam

----
ki Ab-ba-sa$_6$-ga-ta / ba-zi
iti ezem mah
mu En-mah-gal-an-na / en ^{d}Nanna ba-huĝ
left 14 gu$_4$ 115 udu

Obv. 4: Cf. Nisaba 8 129.
Obv. 13: Cf. AnOr 7 104, rev. 4' (lugal Nibru^{ki}-še$_3$ du-ni).

505: SM 1911.10.475 (ŠS2 xi 27)

obv. 2 gu$_4$ lugal Iri-saĝ-rig$_7$(PA.HUB$_2$./DU)^{ki}-še$_3$ du-ni ma$_2$-a ba-a-ĝar
1 gu$_4$ mu aga$_3$-us$_2$-e-ne-še$_3$
šu-gid$_2$ e$_2$ muhaldim u$_4$ 8-kam
1 gu$_4$ šu-gid$_2$ e$_2$ muhaldim
u$_4$ 12-kam
3 gu$_4$ šu-gid$_2$ e$_2$ muhaldim
mu ur-mah-še$_3$
u$_4$ 14-kam
1 gu$_4$ šu-gid$_2$ e$_2$ muhaldim
u$_4$ 26-kam
1 ^{anše}kunga$_2$ munus
rev. 1 dusu$_2$ nita$_2$
šu-gid$_2$ e$_2$ muhaldim
mu ur-mah-še$_3$
u$_4$ 27-kam
====
šu-niĝin$_2$ 8 gu$_4$
šu-niĝin$_2$ 1 ^{anše}kunga$_2$ munus
šu-niĝin$_2$ 1 dusu$_2$ nita$_2$
====
ki ^{d}En-lil$_2$-la$_2$-ta
ba-zi
iti ezem Me-ki-ĝal$_2$
mu ma$_2$-dara$_3$ abzu / ^{d}En-ki ba-ab-du$_8$
left 8 gu$_4$ 2 anše

506: SM 1911.10.476 (AS4 viii 8)

obv. 2 gu$_4$
0 udu
7 maš$_2$ gal
^{d}En-lil$_2$ ^{d}Nin-lil$_2$
[x] udu 2 maš$_2$ gal
[^{d}Luga]l-gu$_4$-si-su
[ĝiri$_3$ Ša]r-ru-um-i$_3$-li$_2$ sagi
[^{d}Nanš]e-ul$_4$-gal maškim
[ ] 1 maš$_2$ gal
[^{d}g]u-za ^{d}Šul-gi-ra
[Ša$_3$-ta]-ku$_3$-zu ra$_2$-gaba maškim
[x] gu$_4$
[I$_3$]-lal$_3$-lum
[x] udu LU$_2$.SU
rev. [ ] LU$_2$.SU
[Lu]gal-ma$_2$-gur$_8$-re
[š]a$_3$ mu-DU-ra-ta
[1] sila$_4$ ^{d}En-lil$_2$
1 sila$_4$ ^{d}Nin-lil$_2$
mu-DU Wa-ta$_2$-ru-um saĝĝa
^{d}Nanše-ul$_4$-gal maškim
u$_4$ 8-kam
ki Ab-ba-sa$_6$-ga-/ta ba-zi
iti šu-eš$_5$-ša
mu En-mah-gal-an-na / en ^{d}Nanna ba-huĝ
left 30+[ ]

507: SM 1911.10.477 (-- xi --)

obv. 1 gu$_4$ niga a-tu$_5$-a / ^{d}Nin-tin-ug$_5$-ga
2 gu$_4$ niga ezem ab-e$_3$
ki-a-naĝ Ur-^{d}Namma-ka
4 gu$_4$ niga Dal-ba-na
10-la$_2$-1 gu$_4$ niga 11 gu$_4$
eš$_3$-eš$_3$ u$_4$-sakar
1 gu$_4$ niga 1 ab$_2$ mu-2 niga
ki ^{d}EN.ZU
6 gu$_4$ niga ezem amar-a-a-si / Ĝir$_2$-su^{ki}-še$_3$

rev. [šu-nigin$_2$ 20]+3 gu$_4$ niga
[šu-nigin$_2$ 1] ab$_2$ niga
[šu-nigin$_2$ 11] gu$_4$
[ki]-ni-ta
[ ]
====
[iti ezem Me-ki-ĝ]al$_2$
[mu]^{ki} / [h]ul

508: SM 1911.10.479 (AS6 vii)

obv. 102 udu
102 sila$_4$
118 u$_8$
201 maš$_2$
230-la$_2$-1 ud$_5$
1 ud$_5$ maš$_2$ nu-a
2 ^{munus}aš$_2$-gar$_3$
iti a$_2$-ki-ti
164 udu
rev. 101 [sila$_4$]
366 maš$_2$-gal
iti ezem ^{d}Šul-gi
bala-a zi-ga
kišib Ka$_5$-a-mu
ki Ur-ku$_3$-nun-na-ta
In-ta-e$_3$-a i$_3$-dab$_5$
mu Ša-aš-ru^{ki} ba-hul
----
left 1386

Obv. 1-8: Cf. CM 26 140.
Obv. 9-rev. 11: Cf. RA 79 27 21; CM 26 140.

509: SM 1911.10.480 (AS5 x)

obv. 41 udu 4 sila$_4$
101 u$_8$ 6 maš$_2$
ki sipa-e-ne-ta
[ ] u$_8$ 1 udu

[ki] LAL$_3$ GA-ta
[ ] ki A-hu-ni-ta
[ĝiri$_3$ Ur-ku$_3$]-nun-na
[ ] sila$_4$
[ ] maš$_2$
rev. kišib A-al-la-mu
zi-ga

šu-niĝin$_2$ 156 udu 25 sila$_4$
šu-niĝin$_2$ 378 u$_8$ 88 maš$_2$
ki In-ta-e$_3$-a-/ta
Ur-ku$_3$-nun-na i$_3$-dab$_5$
iti šu-eš$_5$-ša-ta
iti ezem an-na-še$_3$
mu En-unu$_6$-gal / ^{d}Inana ba-huĝ
left 647

510: SM 1911.10.481 (-- -- --)
obv. 1 gu$_4$
kišib Ur-^{d}Ba-b[a$_6$] / kurušda Nin$_9$-kal-l[a]
ki Ur-^{d}Ba-ba$_6$ / dumu Tur-tur-ta
rev. (*unavailable*)

Note that the tablet, which is preserved by an envelope, is readable only on the obverse, whereas the reverse is illegible, unless the tablet is removed from the envelope.

511: SM 1911.10.482 (Š41 viii 30)
obv. 12 udu u$_4$ 1-kam
300-la$_2$-2 udu u$_4$ 2-kam
180 udu u$_4$ 4-kam
40 udu u$_4$ 10-la$_2$-1-kam
60 udu u$_4$ 10-kam
120 udu u$_4$ 20-la$_2$-2-kam
240 udu u$_4$ 20-la$_2$-1-kam ša$_3$-bi / Lugal-ša$_3$-la$_2$
110 udu u$_4$ 20-kam
60 udu u$_4$ 21-kam

60+[x]+1 udu u$_4$ 22-kam
[x]+25 udu u$_4$ 24-kam
rev. 22 udu u$_4$ 25-kam
600 udu u$_4$ 26-kam
600 udu u$_4$ 27-kam
120 udu u$_4$ 30-la$_2$-2-kam
60 udu u$_4$ 30-la$_2$-1-kam
60 udu u$_4$ 30-kam
====
mu-DU iti šu-eš-ša
mu us$_2$-sa e$_2$ ba-du$_3$-a / mu us$_2$-sa-bi
left šu-niĝin$_2$ 3672 udu

512: SM 1911.10.484 (AS2 xi 20)

obv. 1 amar az e$_2$ uz-ga
mu-DU Šu-^{d}EN.ZU
A-a-kal-la maškim
7 udu
Tu-li$_2$-id-^{d}UTU^{ši} / nin-diĝir ^{d}EN.ZU
u$_4$ du$_6$ babbar$_2$-še$_3$ {ŠE$_3$} i$_3$-ĝen-na
rev. Arad$_2$-ĝu$_{10}$ maškim
2 gu$_4$ 1 gu$_4$ mu-2
5 udu
šu-gid$_2$ e$_2$ muhaldim-še$_3$
[u$_4$] 20-kam
[ki] Ab-ba-sa$_6$-ga-ta
ba-zi
[iti] ezem Me-ki-ĝal$_2$
[mu] ^{d}Amar-^{d}EN.ZU lugal-/e Ur-bi$_2$-lum^{ki} / mu-hul
left 16

This object is preserved together with its envelope (fragment).
Rev. 8: These three oxen are mentioned in Neumann, Fs Pettinato, 215, JH T 104, rev. 11.

513: SM 1911.10.486 (Š42 vi)

obv. 1 amar dusu$_2$ nita$_2$

nam-ra-ak Kara$_2$-har^{ki}
mu Kur-mu-gam-še$_3$
kišib Kur-bi-Er$_3$-ra
iti ezem ^{d}Šul-gi
1 dusu$_2$ nita$_2$
1 dusu$_2$ munus
mu Lu$_2$-bi-mu-še$_3$
[kiš]ib A-ma-ne-en$_6$
[iti] [ez]em mah
rev. [mu us$_2$]-sa e$_2$ PU$_3$.ŠA-iš-/[^{d}D]a-gan ba-du$_3$ mu us$_2$-sa-bi
3 dusu$_2$ nita$_2$
2 dusu$_2$ munus
kišib Ur-^{d}Nin-zu
iti a$_2$-ki-ti
mu Ša-aš-ru^{ki} ba-hul

šu-niĝin$_2$ 8 dusu$_2$ hi-a
niĝ$_2$-ka$_9$-bi ak-de$_3$
kišib lu$_2$ niĝ$_2$-dab$_5$-ke$_4$-ne
Lu$_2$-^{d}Nin-šubur šu ba-ti

514: SM 1911.10.487 (AS8 ii 26)

obv. 1 sila$_4$ e$_2$ uz-ga
mu-DU ME-^{d}Ištaran
Ur-^{d}Ba-ba$_6$ muhaldim maškim
1 šeg$_9$-bar nita$_2$
5 udu niga 2 udu aslum$_x$(A.LUM) niga
1 u$_8$ aslum$_x$(A.LUM) niga 1 ^{munus}aš$_2$-gar$_3$ niga
10-la$_2$-1 sila$_4$ 1 ^{munus}aš$_2$-gar$_3$ a-dara$_4$
1 amar maš-da$_3$ nita$_2$
rev. A-bi$_2$-si$_2$-im-ti
niĝ$_2$-dab$_5$ u$_4$-nu$_2$-a
ša$_3$ mu-DU-ra-ta
u$_4$ 26-kam
ki Lugal-amar-ku$_3$-ta / ba-zi
iti šeš-da-gu$_7$
mu En-nun-e-^{d}/Amar-^{d}EN.ZU-ra-ki-aĝ$_2$ / en Eridu^{ki} ba-huĝ
left 22

515: SM 1911.10.488 (AS8 ix 20)

obv. 2 gu$_4$ niga 10 udu
10 maš$_2$ gal
ME-^{d}Ištaran
3 udu Ra-ba-tum
E-er-be-li$_2$ ra$_2$-gaba / maškim
5 udu Nin-me-du$_{10}$-ga
rev. Arad$_2$-ĝu$_{10}$ maškim
u$_4$ 20-kam
ki Ab-ba-sa$_6$-ga-ta
ba-zi
ĝiri$_3$ Da-a-a-ti dub-sar
iti ezem mah
mu en Eridu^{ki} / ba-huĝ
left 30

Obv. 6: For the similar name Lugal-me-du$_{10}$-ga, cf. TCL 2 5539.

516: SM 1911.10.489 (AS7 iii)

obv. 1 sila$_4$ ša$_3$ 2
10 sila$_4$ a-ša$_3$-ta
bar-ta ĝal$_2$-la
ĝiri$_3$ Id-ni-id
3 sila$_4$ 3 maš$_2$ LU$_2$.SU
ša$_3$-bi 17-ta
1 udu 1 sila$_4$ 1 maš$_2$
kišib Du$_{11}$-ga
1 sila$_4$ kišib Ur-mes
----
rev. 4
zi-ga-am$_3$
13 sila$_4$ ib$_2$-tak$_4$
====
niĝ$_2$-ka$_9$-ak Id-ni-id
iti u$_5$-bi$_2$-gu$_7$
mu Hu-uh$_2$-nu-ri^{ki} / ba-hul

517: SM 1911.10.490 (AS8 vi 12)

obv. 1 ^{munus}aš$_2$-gar$_3$ niga e$_2$ uz-ga
A-a-kal-la muhaldim maškim
1 sila$_4$ ^{d}En-lil$_2$
1 sila$_4$ ^{d}Nin-lil$_2$
A-tu sagi maškim
1 udu lu$_2$-ulu$_3$-um niga sig$_5$-us$_2$
1 maš$_2$ gal a-dara$_4$ niga 3-kam-us$_2$
1 udu aslum$_x$(A.LUM) niga
2 ^{munus}aš$_2$-gar$_3$ niga
2 udu aslum$_x$(A.LUM)
rev. 1 udu ĝiš-du$_3$
1 ^{munus}aš$_2$-gar$_3$ 2 sila$_4$
ME-^{d}Ištaran
niĝ$_2$-dab$_5$ e$_2$-u$_4$-15
ša$_3$ mu-DU-ra-ta
u$_4$ 12-kam
ki Ab-ba-sa$_6$-ga-ta
ba-zi
iti a$_2$-ki-ti
mu En-nun-e-$^{[d]}$Amar-/^{d}EN.ZU-ra-ki-aĝ$_2$ en / Eridu^{ki} ba-huĝ
left 12

518: SM 1911.10.492 (AS3 ix)

obv. 134 [ ]
10 sila$_4$ kin-gi$_4$-a
164 sila$_4$
23 u$_8$
10 kir$_{11}$
88 maš$_2$
4 ^{munus}aš$_2$-gar$_3$
šu-la$_2$-a ĝiri$_3$ Šu-^{d}Da-/gan
rev. [ ] i$_3$-dab$_5$
ki Ab-ba-sa$_6$-ga-/ta ba-zi
iti ezem m[ah]
mu ^{d}gu-za [^{d}En]-/lil$_2$-la$_2$ ba-dim$_2$
====
left 433

519: SM 1911.10.493 (ŠS2 x --)

obv. 10-la$_2$-1 udu 1 maš$_2$ gal
u$_4$ 13-kam
6 gukkal 6 maš$_2$ gal
u$_4$ 14-kam
7 udu [ ]
u$_4$ 20+[x-kam]
1 sila$_4$ [u$_4$ x-kam]
4 udu u$_4$ [x-kam]
rev. ki In-ta-e$_3$-a-/ta
Du$_{11}$-ga i$_3$-dab$_5$
ša$_3$-bi 34-ta
32 udu kišib Al-la-mu
----
iti ezem An-na
mu ma$_2$-dara$_3$ abzu / ba-ab-du$_8$

520: SM 1911.10.495 (Š46 iv)

obv. 75 u$_8$
4 kir$_{11}$
33 udu
7 sila$_4$
[udu] šu-gid$_2$ Iri-saĝ-/rig$_7$^{ki}
rev. ki Ur-mes-ta
====
mu-DU
iti ki-siki ^{d}Nin-a-zu
mu Ki-maš^{ki} / ba-hul
left 120-[la$_2$-1]

This text is a duplicate of OrSP 18 pl. 3 8.

521: SM 1911.10.496 (AS2 ix)

obv. 30 udu
sa$_2$-du$_{11}$ ^{d}Gu-la
ša$_3$ Uri$_5$^{ki}-ma
20 udu 10 maš$_2$

ba-ug$_{7}$ mu ur-gi$_{7}$-ra-še$_{3}$
DIĜIR-ba-ni sipa / ur-gi$_{7}$-ra šu ba-ti
rev. 6 udu sa$_{2}$-du$_{11}$ Inim-/^{d}Nanna dumu lugal
ki Ab-ba-sa$_{6}$-ga-/ta ba-zi
iti ezem mah
mu ^{d}Amar-^{d}EN.ZU / lugal-e Ur-bi$_{2}$-/lum^{ki} mu-hul
left 66

This is the original record for SAT 2 724, rev. iii 35-44.

522: SM 1911.10.497 (AS7 xii 23)

obv. 1 ud$_{5}$ maš$_{2}$ nu-a niga
e$_{2}$ uz-ga
Ur-^{d}Ba-ba$_{6}$ maškim
1 amar maš-da$_{3}$ munus
^{d}En-lil$_{2}$
A-tu sagi / maškim
ša$_{3}$ mu-DU-ra-ta
rev. u$_{4}$ 23-kam
ki Ab-ba-sa$_{6}$-ga-/ta
ba-zi
====
iti še-KIN-ku$_{5}$
mu Hu-uh$_{2}$-nu-ri/^{ki} ba-hul
left 2

523: SM 1911.10.499 (AS8 vii)

obv. 1 ^{munus}aš$_{2}$-gar$_{3}$ ša-ru-mi-/um
e$_{2}$ ^{d}Nusku-še$_{3}$
ki Ab-ba-sa$_{6}$-ga-/ta
Da-da gala
rev. i$_{3}$-dab$_{5}$
====
iti ezem ^{d}Šul-gi
mu En-nun-e-^{d}Amar-/^{d}EN.ZU-ra-ki-aĝ$_{2}$ / en Eridu^{ki} ba-huĝ
left 1

524: SM 1911.10.500 (AS8 vi)

obv. 13 gukkal ĝiš-du$_3$
1 maš$_2$ gal
mu-DU lugal
ki Ab-ba-sa$_6$-ga-/ta
Ur-^{d}Ištaran
rev. i$_3$-dab$_5$
BAD$_3$.AN^{ki}-še$_3$
====
iti a$_2$-ki-ti
mu en Eridu^{ki} / ba-huĝ
left 14

525: SM 1911.10.501 (AS4 x 21)

obv. 1 gu$_4$ 5 udu
Geme$_2$-sa$_6$-ga dam / [Ur-me]s
u$_4$ ^{d}Ištaran / in-da-a
ĝiri$_3$ PU$_3$.ŠA-[tab]-num$_2$ sukkal
rev. Arad$_2$-ĝu$_{10}$ maškim
5 udu
šu-gid$_2$ e$_2$ muhaldim-še$_3$
u$_4$ 21-kam
ki In-ta-e$_3$-a-ta / ba-zi
iti ezem An-na
mu en ^{d}Nanna ba-huĝ
left 1 gu$_4$ 10 udu

Obv. 4: Cf. YOS 4 217 for the variant personal name PU$_3$.ŠA-tab-nu-um.

526: SM 1911.10.502 (ŠS3 viii)

obv. 833 udu / maš$_2$ hi-a
e$_2$ muhaldim u$_4$-da sa$_2$-a
iti ezem An-na
mu en Eridu^{ki} ba-huĝ
81 udu ba-ug$_7$
ad$_6$ kuš-bi e$_2$-gal-še$_3$ / ba-an-ku$_4$
rev. mu en Ga-eš$_5$^{ki} ba-huĝ
27 udu Ga-eš$_5$^{ki}-ta

iti a$_2$-ki-ti
11 udu ba-ug$_7$ gid$_2$-dam
16 udu ĝiri$_3$ Ur-^{d}En-lil$_2$-la$_2$
Ur-mes i$_3$-dab$_5$
iti ezem ^{d}Šu-^{d}EN.ZU
mu Si-ma-num$_2$^{ki} ba-hul
bar-ta ĝal$_2$-la
[x] uz Du$_{11}$-ga-ta
left ki A-ha-an-ni-šu-ta ba-zi
968

Obv. 2: Cf. SAT 2 972; SET 22.

527: SM 1911.10.503 (AS4 viii 24)

obv. 11 u$_8$ 2 udu
1 sila$_4$
11 maš$_2$
u$_4$ 24-kam
ki Ab-ba-sa$_6$-ga-/ta
In-ta-e$_3$-a
rev. i$_3$-[dab$_5$]
====
iti šu-eš$_5$-ša
mu En-mah-gal-/an-na en ^{d}Nanna / ba-huĝ
left 25

528: SM 1911.10.504 (AS4 iii 26)

obv. 5 udu niga
1 sila$_4$
A-bi$_2$-si$_2$-im-/ti
Unug^{ki}-še$_3$ du-ni ma$_2$-a / ba-na-a-gub
ĝiri$_3$ Nu-hi-DIĜIR ra$_2$-/gaba
rev. u$_4$ 26-kam
ki Ab-ba-sa$_6$-ga-/ta
ba-zi
iti u$_5$-bi$_2$-gu$_7$
mu us$_2$-sa gu-za / ^{d}En-lil$_2$-la$_2$ ba-dim$_2$
left 6

529: SM 1911.10.505 (-- -- 7)

obv. (*beginning damaged*)
u$_4$ 7-kam
ki Ur-ku$_3$-nun-na-ta
ba-zi
rev. ĝiri$_3$ Hu-[la-al]
(*ending damaged*)

530: SM 1911.10.506 (AS8 ix 19)

obv. 15 udu u$_4$ 17-kam
4 maš$_2$-gal
u$_4$ 18-kam
3 gu$_4$ niga
[1] udu lu$_2$-ulu$_3$-um niga
[4]+1 maš$_2$-gal lu$_2$-ul[u$_3$-um] niga
rev. u$_4$ 20-la$_2$-1-kam
ki Ab-ba-sa$_6$-ga-ta
U$_2$-ta$_2$-mi-[šar-ra-am]
i$_3$-dab$_5$
iti ezem mah
mu en Eridu^{ki} ba-/huĝ

This object's accession number SM 1911.10.506 is the museum number for the tablet and its envelope (wholly preserved).
Obv. 4-6: The number of livestock is restored from TRU 84 (AS 8 ix 19).

531: SM 1911.10.507 (ŠS3 iii)

obv. 40 udu 10+[ ]
7 sila$_4$ [ ]
šu-[gid$_2$]
ki A-hu-[šu]-ni-ta
Du$_{11}$-ga i$_3$-dab$_5$
rev. ====
iti u$_5$-bi$_2$-gu$_7$
mu us$_2$-sa ma$_2$-dara$_3$ / abzu ^{d}En-ki ba-ab-/du$_8$
seal Ur-mes
dumu La-na kurušda

532: SM 1911.10.509 (ŠS9 i)

obv. 80 udu niga
bala ensi$_2$ / Zimbir^{ki}
ki A-ba-^{d}En-lil$_2$-gin$_7$-/ta
Ur-ku$_3$-nun-na
rev. i$_3$-dab$_5$
kišib Du$_{11}$-ga
====
iti še-KIN-ku$_5$
mu ^{d}Šu-^{d}EN.ZU / lugal Uri$_5$^{ki}-ma-ke$_4$ / e$_2$ ^{d}Šara$_2$ Umma^{ki}-ka / mu-du$_3$
seal Du$_{11}$-ga [dub-sar]
dumu Lu$_2$-[^{d}Nin-ĝir$_2$-su]
sipa na-[gab$_2$-tum]

533: SM 1911.10.510 (ŠS9 x 13)

obv. 2 sila$_4$ ĝiri$_3$ Lugal-amar-ku$_3$
5 sila$_4$ 4 maš$_2$
u$_4$ 12-kam
8 udu 3 sila$_4$
u$_4$ 13-kam
ki In-ta-e$_3$-a-ta
Ur-ku$_3$-nun-na i$_3$-dab$_5$
rev. ==== (*seal*)
iti ezem mah
mu ^{d}Šu-^{d}EN.ZU / lugal Uri$_5$^{ki}-ma-ke$_4$ / e$_2$ ^{d}Šara$_2$ Umma^{ki}-ka / mu-du$_3$
seal Du$_{11}$-ga dub-[sar]
dumu Lu$_2$-^{d}Nin-ĝir$_2$-[su]
sipa na-gab$_2$-[tum]

This text is a duplicate of No. 534.

534: SM 1911.10.511 (ŠS9 x 13)

obv. 2 sila$_4$ ĝiri$_3$ Lugal-amar-[k]u$_3$
5 sila$_4$ 4 maš$_2$
u$_4$ 12-kam
8 udu 3 sila$_4$

u$_4$ 13-kam
ki In-ta-e$_3$-a-ta
Ur-ku$_3$-nun-na i$_3$-dab$_5$
rev. ==== (*seal*)
iti e[zem] mah
mu ^{d}Šu-^{d}EN.ZU / lugal Uri$_5$^{ki}-ma-ke$_4$ / e$_2$ ^{d}Šara$_2$ Umma^{ki}-ka / mu-du$_3$
seal Du$_{11}$-ga [dub-sar]
dumu [Lu$_2$-^{d}Nin-ĝir$_2$-su]
sipa [na-gab$_2$-tum]

This text is a duplicate of No. 533.

535: SM 1911.10.512 (ŠS2 i)

obv. 7 udu
1 gukkal
2 maš$_2$-gal
10 ud$_5$
šu-gid$_2$
rev. ki A-hu-We-er-ta
Du$_{11}$-ga i$_3$-dab$_5$
ĝiri$_3$ Ur-uš-gid$_2$-da
==== (*seal*)
iti maš-da$_3$-gu$_7$
mu us$_2$-sa ^{d}Šu-^{d}EN./ZU lugal
seal Ur-mes
dumu La-na kurušda

536: SM 1911.10.513 (ŠS9 viii 14)

obv. 9 gu$_4$
u$_4$ 14-kam
ki In-ta-e$_3$-a-/ta
Ur-ku$_3$-nun-na
i$_3$-dab$_5$
rev. gu$_4$ ME-^{d}Ištaran
iti ezem ^{d}Šul-gi
mu e$_2$ ^{d}Šara$_2$ / ba-du$_3$
seal i ^{d}Šu-^{d}EN.ZU

lugal kala-ga
lugal Uri$_5$/^{ki}-ma
lugal an ub-/da limmu$_2$-ba
ii Ur-ku$_3$-nun-na
dub-sar
dumu Lu$_2$-^{d}Nin-ĝir$_2$-/su kurušda
arad$_2$-zu

537: SM 1911.10.514 (ŠS9 vii 13)

obv. 2 udu saĝ sila$_4$
28 sila$_4$ saĝ sila$_4$
100 sila$_4$
45 udu maš$_2$ hi-a
e$_2$ ^{d}En-lil$_2$-la$_2$-še$_3$
Za-zi i$_3$-dab$_5$
ĝiri$_3$ Ab-ba-kal-[la]
ša$_3$ Nibru$^{[ki]}$
rev. 7 sila$_4$ ba-ug$_7$
u$_4$ 13-kam
ša$_3$ PU$_3$.ŠA-iš-^{d}Da-gan
ki A-a-diĝir-ta
Ab-ba-kal-la i$_3$-dab$_5$
==== (*seal*)
iti a$_2$-ki-ti
mu e$_2$ ^{d}Šara$_2$ Umma^{ki}-/ka ba-du$_3$
left 182
seal Ab-ba-kal-la
dub-sar
dumu Lu$_2$-^{d}Nin-/ĝir$_2$-su

538: SM 1911.10.515 (ŠS8 iii 20)

obv. 4 gu$_4$ u$_2$
šu-gid$_2$
u$_4$ 20-kam
ki PU$_3$.ŠA-^{d}En-lil$_2$-/ta
Ur-ku$_3$-nun-na
rev. i$_3$-dab$_5$

==== (*seal*)
iti šeš-da-gu$_7$
mu ^{d}Šu-^{d}EN.ZU / lugal Uri$_5$^{ki}-ma-ke$_4$ / ma$_2$-gur$_8$ mah / ^{d}En-lil$_2$ ^{d}Nin-lil$_2$-ra / mu-ne-dim$_2$
seal Ab-ba-kal-la
dub-sar
dumu Lu$_2$-[^{d}Nin-ĝir$_2$-su]

539: SM 1911.10.516 (ŠS9)

obv. 26 maš$_2$
[ki] Lu$_2$-^{d}EN.ZU-/ta
Ur-ku$_3$-nun-na / i$_3$-dab$_5$
rev. ==== (*seal*)
mu [^{d}Šu]-^{d}EN.ZU / lugal-e e$_2$ ^{d}Šara$_2$ / Umma^{ki}-ka / mu-du$_3$
seal i ^{d}Šu-^{d}EN.ZU
lugal kala-ga
lugal Uri$_5$/^{ki}-ma
lugal an ub-/da limmu$_2$-da
ii Ur-ku$_3$-nun-na
dub-sar
dumu Lu$_2$-^{d}Nin-/ĝir$_2$-su kurušda
arad$_2$-zu

540: SM 1911.10.517 (ŠS9 iv 15)

obv. 723 udu / maš$_2$ hi-a
ki In-ta-e$_3$-a-/ta
Ur-ku$_3$-nun-na
i$_3$-dab$_5$
rev. u$_4$ 15-kam
==== (*seal*)
iti u$_5$-[bi$_2$]-gu$_7$
mu e$_2$ ^{d}Šara$_2$ / ba-du$_3$
seal Du$_{11}$-ga dub-sar
dumu Lu$_2$-^{d}Nin-ĝir$_2$-su
sipa na-gab$_2$-tum

541: SM 1911.10.518 (ŠS9 vii)

obv. 1 sila$_4$ ša$_3$ 151
[x] GU [x] LUGAL e$_3$ KI
[x] sila$_4$
[ ] ^{d}Dumu-zi-da
[x] sila$_4$ kin-[gi$_4$]-a
2 ud$_5$ maš$_2$ [nu-a]
Ib$_2$-ru-^{d}Lamma
20-la$_2$-1 u$_8$ sila$_4$ nu-a
rev. [ ] sipa [ ]
[ ]
==== (*seal*)
ki Du$_{11}$-ga-ta ba-zi
iti a$_2$-ki-ti
mu ^{d}Šu-^{d}EN.ZU / lugal Uri$_5$^{ki}-ma / e$_2$ ^{d}Šara$_2$ Umma^{ki}-ka / mu-du$_3$
left 50-la$_2$-1
seal i ^{d}Šu-^{d}EN.ZU
lugal kala-ga
lugal Uri$_5$/^{ki}-ma
[lugal an ub-da limmu$_2$-ba]
ii Ur-ku$_3$-nun-na
dub-sar
dumu Lu$_2$-^{d}[Nin-ĝir$_2$]-/su kurušda
[arad$_2$-zu]

542: SM 1911.10.519 (ŠS9 i 11)

obv. 5 udu 31 u$_8$
13 ud$_5$ 24 sila$_4$
18 maš$_2$
mu ma$_2$-gur$_8$ mah ba-dim$_2$
4 udu niga 7 udu 3 sila$_4$
ki ^{d}Šul-gi-i$_3$-li$_2$-ta
11 udu ki Ur-tur-ta
23 udu saĝ sila$_4$
6 maš$_2$ gal saĝ maš$_2$
rev. 6 udu šu-gid$_2$ 6 sila$_4$
u$_4$ 11-kam
1 sila$_4$ u$_4$ 7-kam

ki In-ta-e$_3$-a-ta
====
gaba-ri kišib Du$_{11}$-ga
iti še-KIN-ku$_5$
mu e$_2$ ^{d}Šara$_2$-ka [ba-du$_3$]

543: SM 1911.10.520 (ŠS3 i 24)

obv. 7 udu 5 sila$_4$
2 amar maš-da$_3$ munus
u$_4$ 23-kam
6 sila$_4$
1 amar maš-da$_3$ munus
u$_4$ 24-kam
rev. ki In-ta-e$_3$-a-ta
Du$_{11}$-ga i$_3$-dab$_5$
==== (*seal*)
iti maš-da$_3$-gu$_7$
mu us$_2$-sa ma$_2$-dara$_3$ / abzu ba-ab-du$_8$
seal Ur-[mes]
dumu La-na [kurušda]

544: SM 1911.10.521 (ŠS8 x)

obv. 78 udu maš$_2$ hi-a
ĝiri$_3$ Du-du
ki A-al-la-mu-/ta [ba]-zi
ša$_3$ Uri$_5$^{ki}-ma
rev. ==== (*seal*)
iti ezem mah
mu ma$_2$-gur$_8$ mah / ba-dim$_2$
seal i ^{d}Šu-^{d}EN.ZU
lugal kala-ga
lugal Uri$_5$/^{ki}-ma
lugal an ub-/da limmu$_2$-ba
ii Ur-ku$_3$-nun-na
dub-sar
dumu Lu$_2$-^{d}Nin-ĝir$_2$-/su kurušda
arad$_2$-zu

545: SM 1911.10.522 (IS1 xiid)

obv. 3 udu
ĝiri$_3$ Ma-šum i$_3$-du$_8$
1 udu ĝiri$_3$ Lu$_2$-^{d}Nanna / sagi
6 udu ĝiri$_3$ Ur-^{d}Lamma / lu$_2$-niĝ$_2$-ke$_4$
ki Ur-ku$_3$-nun-na-ta
rev. Du$_{11}$-ga i$_3$-dab$_5$
==== (*seal*)
iti diri ezem ^{d}Me-ki-/ĝal$_2$
mu ^{d}I-bi$_2$-/^{d}EN.ZU lugal
left 10
seal Du$_{11}$-ga dub-[sar]
dumu Lu$_2$-^{d}Nin-ĝir$_2$-su
sipa na-gab$_2$-tum

546: SM 1911.10.523 (ŠS3 viii 25)

obv. 3 sila$_4$
u$_4$ 24-kam
1 sila$_4$
u$_4$ 25-kam
rev. ki In-ta-e$_3$-a-ta
Du$_{11}$-ga i$_3$-dab$_5$
==== (*seal*)
iti ezem ^{d}Šu-^{d}EN.ZU
mu Si-ma-num$_2$[^{ki} ba-hul]
seal Ur-[mes]
dumu La-na kurušda

547: SM 1911.10.524 (IS1)

obv. 9 udu u$_2$
2 sila$_4$
ki ^{d}Šul-gi-/iri-ĝu$_{10}$-ta
rev. Ur-ku$_3$-nun-na
i$_3$-dab$_5$
==== (*seal*)
mu ^{d}I-bi$_2$-/^{d}EN.ZU lugal
seal Du$_{11}$-ga dub-[sar]
dumu Lu$_2$-^{d}Nin-[ĝir$_2$-su]
sipa na-gab$_2$-tum

548: SM 1911.10.525 (ŠS1 xiid)

obv. 27 sila$_4$
ĝiri$_3$ DIĜIR-su$_2$-ba-ni
1 udu Ur-^{d}Šul-pa-/e$_3$
[ ] Du$_{11}$-ga
[ ] Šu-Eš$_{18}$-tar$_2$
[ ]
rev. 10 udu kišib MI$_2$-[ ]
==== (*seal*)
ki Ur-mes-ta ba-zi
iti diri še-KIN-ku$_5$
mu ^{d}Šu-^{d}EN.ZU / lugal
seal Du$_{11}$-ga dub-sar
dumu Lu$_2$-^{d}Nin-ĝir$_2$-su
sipa na-gab$_2$-tum

549: SM 1911.10.526 (AS8 xii)

obv. 1528 / udu maš$_2$ hi-a
mu-DU ir$_2$-su$_3$-a
iti ezem An-na
0 udu Be-li$_2$-i$_3$-li$_2$
0 udu ša$_3$ Ga-eš^{ki}
0 maš$_2$ ĝiri$_3$ Ur-^{d}Nanše
rev. 11 udu diri kišib U-bar / u$_3$ Ur-^{d}[Ba-ba$_6$]
iti še-KIN-[ku$_5$]
ki Du$_{11}$-ga-t[a]
Ur-ku$_3$-nun-na i$_3$-da[b$_5$]
====
mu en Eridu^{ki} ba-huĝ
seal Ur-ku$_3$-nun-na
dub-sar
dumu Lu$_2$-^{d}Nin-ĝir$_2$-su
sipa na-gab$_2$-tum

550: SM 1911.10.527 (IS1 xiid)

obv. 20-la$_2$-1 udu ĝiri$_3$ Lu$_2$-/^{d}Da-mu
A-a-diĝir i$_3$-dab$_5$
1 udu 1 maš$_2$
Ib-ni-DIĜIR i$_3$-dab$_5$

1 maš$_2$ Ab-ba-kal-la / i$_3$-dab$_5$
rev. ĝiri$_3$ Un-sig$_5$
3 maš$_2$ Ur-^{d}Dumu-zi-da / sipa i$_3$-dab$_5$
6 udu 5 maš$_2$
saĝ sila$_4$-še$_3$
Za-zi i$_3$-dab$_5$
ki Iš-me-DIĜIR-ta ba-zi
ĝiri$_3$ Lugal-ezem
iti diri ezem Me-ki-ĝal$_2$
mu ^{d}I-bi$_2$-/^{d}EN.ZU lugal
left 36
seal i ^{d}Šu-^{d}EN.ZU
lugal kala-ga
lugal Uri$_5$/^{ki}-ma
lugal an ub-/da limmu$_2$-ba
ii Ur-ku$_3$-nun-[na]
dub-[sar]
dumu Lu$_2$-^{d}Nin-ĝir$_2$-/su kuru[šda]
arad$_2$-[zu]

551: SM 1911.10.528 (ŠS7 vii)

obv. 1 udu u$_2$
la$_2$-ia$_3$ mu-DU
maš$_2$-da-re-a a$_2$-ki-/ti šu-numun-na
[ki In-t]a-e$_3$-a-/ta
rev. Ku$_3$-^{d}Nanna ensi$_2$ / i$_3$-dab$_5$
kišib Ša$_3$-bi
====
iti a$_2$-ki-ti
mu ^{d}Šu-^{d}EN.ZU / lugal Uri$_5$^{ki}-ma / ma-da Za-ab-ša-/li^{ki} mu-hul
seal Ša$_3$-bi
dub-sar
dumu Ba-sa$_6$

552: SM 1911.10.529 (ŠS3 viii 18)

obv. 22 sila$_4$
20 maš$_2$

u$_4$ 18-kam
ki In-ta-e$_3$-a-ta
Du$_{11}$-ga i$_3$-dab$_5$
rev. ====
iti ezem ^{d}Šu-^{d}EN.ZU
mu Si-ma-[num$_2$]^{ki} / ba-hul
seal Ur-ku$_3$-[nun-na]
dumu Lu$_2$-^{d}Nin-[ĝir$_2$-su]
sipa [na-gab$_2$-tum]

553: SM 1911.10.530 (ŠS2 iii)

obv. 6 udu
šu-gid$_2$
ki Na-lu$_5$-ta
Du$_{11}$-ga
i$_3$-dab$_5$
rev. kišib Ur-mes
====
iti u$_5$-bi$_2$-gu$_7$
mu ma$_2$-dara$_3$-abzu / [ba-ab-d]u$_8$
seal Ur-mes
dumu La-[na kurušda]

554: SM 1911.10.531 (ŠS2 viii)

obv. 31 udu
ĝiri$_3$ Ur-^{d}Nanše
2 udu ĝiri$_3$ Ur-ĝar
16 <udu> ĝiri$_3$ Ur-^{d}Ba-ba$_6$
3 udu ba-ug$_7$ ĝiri$_3$ I-pa$_2$-/li$_2$-is
16 udu ĝiri$_3$ A-DIĜIR
3 udu ĝiri$_3$ Ur-mes
rev. ki Ur-^{d}Nanše-ta
Ur-mes i$_3$-dab$_5$
==== (*seal*)
iti šu-eš-ša
mu ma$_2$-dara$_3$-abzu / ba-ab-du$_8$
seal Ur-mes
dumu La-na kurušda

555: SM 1911.10.533 (ŠS9 vii)

obv. 0.0.1 5 sila$_3$ 16 gin$_2$ / i$_3$-nun
mu bala ensi$_2$ Babila^{ki}-še$_3$
ki Lu$_2$-kal-la-ta
Ur-ku$_3$-nun-na
šu ba-an-ti
niĝ$_2$-dab$_5$ ma$_2$ An-na
rev. ====
iti a$_2$-ki-ti
mu ^{d}[Šu]-^{d}EN.ZU / lugal Uri$_5$^{ki}-ma-/ke$_4$
e$_2$ ^{d}Šara$_2$ Umma^{ki}-/ka mu-du$_3$
seal i ^{d}Šu-^{d}EN.ZU
lugal kala-ga
lugal Uri$_5$/^{ki}-ma
lugal an ub-/da limmu$_2$-ba
ii Ur-ku$_3$-nun-na
dub-sar
dumu Lu$_2$-^{d}Nin-ĝir$_2$-/su kurušda
arad$_2$-zu

556: SM 1911.10.534 (ŠS3 vii 1)

obv. 5 sila$_4$ u$_4$ 30-la$_2$-1-kam
1 sila$_4$ 1 maš$_2$
u$_4$ 30-kam
iti a$_2$-ki-ti
23 udu maš$_2$ hi-a
ĝiri$_3$ Nu-ur$_2$-^{d}EN.ZU
4 udu 1 sila$_4$ 2 maš$_2$
rev. ĝiri$_3$ Ur-^{d}Ba-ba$_6$
u$_4$ 1-kam
iti ezem ^{d}Šul-gi
ki In-ta-e$_3$-a-ta
Du$_{11}$-ga i$_3$-dab$_5$
====
mu Si-ma-num$_2$^{ki} / ba-hul
seal Ur-mes
dumu La-na kurušda

557: SM 1911.10.535 (ŠS1 xiid 16)

obv. 7 udu
4 u$_8$
8 maš$_2$-gal
6 ud$_5$
šu-gid$_2$ u$_4$ 16-kam
rev. ki Kur-bi-la-ak-/ta
Du$_{11}$-ga i$_3$-dab$_5$
kišib Ur-mes
iti diri še-KIN-ku$_5$
mu ^{d}Šu-^{d}EN.ZU / lugal
seal Ur-mes
dumu La-na kurušda

558: SM 1911.10.536 (ŠS9 viii)

obv. 1 gu$_4$ šu-gid$_2$
ki PU$_3$.ŠA-^{d}En-lil$_2$-/ta
Ur-ku$_3$-nun-na
i$_3$-dab$_5$
rev. iti ezem ^{d}Šul-gi
==== (*seal*)
mu ^{d}Šu-^{d}EN.ZU / lugal Uri$_5$^{ki}-ma / e$_2$ ^{d}Šara$_2$ Umma^{ki}-/ka mu-du$_3$
seal i ^{d}Šu-^{d}EN.ZU
lugal kala-ga
lugal Uri$_5$/^{ki}-ma
lugal an ub-/da limmu$_2$-ba
ii Ur-ku$_3$-nun-na
dub-sar
dumu Lu$_2$-^{d}Nin-ĝir$_2$-/su kurušda
arad$_2$-zu

559: SM 1911.10.537 (IS1 xi)

obv. 1 udu ša$_3$ 2 Šar-ru-/i$_3$-li$_2$
1 udu Šal-mah muhaldim
ki A-a-diĝir-[ta]
ba-z[i]
rev. ==== (*seal*)

iti ezem An-na
mu ^{d}I-bi$_2$-/^{d}EN.ZU lugal
seal i [^{d}Šu]-^{d}EN.ZU
lugal kala-ga
lugal Uri$_5$/^{ki}-ma
lugal an ub-/da limmu$_2$-ba
ii Ur-ku$_3$-nun-na
dub-sar
dumu Lu$_2$-^{d}Nin-[ĝir$_2$]-/su kurušda
arad$_2$-[zu]

560: SM 1911.10.539 (AS1-29)

obv. 3 gu$_4$ mu-DU u$_4$ 2-kam
3 gu$_4$ u$_4$ 7-kam
2 gu$_4$ u$_4$ 10-kam
1 gu$_4$ u$_4$ 14-kam
1 gu$_4$ u$_4$ 18-kam
1 gu$_4$ u$_4$ 25-kam
1 gu$_4$ u$_4$ 26-kam
1 gu$_4$ u$_4$ 30-la$_2$-1-kam
mu-DU lugal
rev. 40 gu$_4$ ki Al-la-mu kuš$_7$-ta
4 gu$_4$ a-ra$_2$ 1-kam
4 gu$_4$ 1 ab$_2$ a-ra$_2$ 2-kam
4 gu$_4$ a-ra$_2$ 3-kam
la$_2$-ia$_3$ su-ga A-hu-ni

šu-niĝin$_2$ 65 gu$_4$ 1 ab$_2$
[ki] Na-sa$_6$-ta
[^{d}En]-lil$_2$-l[a$_2$ i$_3$]-dab$_5$
[iti]
[mu ^{d}Ama]r-^{d}EN.ZU / lugal
left 66

561: SM 1911.10.540 (ŠS2 x 24)

obv. 1 udu aslum$_x$(A.LUM) niga 3-kam-us$_2$
u$_4$ 23-kam
2 udu aslum$_x$(A.LUM) niga 3-kam-/us$_2$

u$_4$ 24-kam
rev. Be-li$_2$-i$_3$-li$_2$
i$_3$-dab$_5$
====
iti ezem An-na
mu ma$_2$-dara$_3$ abzu / ba-ab-du$_8$
seal Li-bur-^{d}[Šul-gi]
dub-sar
dumu Kal-[la-mu]

For the seal impression, cf. BPOA 7 1861.

562: SM 1911.10.541 (IS1 xiid)

obv. 10 udu kin-gi$_4$-a
ki A-ba-^{d}En-lil$_2$-/gin$_7$-ta
Ur-ku$_3$-nun-na
i$_3$-dab$_5$
rev. Unug^{ki}-še$_3$
====
iti diri ezem ^{d}Me-ki-ĝal$_2$
mu ^{d}I-bi$_2$-/^{d}EN.ZU lugal
seal i ^{d}Šu-^{d}EN.ZU
lugal kala-ga
lugal Uri$_5$/^{ki}-ma
lugal an ub-/da limmu$_2$-ba
ii Ur-ku$_3$-nun-na
dub-sar
dumu Lu$_2$-^{d}Nin-ĝir$_2$-/su kurušda
arad$_2$-zu

563: SM 1911.10.542 (IS1 ii)

obv. 1 gu$_4$ u$_2$
ki In-ta-e$_3$-a-/ta
Ur-ku$_3$-nun-na
i$_3$-dab$_5$
rev. ==== (*seal*)
iti maš-da$_3$-gu$_7$

mu ^{d}I-bi$_{2}$-/^{d}EN.ZU lugal
seal Du$_{11}$-ga dub-sar
dumu Lu$_{2}$-^{d}Nin-ĝir$_{2}$-su
sipa na-gab$_{2}$-tum

564: SM 1911.10.543 (ŠS9)

obv. 515 udu / maš$_{2}$ hi-a
kišib sipa-e-ne
ki Du$_{11}$-ga-ta
kišib Ab-ba-kal-la
rev. ==== (*seal*)
mu e$_{2}$ ^{d}Šara$_{2}$ / ba-du$_{3}$
seal Ab-ba-kal-la
dub-sar
dumu Lu$_{2}$-^{d}Nin-/ĝir$_{2}$-su

565: SM 1911.10.544 (ŠS3 viii 17)

obv. 10 maš$_{2}$-gal u$_{2}$
u$_{4}$ 17-kam
ki In-ta-e$_{3}$(UD./DU)-a-ta
rev. Du$_{11}$-ga
i$_{3}$-dab$_{5}$
====
iti ezem ^{d}Šu-^{d}EN.ZU
mu Si-ma-num$_{2}$^{ki} / ba-hul
seal Ur-[mes]
dumu La-na kurušda

566: SM 1911.10.545 (ŠS9 vii)

obv. 2 udu niga
sa$_{2}$-du$_{11}$ ^{d}En-ki
ki ^{d}Šul-gi-/i$_{3}$-li$_{2}$-[ta]
rev. ensi$_{2}$ Adab^{ki}
i$_{3}$-dab$_{5}$
kišib Ur-ku$_{3}$-nun-na
----

iti a$_2$-ki-ti
mu e$_2$ ^{d}Šara$_2$ / ba-du$_3$
seal i [^{d}Šu-^{d}EN.ZU]
lugal kala-ga
lugal Uri$_5$/^{ki}-ma
lugal an ub-/da limmu$_2$-ba
ii Ur-[ku$_3$-nun-na]
dub-[sar]
dumu [Lu$_2$-^{d}Nin-ĝir$_2$-su kurušda]
arad$_2$-[zu]

567: SM 1911.10.546 (ŠS1 vi)
obv. 5 udu
udu kin-gi$_4$-še$_3$
ki PU$_3$.ŠA-^{d}En-lil$_2$-/ta
Ur-ku$_3$-nun-na
rev. i$_3$-dab$_5$
====
iti a$_2$-ki-ti
[mu] ^{d}Šu-/^{d}EN.ZU lugal
seal i ^{d}Šu-^{d}EN.ZU
lugal kala-ga
lugal Uri$_5$/^{ki}-ma
lugal an ub-/da limmu$_2$-ba
ii Ur-ku$_3$-nun-na
dub-sar
dumu Lu$_2$-^{d}Nin-/ĝir$_2$-su kurušda
arad$_2$-zu

568: SM 1911.10.547 (AS5 x)
obv. 4 maš$_2$-gal
ki Ur-^{d}Ba-ba$_6$-ta
Ur-ku$_3$-nun-na
i$_3$-dab$_5$
rev. ====
iti ezem An-na
mu en ^{d}Inana / ba-huĝ-ĝa$_2$
seal (*illegible*)

Note that the ending -ĝa$_2$ in the year name mu en ^{d}Inana / ba-huĝ-ĝa$_2$ (AS5) is not attested in Drehem texts.

569: SM 1911.10.548 (IS1)

obv. 1 2/3 gin$_2$ ku$_3$-babbar
šа$_3$ 3 gin$_2$ ib$_2$-tak$_4$
maš$_2$ nu-tuku
ĝiri$_3$ Ur-^{d}IŠKUR
ki Igi-sa$_6$-sa$_6$-ta
rev. Ur-ku$_3$-nun-na
šu ba-ti
====
mu ^{d}I-bi$_2$-/^{d}EN.ZU lugal
seal i ^{d}Šu-^{d}EN.ZU
lugal kala-ga
lugal Uri$_5$/^{ki}-ma
lugal an ub-/da limmu$_2$-ba
ii Ur-ku$_3$-nun-na
dub-sar
dumu Lu$_2$-^{d}Nin-ĝir$_2$-/su kurušda
arad$_2$-zu

570: SM 1911.10.549 (ŠS9 viii)

obv. 3 gu$_4$ šu-gid$_2$
ki In-ta-e$_3$-a-/ta
Ur-ku$_3$-nun-na
i$_3$-dab$_5$
iti ezem ^{d}Šul-gi
rev. mu e$_2$ ^{d}Šara$_2$ / ba-du$_3$
ĝiri$_3$ U$_4$-de$_3$-niĝ$_2$-saga
seal i ^{d}Šu-^{d}EN.ZU
lugal kala-ga
lugal Uri$_5$/^{ki}-ma
lugal an ub-/da limmu$_2$-ba
ii Ur-ku$_3$-nun-na
dub-sar
dumu Lu$_2$-^{d}Nin-ĝir$_2$-/su kurušda
arad$_2$-zu

571: SM 1911.10.550 (ŠS3 i 1)

obv. 5 maš$_2$-gal
1 sila$_4$
u$_4$ 1-kam
ki In-ta-e$_3$-a-/ta
rev. Du$_{11}$-ga i$_3$-dab$_5$
====
iti maš-da$_3$-gu$_7$
mu us$_2$-sa ma$_2$-dara$_3$ / abzu ba-ab-du$_8$
seal (*illegible*)

572: SM 1911.10.551 (AS9 iv)

obv. 1 maš$_2$
ki Ab-ba-sa$_6$-ga-/ta
Ur-^{d}Ig-alim i$_3$-dab$_5$
iti ki-siki ^{d}Nin-a-zu
rev. mu en ^{d}Nanna / Kar-zi-da ba-/huĝ
seal (*illegible*)

573: SM 1911.10.552 (ŠS3 xi 21)

obv. [ ]
[ ]
[ ]
1 sila$_4$
A-gu-a
u$_4$ 21-kam
mu-DU lugal
rev. [In]-ta-e$_3$-a
i$_3$-dab$_5$
ĝiri$_3$ Nu-ur$_2$-^{d}EN.ZU / dub-sar
[it]i ezem Me-ki-ĝal$_2$
[m]u ^{d}Šu-^{d}EN.ZU / lugal-e
[Si-ma-num$_2$]^{ki} mu-/hul
seal (*illegible*)

574: SM 1911.10.553 (ŠS2 iii)

obv. 16 udu
5 maš$_2$-gal
1 ud$_5$
3 maš$_2$ gaba
šu-gid$_2$
rev. ki Kur-bi-la-ak-ta
Du$_{11}$-ga i$_3$-dab$_5$
kišib Ur-mes
----
iti u$_5$-bi$_2$-gu$_7$
mu ma$_2$-dara$_3$ abzu / ^{d}En-ki ba-ab-du$_8$
seal Ur-mes
dumu La-na kurušda

575: SM 1911.10.554 (ŠS1 xiid)

obv. 14 udu
kišib Šu-^{d}Nisaba
ki Ur-mes-ta
ba-zi
iti diri še-KIN-ku$_5$
rev. mu ^{d}Šu-^{d}EN.ZU / lugal
==== (*seal*)
seal Du$_{11}$-ga dub-sar
dumu Lu$_2$-^{d}Nin-ĝir$_2$-su
sipa na-gab$_2$-tum

576: SM 1911.10.555 (AS7 x)

obv. 10 udu
la$_2$-ia$_3$ mu-DU
ir$_2$-su$_3$-a
ki Ab-ba-sa$_6$-/ga-ta
Ur-sa$_6$-sa$_6$-ga
rev. i$_3$-dab$_5$
kišib A-hu-šu-ni
==== (*seal*)
iti ezem An-na

mu Hu-uh$_2$-nu-/ri^{ki} ba-hul
seal A-hu-šu-ni
dumu [ ]

For the seal, cf. the Girsu text HLC 71 (pl. 82) (ŠS1 xii): A-hu-šu-ni dumu Šu-i$_3$-li$_2$.

577: SM 1911.10.556 (ŠS3 ix)

obv. 2 udu
1 maš$_2$-gal
šu-gid$_2$
ki Na-lu$_5$-ta
Du$_{11}$-ga i$_3$-dab$_5$
rev. kišib Ur-mes
====
iti ezem mah
mu Si-ma-num$_2$^{ki} / ba-hul
seal Ur-mes
dumu La-na kurušda

578: SM 1911.10.557 (ŠS8 xi)

obv. 1007 u[du?]
kišib lu$_2$-niĝ$_2$-dab$_5$-ba-ke$_4$-ne
u$_3$ kišib šu-la$_2$-a didli
ki Du$_{11}$-ga-ta
Ab-ba-kal-la
rev. šu ba-ti
====
iti ezem An-na
mu ^{d}Šu-^{d}EN.ZU / lugal Uri$_5$^{ki}-ma-ke$_4$ / ma$_2$-gur$_8$ mah ^{d}En-lil$_2$ / ^{d}Nin-lil$_2$-ra mu-/ne-[dim$_2$]
seal Ab-ba-kal-la
dub-sar
dumu Lu$_2$-^{d}Nin-ĝir$_2$-su

579: SM 1911.10.558 (ŠS9 i)

obv. 33 udu
7 u$_8$ sila$_4$ nu-a
2 ud$_5$ maš$_2$ nu-a
Za-zi i$_3$-dab$_5$
1 udu
rev. Lugal-^{d}Utu
ki A-la-mu-ta
ba-zi
==== (*seal*)
iti še-KIN-ku$_5$
mu e$_2$ ^{d}Šara$_2$ / ba-du$_3$
seal Ab-ba-kal-la
dub-sar
dumu Lu$_2$-^{d}Nin-ĝir$_2$-su

580: SM 1911.10.559 (ŠS2 iv)

obv. 2 [x]
ki Na-lu$_5$-t[a]
Du$_{11}$-ga i$_3$-dab$_5$
kišib Ur-mes
rev. ====
iti ki-siki ^{d}Nin-a-zu
mu ma$_2$-dara$_3$ abzu / ba-ab-du$_8$
seal Ur-mes
dumu La-na kurušda

581: SM 1911.10.560 (IS2 x)

obv. 2 maš$_2$
ki E$_2$-a-šar-ta
Ur-ku$_3$-nun-na
i$_3$-dab$_5$
rev. ĝiri$_3$ Lu$_2$-^{d}Nanna
====
iti ezem mah
mu en ^{d}Inana / Unug^{ki}-ga maš$_2$-e / i$_3$-pad$_3$
seal i ^{d}Šu-^{d}EN.ZU

lugal kala-ga
lugal Uri$_5$/^{ki}-ma
lugal an ub-/da limmu$_2$-ba
ii Ur-ku$_3$-nun-na
dub-sar
dumu Lu$_2$-^{d}Nin-/ĝir$_2$-su kurušda
arad$_2$-zu

582: SM 1911.10.561 (AS4 x 7)

obv. 1 gu$_4$ niga
3 udu niga
2 gukkal
1 sila$_4$ 4 maš$_2$
Ur-^{d}Nin-gublaga nar
mu-DU En-ša$_3$-ku$_3$-ge / en ^{d}Nanše
Tah-ša-tal ra$_2$-gaba / maškim
rev. u$_4$ 7-kam
ki Ab-ba-sa$_6$-ga-/ta ba-zi
----
iti ezem An-na
mu En-mah-gal-/an-na en ^{d}Nanna / ba-huĝ
left 11

583: SM 1911.10.562 (AS1 vi)

obv. 21 gu$_4$ niga
ab$_2$ 2-ta
ki-ba ĝa$_2$-ĝa$_2$
10-la$_2$-1 gu$_4$
100 udu
šu-la$_2$-a
rev. ki Na-sa$_6$-ta
Be-li$_2$-a-zu
i$_3$-dab$_5$
====
iti a$_2$-ki-ti
mu ^{d}Amar-^{d}EN.ZU / lugal
left 130

584: SM 1911.10.563 (ŠS4 xi)

obv.	1 maš$_2$
	ki Ur-mes-ta
	Ar-ši-ah
	i$_3$-dab$_5$
rev.	iti ezem An-na
	==== (*seal*)
	mu bad$_3$ mar-/tu ba-du$_3$
seal	(*illegible*)

585: SM 1911.10.564 (-- -- --)

obv.	25 udu
	ki Ur-^{d}Nanše-/ta
	Ur-mes
rev.	i$_3$-dab$_5$
	==== (*seal*)
seal	Ur-mes
	dumu La-na kurušda

586: SM 1911.10.565 (AS6 v 26)

obv.	2 udu aslum$_x$(A.LUM)
	u$_4$ 26-kam
	ki Ab-ba-sa$_6$-ga-/ta
	U$_2$-ta$_2$-mi-šar-ra-am / i$_3$-dab$_5$
rev.	iti ezem ^{d}Nin-a-zu
	mu Ša-aš-ru^{ki} / ba-hul
	====
left	2

587: SM 1911.10.567 (ŠS1 xii 29)

obv.	2 sila$_4$
	u$_4$ 30-la$_2$-1-kam
	ki In-ta-e$_3$-a-/ta
	Du$_{11}$-ga i$_3$-dab$_5$
rev.	kišib Ur-mes
	==== (*seal*)
	iti še-KIN-ku$_5$

mu ^{d}Šu-^{d}EN./ZU lugal
seal Ur-mes
dumu La-na kurušda

588: SM 1911.10.568 (AS8 ix 8)

obv. 1 gu$_4$ niga
1 gu$_4$
u$_4$ 8-kam
ki Ab-ba-sa$_6$-ga-/ta
Ur-tur
rev. i$_3$-dab$_5$
====
iti ezem mah
mu en Eridu/^{ki} ba-huĝ
left 2

589: SM 1911.10.569 (AS4 i 11)

obv. 6 udu niga
1 sila$_4$ niga
1 gukkal
u$_4$ 11-kam
ki Ab-ba-sa$_6$-ga-/ta
rev. Na-lu$_5$ i$_3$-dab$_5$
====
iti maš-da$_3$-gu$_7$
mu us$_2$-sa ^{d}gu-/za ^{d}En-lil$_2$-la$_2$ / ba-dim$_2$
left 8

This text is a duplicate of TCS 332 (AS4 i 11).

590: SM 1911.10.570 (ŠS2 x 25)

obv. 6 gu$_4$
55 udu
7 u$_8$
53 maš$_2$-gal
12 ud$_5$

šu-gid$_2$
rev. ki Kur-bi-la-ak-ta
Du$_{11}$-ga i$_3$-dab$_5$
u$_4$ 25-kam
----
iti ezem An-na
mu ma$_2$-dara$_3$ abzu / ^{d}En-ki-ka ba-ab-/du$_8$
left 6 gu$_4$ 127 udu

591: SM 1911.10.571 (AS2 ii 8)

obv. 1 udu aslum$_x$(A.LUM) niga
1 gukkal niga
1 udu
15 maš$_2$-gal babbar
5 maš$_2$-gal
u$_4$ 8-kam
rev. ki Ab-ba-sa$_6$-/ga-ta
^{d}Šul-gi-a-a-ĝu$_{10}$ / i$_3$-dab$_5$
iti šeš-da-gu$_7$
mu Ur-bi$_2$-lum^{ki} / ba-hul
left 23

592: SM 1911.10.572 (AS8 xi 23)

obv. 2 amar az
e$_2$ uz-ga
Ur-^{d}Ba-ba$_6$ / muhaldim maškim
ša$_3$ mu-DU-ra-/ta
rev. u$_4$ 23-kam
ki Ab-ba-sa$_6$-ga-/ta ba-zi
ĝiri$_3$ Da-a-a-ti / dub-sar
iti ezem Me-ki-ĝal$_2$
mu en Eridu^{ki} ba-huĝ
left 2

593: SM 1911.10.576 (AS4 vi 23)

obv. 4 udu niga
2 sila$_4$ niga

2 sila$_4$
u$_4$ 23-kam
ki Ab-ba-sa$_6$-ga-/ta
rev. Na-lu$_5$ i$_3$-dab$_5$
====
iti a$_2$-ki-ti
mu en ^{d}Nanna / ba-huĝ
left 8

594: SM 1911.10.578 (AS8 iv 14)

obv. 8 udu
u$_4$ 14-kam
ki Lugal-amar-ku$_3$-ta
Ta$_2$-hi-iš-a-tal
i$_3$-dab$_5$
rev. ====
iti ki-siki ^{d}Nin-a-zu
mu En-nun-e-/^{d}Amar-^{d}EN.ZU-ra-ki-/aĝ$_2$ en Eridu^{ki} / ba-huĝ
left 8

595: SM 1911.10.579 (AS8 ii 25)

obv. 2 gukkal
1 maš$_2$-gal
u$_4$ 25-kam
ki Lugal-amar-ku$_3$-ta
A-hu-We-er
i$_3$-dab$_5$
rev. ====
iti šeš-da-gu$_7$
mu En-nun-e-/^{d}Amar-^{d}EN.ZU-ra-/ki-aĝ$_2$ en Eridu^{ki} / ba-huĝ
left 3

596: SM 1911.10.580 (AS8 i 19)

obv. 1 udu niga
u$_4$ 20-la$_2$-1-kam
ki Lugal-amar-ku$_3$-ta

Šu-Ma-ma
i$_3$-dab$_5$
rev. ====
iti maš-da$_3$-gu$_7$
mu En-nun-e-/^{d}Amar-^{d}EN.ZU-ra-ki-/aĝ$_2$ en Eridu^{ki} ba-huĝ
left 1

597: SM 1911.10.581 (AS8 ii 30)

obv. 46 udu niga sa$_2$-du$_{11}$
u$_4$ 30-kam
ki Lugal-amar-ku$_3$-/ta
A-hu-We-er
i$_3$-dab$_5$
rev. ====
iti šeš-da-gu$_7$
mu En-nun-e-/^{d}Amar-^{d}EN.ZU-ra-/ki-aĝ$_2$ en Eridu^{ki} / ba-huĝ
left 46

598: SM 1911.10.582 (AS6 iii 27)

obv. 8 sila$_4$
u$_4$ 27-kam
ki Ab-ba-sa$_6$-/ga-ta
In-ta-e$_3$-a
rev. i$_3$-dab$_5$
====
iti u$_5$-bi$_2$-gu$_7$
mu Ša-aš-ru^{ki} / ba-hul
left 8

Obv. 1: Cf. SAT 2 996 (AS6 iii 27).

599: SM 1911.10.583 (AS6 iii 6)

obv. 3 sila$_4$
u$_4$ 6-kam
ki Ab-ba-sa$_6$-ga-/ta
In-ta-e$_3$-a

rev. i$_3$-dab$_5$
====
iti u$_5$-bi$_2$-gu$_7$
mu Ša-aš-ru^{ki} / ba-hul
left 3

600: SM 1911.10.584 (AS4 viii 1)

obv. 4 udu [xx]
1 udu LU$_2$.SU^{ki}
1 udu ĝiš-du$_3$ LU$_2$.SU^{ki}
2 u$_8$ LU$_2$.SU^{ki}
4 maš$_2$-gal LU$_2$.SU^{ki}
1 ud$_5$ LU$_2$.SU^{ki}
rev. 1 ^{munus}aš$_2$-gar$_3$ LU$_2$.SU^{ki}
u$_4$ 1-kam
ki Ab-ba-sa$_6$-ga-/ta
En-diĝir-ĝu$_{10}$ i$_3$-dab$_5$
iti šu-eš-ša
mu En-mah-gal-an-na / en ^{d}Nanna [ba-huĝ]
left 14

601: SM 1911.10.585 (AS8 vii)

obv. 1 [gu$_4$]
bala Arad$_2$-ĝu$_{10}$ / ensi$_2$ Ĝir$_2$-su^{ki}-/ka ba-an-zi
ki Ta$_2$-hi-iš-a-tal-ta
rev. Lu$_2$-sa$_6$-ga
i$_3$-dab$_5$
====
iti ezem ^{d}Šul-gi
mu en Eridu^{ki} ba-huĝ
left 1 gu$_4$

602: SM 1911.10.586 (AS8 i 20)

obv. 7 amar maš-da$_3$ nita$_2$
1 amar maš-da$_3$ munus
u$_4$ 20-kam

ki Lugal-amar-ku$_3$-ta
Lu$_2$-diĝir-ra
i$_3$-dab$_5$
rev. ====
iti maš-da$_3$-gu$_7$
mu En-nun-e-/^{d}Amar-^{d}EN.ZU-ra-/ki-aĝ$_2$ en Eridu/^{ki} ba-huĝ
left 8

603: SM 1911.10.587 (AS6 ix 9)

obv. 1 sila$_4$
e$_2$ uz-ga
mu-DU Du-uk-ra
A-a-kal-la maškim
u$_4$ 10-la$_2$-1-kam
rev. ki Ab-ba-sa$_6$-ga-/ta ba-zi
----
iti ezem mah
mu Ša-aš-ru/^{ki} ba-hul
left 1

604: SM 1911.10.588 (AS8 i 21)

obv. 1 amar az
u$_4$ 21-kam
ki Lugal-amar-ku$_3$-ta
Lu$_2$-diĝir-ra
i$_3$-dab$_5$
rev. ====
iti maš-da$_3$-gu$_7$
mu En-nun-e-/^{d}Amar-^{d}EN.ZU-ra-/ki-aĝ$_2$ en Eridu^{ki} / ba-huĝ
left 1

605: SM 1911.10.589 (AS6 xi 13)

obv. 1 udu aslum$_x$(A.LUM) niga
u$_4$ 13-kam
ki Ab-ba-sa$_6$-/ga-ta
Ta$_2$-hi-iš-a-/tal

rev. i$_3$-dab$_5$
====
iti ezem Me-ki-ĝal$_2$
mu Ša-aš-ru^{ki} / ba-hul
left 1

606: SM 1911.10.590 (AS6 iii 8)

obv. 1 dusu$_2$ nita$_2$
u$_4$ 8-kam
ki Ab-ba-sa$_6$-/ga-ta
Šu-Er$_3$-ra
rev. i$_3$-dab$_5$
====
iti u$_5$-bi$_2$-gu$_7$
mu Ša-aš-ru^{ki} / ba-hul
left 1

607: SM 1911.10.591 (AS8 xii 29)

obv. 11 gu$_4$
u$_4$ 30-la$_2$-1-kam
ki Ab-ba-sa$_6$-ga-/ta
^{d}En-lil$_2$-la$_2$
rev. i$_3$-dab$_5$
====
iti še-KIN-ku$_5$
mu en Eridu^{ki} / ba-huĝ
left 11 gu$_4$

608: SM 1911.10.592 (AS8 i 16)

obv. 4 maš$_2$-gal LU$_2$.SU
u$_4$ 16-kam
ki Lugal-amar-ku$_3$-ta
Ta$_2$-hi-iš-a-tal
i$_3$-dab$_5$
rev. ====
iti maš-da$_3$-gu$_7$
mu En-nun-e-/^{d}Amar-^{d}EN.ZU-ra-/ki-aĝ$_2$ en Eridu^{ki} / ba-huĝ
left 4

609: SM 1911.10.593 (AS8 vii 12)

obv. 25 udu
15 maš$_2$-gal
šu-gid$_2$
u$_4$ 12-kam
ki Ab-ba-sa$_6$-ga-ta
rev. Du$_{11}$-ga
i$_3$-dab$_5$
----
iti ezem ^{d}Šul-gi
mu en Eridu^{ki} / ba-huĝ
left 40

610: SM 1911.10.594 (AS8 v 24)

obv. 2 udu
Ur-^{d}Nin-gublaga nar
^{d}En-lil$_2$-zi-ša$_3$-ĝal$_2$ / maškim
ša$_3$ mu-DU-ra-ta
rev. u$_4$ 24-kam
ki Ab-ba-sa$_6$-ga-ta / ba-zi
iti ezem ^{d}Nin-a-/zu
mu en Eridu^{ki} / ba-huĝ
left 2

611: SM 1911.10.595 (AS8 vi 4)

obv. 3 udu
u$_4$ 4-kam
ki Ab-ba-sa$_6$-ga-ta
Na-lu$_5$
i$_3$-dab$_5$
rev. ====
iti a$_2$-ki-ti
mu En-nun-e-/^{d}Amar-^{d}EN.ZU-ra-ki-/aĝ$_2$ en Eridu^{ki} / ba-huĝ
left 3

612: SM 1911.10.596 (ŠS1 xii 1)

obv. 4 sila$_4$
u$_4$ 1-kam
ki In-ta-e$_3$-/a-ta
rev. Ur-mes i$_3$-dab$_5$
==== (*seal*)
iti še-[KIN-ku$_5$]
mu ^{d}[Šu-^{d}EN.ZU] / lugal
seal Ur-[mes]
dumu La-[na kurušda]

613: SM 1911.10.597 (AS8 iii 18)

obv. 1 amar maš-da$_3$ munus
e$_2$ uz-ga
mu-DU Wa-ta$_2$-ru-/um saĝĝa
Ur-^{d}Ba-ba$_6$ muhaldim / maškim
rev. u$_4$ 18-kam
ki Lugal-amar-ku$_3$-ta
ba-zi
----
iti u$_5$-bi$_2$-gu$_7$
mu En-nun-e-/^{d}Amar-^{d}EN.ZU-ra-/ki-aĝ$_2$ en Eridu^{ki} / ba-huĝ
left 1

614: SM 1911.10.598 (AS8 vi 15)

obv. 3 gu$_4$ niga
u$_4$ 15-kam
ki Ab-ba-sa$_6$-/ga-ta
Igi-^{d}En-lil$_2$-še$_3$
rev. i$_3$-dab$_5$
====
iti a$_2$-ki-ti
mu en Eridu^{ki} / ba-huĝ
left 3

615: SM 1911.10.600 (AS8 iv 9)

obv. 1 udu aslum$_x$(A.LUM) niga
u$_4$ 10-la$_2$-1-kam
ki Lugal-amar-ku$_3$-ta
U$_2$-ta$_2$-mi-šar-ra-/am
i$_3$-dab$_5$
rev. ====
iti ki-siki ^{d}Nin-a-zu
mu En-nun-e-/^{d}Amar-^{d}EN.ZU-ra-/ki-aĝ$_2$ en Eridu^{ki} / ba-huĝ
left 1

616: SM 1911.10.601 (AS8 iv 17)

obv. 10-la$_2$-1 gu$_4$
1 gu$_4$ ĝiš-du$_3$
u$_4$ 17-kam
ki Lugal-amar-ku$_3$-/ta
rev. Ur-tur i$_3$-dab$_5$
iti ki-siki ^{d}Nin-a-/zu
mu En-nun-e-/^{d}Amar-^{d}EN.ZU-/ki-aĝ$_2$ en Eridu^{ki} / ba-huĝ
left 10

This text is a duplicate of BCT 1 51 (AS8 iv 17).

617: SM 1911.10.602 (AS8 ii 3)

obv. 1 maš$_2$ gal šu-gid$_2$
u$_4$ 3-kam
ki Lugal-amar-ku$_3$-/ta
Du$_{11}$-ga
rev. i$_3$-dab$_5$
----
iti šeš-da-gu$_7$
mu En-nun-e-^{d}/Amar-^{d}EN.ZU-ra-ki-aĝ$_2$ / en Eridu^{ki} ba-huĝ
left 1

618: SM 1911.10.603 (AS6 iv 26)

obv. 8 udu
u$_4$ 26-kam
ki Ab-ba-sa$_6$-/ga-ta

Šu-Ma-ma
rev. i$_3$-dab$_5$
====
iti ki-siki ^{d}Nin-a-zu
mu Ša-aš-ru^{ki} / ba-hul
left 8

Cf. SACT 1 187, ii 30'-31'.

619: SM 1911.10.604 (AS1 v 21)

obv. 3 udu niga lu$_2$-ulu$_3$-um
u$_4$ 20-la$_2$-1-kam
4 udu niga lu$_2$-ulu$_3$-um
u$_4$ 21-kam
ki Na-sa$_6$-ta
rev. Na-lu$_5$ i$_3$-dab$_5$
iti ezem ^{d}Nin-a-zu
mu ^{d}Amar-^{d}EN.ZU / lugal

620: SM 1911.10.605 (AS2 i 9)

obv. 6 gu$_4$
u$_4$ 5-kam
11 gu$_4$
u$_4$ 10-la$_2$-1-kam
1 ab$_2$ u$_4$ 30-kam
e$_2$ muhaldim
rev. zi-ga
ki ^{d}En-lil$_2$-la$_2$
iti maš-da$_3$-gu$_7$
mu Ur-bi$_2$-lum/^{ki} ba-hul

Obv. 3-4: See No. 492 (AS2 i 9) in this volume.
Obv. 5: Cf. For 1 ab$_2$, see CT 32 48 BM 103448.

621: SM 1911.10.606 (AS4 vi 20)

obv. 10 udu niga
1 sila$_4$ niga
2 udu

2 sila$_4$
u$_4$ 20-kam
ki Ab-ba-sa$_6$-/ga-ta
rev. Na-lu$_5$ i$_3$-dab$_5$
====
iti a$_2$-ki-ti
mu en ^{d}Nanna / ba-huĝ
left 15

622: SM 1911.10.607 (AS8 ix 11)

obv. 27 gu$_4$
3 ab$_2$
u$_4$ 11-kam
ki Ab-ba-sa$_6$-/ga-ta
rev. Ur-tur i$_3$-dab$_5$
----
iti ezem mah
mu en Eridu^{ki} / ba-huĝ
left 30 gu$_4$

623: SM 1911.10.608 (AS3 v 27)

obv. 11 u$_8$
4 udu
šu-gid$_2$ e$_2$ muhaldim-še$_3$
u$_4$ 27-kam
ki Ab-ba-sa$_6$-/ga-ta
rev. ba-zi
iti ezem ^{d}Nin-a-zu
mu ^{d}gu-za / ^{d}En-lil$_2$-la$_2$ / ba-dim$_2$
left 15

624: SM 1911.10.609 (AS8 vii 25)

obv. 1 udu niga
u$_4$ 25-kam
ki Ab-ba-sa$_6$-ga-/ta
U$_2$-ta$_2$-mi-šar-/ra-am

rev. i$_3$-dab$_5$
----
iti ezem ^{d}Šul-/gi
mu en Eridu^{ki} / ba-huĝ
left 1

625: SM 1911.10.610 (AS7 ix 26)

obv. 1 maš$_2$-gal LU$_2$.[SU]
1 kir$_{11}$ gukkal
u$_4$ 26-kam
ki Ab-ba-sa$_6$-/ga-ta
rev. Šu-Ma-ma i$_3$-dab$_5$
====
iti ezem mah
mu Hu-uh$_2$-nu-/ri^{ki} ba-hul
left 2

626: SM 1911.10.611 (AS4 x 10)

obv. 1 sila$_4$
u$_4$ 10-kam
ki Ab-ba-sa$_6$-ga-/ta
Na-lu$_5$
i$_3$-dab$_5$
rev. ====
iti ezem An-na
mu En-mah-⟨gal⟩-an-na / en ^{d}Nanna / ba-huĝ
left 1

627: SM 1911.10.612 (-- xi)

obv. 1 sila$_4$
ki In-ta-/e$_3$-a-ta
kišib Du$_{11}$-ga
rev. iti ezem ^{d}Me-ki-/ĝal$_2$
seal Du$_{11}$-ga
dumu Lu$_2$-^{d}Nin-ĝir$_2$-su
sipa na-gab$_2$-tum

628: SM 1911.10.613 (AS8 iii 16)

obv. 10 maš$_2$-gal
u$_4$ 16-kam
ki Lugal-amar-ku$_3$-ta
Na-lu$_5$
i$_3$-dab$_5$
rev. ====
iti u$_5$-bi$_2$-gu$_7$
mu En-nun-e-/^{d}Amar-^{d}EN.ZU-ra-/ki-aĝ$_2$ en Eridu^{ki} / ba-huĝ
left 10

629: SM 1911.10.614 (AS8 xi 14)

obv. 1 udu
1 maš$_2$-gal
šu-gid$_2$
u$_4$ 14-kam
ki Ab-ba-sa$_6$-ga-ta
rev. Du$_{11}$-ga
i$_3$-dab$_5$
iti ezem Me-ki-ĝal$_2$
mu en Eridu/^{ki} ba-huĝ
left 2

630: SM 1911.10.615 (AS8 ii 23)

obv. 1 udu niga
u$_4$ 23-kam
ki Lugal-amar-ku$_3$-ta
Na-lu$_5$ / i$_3$-dab$_5$
rev. ====
iti šeš-da-gu$_7$
mu En-nun-ne$_2$-^{d}/Amar-^{d}EN.ZU-ra-ki-aĝ$_2$ / en Eridu^{ki} ba-huĝ
left 1

631: SM 1911.10.616 (AS8 iii 19)

obv. 1 maš$_2$ a-dara$_4$
1 ^{munus}aš$_2$-gar$_3$ a-dara$_4$
u$_4$ 20-la$_2$-1-kam

ki Lugal-amar-ku$_3$-ta

[L]u$_2$-diĝir-ra

rev. i$_3$-dab$_5$

iti u$_5$-bi$_2$-gu$_7$

mu En-nun-e-/^{d}Amar-^{d}EN.ZU-ra-/ki-aĝ$_2$ en Eridu/^{ki} ba-huĝ

left 2

632: SM 1911.10.617 (AS4 vi 23)

obv. 2 sila$_4$

u$_4$ 23-kam

ki Ab-ba-sa$_6$-ga-/ta

In-ta-e$_3$-a

rev. i$_3$-dab$_5$

====

iti a$_2$-ki-ti

mu en [^{d}Nan]na / [ba-huĝ]

left 2

633: SM 1911.10.618 (AS4 vi 21)

obv. 3 udu niga

2 sila$_4$ niga

2 udu

1 ^{munus}aš$_2$-gar$_3$

u$_4$ 21-kam

rev. ki Ab-ba-sa$_6$-/ga-ta

Na-lu$_5$ i$_3$-dab$_5$

iti a$_2$-ki-ti

mu en ^{d}Nanna / ba-huĝ

left 8

634: SM 1911.10.619 (AS8 xi 6)

obv. 1 udu aslum$_x$(A.LUM) niga

u$_4$ 6-kam

[k]i Ab-ba-sa$_6$-ga-/ta

Ta$_2$-hi-iš-a-tal

rev. i$_3$-dab$_5$
====
iti ezem Me-ki-ĝal$_2$
mu en Eridu^{ki} / ba-huĝ

635: SM 1911.10.620 (Š45 iv)

obv. 5 udu
7 maš$_2$
didli mu maš-da$_3$-še$_3$
ki sagi-ne-ta
ĝiri$_3$ Ur-^{d}Šul-pa-e$_3$
rev. mu-DU
iti šeš-da-gu$_7$ / u$_3$ iti ki-siki ^{d}Nin-a-zu
mu Ur-bi$_2$-lum^{ki} / ba-hul
left 12

636: SM 1911.10.621 (AS4 vi 18)

obv. 3 maš$_2$ gal a-dara$_4$ / ĝiš-du$_3$
u$_4$ 18-kam
ki Ab-ba-sa$_6$-/ga-ta
rev. Lu$_2$-diĝir-ra
i$_3$-dab$_5$
iti a$_2$-ki-ti
mu en ^{d}Nanna / ba-huĝ
left 3

637: SM 1911.10.622 (AS8 viii 18)

obv. 1 maš$_2$-gal
gu-za ^{d}Šul-gi-/ra
Ur-^{d}Šul-pa-e$_3$ / muhaldim maškim
rev. ša$_3$ mu-DU-ra-ta
u$_4$ 18-kam
ki Ab-ba-sa$_6$-/ga-ta ba-zi
iti šu-eš$_5$-ša
mu en Eridu^{ki} / ba-huĝ
left 1 udu

638: SM 1911.10.623 (AS4 ix 10)

obv. 1 sila$_4$
e$_2$ uz-ga
mu-DU Ṣe-lu-uš-/^{d}Da-gan
Ur-^{d}Ba-ba$_6$ maškim
rev. u$_4$ 10-kam
ki Ab-ba-sa$_6$-/ga-ta
ba-zi
iti ezem mah
mu En-mah-gal-an-na / en ^{d}Nanna ba-huĝ
left 10 1

639: SM 1911.10.624 (AS4 vii 8)

obv. 5 udu niga
1 sila$_4$
u$_4$ 8-kam
ki Ab-ba-sa$_6$-/ga-ta
rev. Na-lu$_5$ i$_3$-dab$_5$
----
iti ezem ^{d}Šul-gi
mu En-mah-⟨gal⟩-an-/na en ^{d}Nanna / ba-huĝ
left 6

This text is a duplicate of CST 288 (AS4 vii 8).

640: SM 1911.10.625 (AS2 iv 27)

obv. 1 gu$_4$ gun$_3$-a niga
2 udu niga
3 maš$_2$-gal LU$_2$.SU
u$_4$ 27-kam
mu-DU lugal
rev. ki Ab-ba-sa$_6$-ga-ta
^{d}Šul-gi-a-a-ĝu$_{10}$ / i$_3$-dab$_5$
iti ki-siki ^{d}Nin-a-zu
mu ^{d}Amar-^{d}EN./ZU lugal-e Ur-bi$_2$-/lum^{ki} mu-hul
left 6

For these animals, see OIP 121 76.

641: SM 1911.10.626 (AS2 v 9)

obv. 2 udu niga
u$_4$ 10-la$_2$-1-kam
ki Ab-ba-sa$_6$-/ga-ta
rev. ^{d}Šul-gi-a-a-/ĝu$_{10}$ i$_3$-dab$_5$
iti ezem ^{d}Nin-a-zu
mu ^{d}Amar-^{d}EN.ZU / lugal-e Ur-bi$_2$-/lum^{ki} mu-hul
left 2

642: SM 1911.10.627 (AS6 i 13)

obv. 1 sila$_4$ niga
u$_4$ 13-kam
ki Ab-ba-sa$_6$-/ga-ta
Na-lu$_5$
rev. i$_3$-dab$_5$
ša$_3$ Uri$_5$^{ki}-ma
----
iti maš-da$_3$-gu$_7$
mu Ša-aš-ru^{ki} / ba-hul
left 1

This text is a duplicate of TRU 151 (AS6 i 13).

643: SM 1911.10.628 (Š47 viii 6)

obv. 7 gu$_4$
4 ab$_2$
e$_2$ muhaldim
u$_4$ 6-kam
zi-ga
rev. ki ^{d}En-lil$_2$-la$_2$
iti šu-eš-ša
mu us$_2$-sa Ki-maš^{ki} / ba-hul

644: SM 1911.10.629 (Š47 vi 2)

obv. 2 udu
3 u$_8$

4 maš$_2$
6 ud$_5$
e$_2$ muhaldim
rev. u$_4$ 2-kam
zi-ga
ki Ur-ku$_3$-nun-na
iti a$_2$-ki-ti
mu us$_2$-sa / Ki-maš^{ki} ba-hul

645: SM 1911.10.630 (Š47 vii 19)

obv. 18 udu
14 u$_8$
24 maš$_2$
64 ud$_5$
e$_2$ muhaldim
rev. u$_4$ 20-la$_2$-1-kam
zi-ga
ki Ur-ku$_3$-nun-na
iti ezem ^{d}Šul-gi
mu us$_2$-sa Ki-maš^{ki} / ba-hul

646: SM 1911.10.632 (-- -- 12)

obv. (*beginning damaged*)
u$_4$ 12-kam
ki Na-sa$_6$-/ta
rev. A-hu-ni i$_3$-dab$_5$
====
(*ending damaged*)

647: SM 1918.01.007 (AS4 iv 29)

obv. 10-la$_2$-1 gu$_4$
2 udu
5 sila$_4$
1 maš$_2$
u$_4$ 30-la$_2$-1-kam

ki Ab-ba-sa$_6$-ga-/ta
rev. In-ta-e$_3$-a
i$_3$-dab$_5$
----
iti ki-siki ^{d}Nin-a-zu
mu en ^{d}Nanna / ba-huĝ
left 17

648: SM 1918.01.008 (AS7 vii 14)

obv. 6 sila$_4$
u$_4$ 14-kam
ki Ab-ba-sa$_6$-ga-/ta
In-ta-e$_3$-a
i$_3$-dab$_5$
rev. ====
iti ezem ^{d}Šul-gi
mu Hu-uh$_2$-nu-/ri^{ki} ba-hul
left 6

649: SM 1918.01.009 (Š47 ix)

obv. 1 gu$_4$
ki Lu$_2$-^{d}Nin-/šubur-ta
^{d}En-lil$_2$-la$_2$ i$_3$-dab$_5$
kišib Ur-sa$_6$-ga / dub-sar
==== (*seal*)
iti ezem mah
mu us$_2$-<sa> Ki-maš^{ki} / ba-hul
seal Lugal-he$_2$-ĝal$_2$
dumu ^{d}En-lil$_2$-la$_2$
sipa gu$_4$ [niga]

650: SM 1918.01.010 (AS7 xi 8)

obv. 1 maš$_2$-gal
u$_4$ 8-kam
ki Ab-ba-sa$_6$-/ga-ta
In-ta-e$_3$-a

rev. i$_3$-dab$_5$
====
iti ezem Me-ki-ĝal$_2$
mu Hu-uh$_2$-nu-ri/^{ki} ba-hul
left 1

651: SM 1918.01.011 (AS7 xi 9)
obv. 3 gu$_4$ niga
u$_4$ 10-la$_2$-1-kam
ki Ab-ba-sa$_6$-ga-/ta
Ur-tur
rev. i$_3$-dab$_5$
====
iti ezem Me-ki-ĝal$_2$
mu Hu-uh$_2$-nu-ri/^{ki} ba-hul
left 3 gu$_4$

652: SM 1918.01.012 (AS7 i 29)
obv. 2 u$_8$ sila$_4$ nu-a
2 ud$_5$ maš$_2$ nu-a
u$_4$ 30-la$_2$-1-kam
ki Ab-ba-sa$_6$-/ga-ta
A-hu-We-er
rev. i$_3$-dab$_5$
====
iti maš-da$_3$-gu$_7$
mu Hu-uh$_2$-nu-/ri^{ki} ba-hul
left 4

653: SM 1918.01.013 (AS7 ii 3)
obv. 4 udu niga 3-kam-us$_2$
6 udu niga gu$_4$-e-/us$_2$-sa
u$_4$ 3-kam
ki Ab-ba-sa$_6$-/ga-ta
rev. Na-lu$_5$ i$_3$-dab$_5$

====
iti šeš-da-gu$_7$
mu Hu-uh$_2$-/nu-ri^{ki} ba-hul
left 10

654: SM 1918.01.016 (Š46 viii)

obv. 128 udu
74 maš$_2$
40-la$_2$-1 ^{munus}aš$_2$-gar$_3$
kišib ^{d}Lamma-igi-du
rev. zi-ga
ki Ur-ku$_3$-nun-na
====
iti šu-eš-ša
mu Ki-maš^{ki} / ba-hul
left 241

655: SM 1918.01.017 (AS3 x 28)

obv. 2 gu$_4$
12 udu
10 sila$_4$
11 maš$_2$
u$_4$ 28-kam
rev. ki Ab-ba-sa$_6$-ga-/ta
In-ta-e$_3$-a / i$_3$-dab$_5$
iti ezem An-na
mu ^{d}gu-za ša$_3$-hul$_2$-/la ^{d}En-lil$_2$-la$_2$ ba-dim$_2$
left 35

656: SM 1918.01.018 (AS4 x 29)

obv. 30 udu niga
u$_4$ 30-la$_2$-1-kam
ki Ab-ba-sa$_6$-ga-/ta
Na-lu$_5$
rev. i$_3$-dab$_5$
====
iti ezem An-na

mu En-mah-gal-an-/na en ^{d}Nanna / ba-huĝ
left 30

657: SM 1918.01.019 (AS6 vii 27)

obv. 2 sila$_4$
1 maš$_2$
u$_4$ 27-kam
ki Ab-ba-sa$_6$-ga-ta
In-ta-e$_3$-a / i$_3$-dab$_5$
rev. iti ezem ^{d}Šul-/gi
mu Ša-aš-ru^{ki} / ba-hul
====
left 3

658: SM 1918.01.020 (AS7 vii 13)

obv. 2 udu
u$_4$ 13-kam
ki Ab-ba-sa$_6$-/ga-ta
Na-lu$_5$ i$_3$-dab$_5$
rev. ša$_3$ Uri$_5$^{ki}-ma
----
iti ezem ^{d}Šul-gi
mu Hu-uh$_2$-nu-/ri^{ki} ba-hul
left 2

659: SM 1918.01.021 (AS6 ix 1)

obv. 3 gu$_4$ niga
u$_4$ 1-kam
ki Ab-ba-sa$_6$-/ga-ta
Tah-ša-tal i$_3$-dab$_5$
rev. ====
[it]i ezem [ma]h
mu Ša-aš-ru^{ki} / ba-hul
left 3

660: SM 1918.01.022 (AS7 i 28)

obv. 2 gukkal
1 u$_8$ gukkal
1 sila$_4$ aslum$_x$(A.LUM)
u$_4$ 28-kam
ki Ab-ba-sa$_6$-/ga-ta
rev. Na-lu$_5$ i$_3$-dab$_5$
====
iti maš-da$_3$-gu$_7$
mu Hu-uh$_2$-/nu-ri^{ki} ba-hul
left 4

661: SM 1918.01.023 (-- -- --)

obv. 3 gu$_4$
96 udu
ki In-ta-e$_3$-/a-ta
Ab-ba-sa$_6$-ga i$_3$-dab$_5$
rev. [ga]ba-ri kišib-ba
====

662: SM 1918.01.024 (AS3 x 22)

obv. 7 gu$_4$
60 udu
7 sila$_4$
4 maš$_2$
u$_4$ 22-kam
rev. ki Ab-ba-sa$_6$-/ga-ta
In-ta-e$_3$-a
i$_3$-dab$_5$
iti ezem An-na
mu ^{d}gu-za ša$_3$-/hul$_2$-la ^{d}En-lil$_2$-la$_2$ / ba-dim$_2$
left 78

663: SM 1918.01.025 (AS7 ii 21)

obv. 5 sila$_4$
1 maš$_2$

u$_4$ 21-kam
ki Ab-ba-sa$_6$-ga-/ta
In-ta-e$_3$-a
rev. i$_3$-dab$_5$
====
iti šeš-da-gu$_7$
mu Hu-uh$_2$-<nu-ri>^{ki} / ba-hul
left 6

664: SM 1918.01.026 (AS4 viii 30)

obv. 1 maš$_2$
u$_4$ 30-kam
ki Ab-ba-sa$_6$-/ga-ta
^{d}Šul-gi-a-a-/ĝu$_{10}$
rev. i$_3$-dab$_5$
====
iti šu-eš$_5$-ša
mu En-mah-gal-an-na / en ^{d}Nanna ba-huĝ
left 1

For this animal, see Nisaba 8 37: ii 7.

665: SM 1918.01.027 (AS6 iv 18)

obv. 1 sila$_4$
u$_4$ 18-kam
ki Ab-ba-sa$_6$-/ga-ta
In-ta-e$_3$-a
rev. i$_3$-dab$_5$
====
iti ki-siki ^{d}Nin-a-zu
mu Ša-aš-ru^{ki} / ba-hul
left 1

666: SM 1918.01.028 (AS2 v 9)

obv. 2 udu niga
u$_4$ 10-la$_2$-1-kam

ki Ab-ba-sa$_{6}$-/ga-ta
Lu$_{2}$-diĝir-ra i$_{3}$-dab$_{5}$
rev. [iti] ezem ^{d}Nin-/a-zu
mu ^{d}Amar-^{d}EN.ZU / lugal-e Ur-bi$_{2}$-/lum^{ki} mu-hul
left 2

667: SM 1918.01.029 (AS4 vii 4)

obv. 2 sila$_{4}$
u$_{4}$ 4-kam
ki Ab-ba-sa$_{6}$-/ga-ta
rev. In-ta-e$_{3}$-a
i$_{3}$-dab$_{5}$
iti ezem ^{d}Šul-/gi
mu en ^{d}/Nanna ba-huĝ
left 2

668: SM 1918.01.030 (AS4 ii 25)

obv. 8 gu$_{4}$
2 udu niga
u$_{4}$ 25-kam
ki Ab-ba-sa$_{6}$-/ga-ta
rev. A-hu-We-er
i$_{3}$-dab$_{5}$
iti šeš-da-/gu$_{7}$
mu en ^{d}Nanna / ba-huĝ
left 10

669: SM 1918.01.031 (AS7 vii 29)

obv. 4 udu niga
u$_{4}$ 30-la$_{2}$-1-kam
ki Ab-ba-sa$_{6}$-/ga-ta
rev. Na-lu$_{5}$
i$_{3}$-dab$_{5}$
----
iti ezem ^{d}Šul-gi
mu Hu-uh$_{2}$-nu-/ri^{ki} ba-hul
left 4

670: SM 1918.01.032 (AS2 iii 12)

obv. 4 udu niga 2 sila$_4$ niga
2 maš$_2$ 1 ^{munus}aš$_2$-gar$_3$
u$_4$ 12-kam
ki Ab-ba-sa$_6$-/ga-ta
rev. Na-lu$_5$ i$_3$-dab$_5$
iti u$_5$-bi$_2$-gu$_7$
mu ^{d}Amar-^{d}EN.ZU / lugal-e Ur-bi$_2$-/lum^{ki} mu-/hul
left 10-la$_2$-1

671: SM 1918.01.033 (AS6 xi 26)

obv. 3 sila$_4$
u$_4$ 26-kam
ki Ab-ba-sa$_6$-ga-/ta
In-ta-e$_3$-a
rev. i$_3$-dab$_5$
====
iti ezem Me-ki-ĝal$_2$
mu Ša-aš-ru^{ki} / ba-hul
left 3

672: SM 1918.01.034 (AS2 xi 17)

obv. 8 udu
4 maš$_2$-gal
1 maš$_2$
u$_4$ 17-kam
ki Ab-ba-sa$_6$-ga-/ta
rev. Na-lu$_5$ i$_3$-dab$_5$
----
iti ezem Me-ki-ĝal$_2$
mu ^{d}Amar-^{d}EN.ZU / lugal-e Ur-bi$_2$-/lum^{ki} mu-hul
left 13

673: SM 1918.01.035 (AS2 v 30)

obv. 11 udu niga
u$_4$ 30-kam

ki Ab-ba-sa$_6$-ga-/ta
Lu$_2$-diĝir-ra
rev. i$_3$-dab$_5$
====
iti ezem ^{d}Nin-a-zu
mu ^{d}Amar-^{d}EN.ZU / lugal-e Ur-bi$_2$-lum/^{ki} mu-hul
left 11

For these animals, see JCS 14 108, rev. 2.

674: SM 1918.01.036 (AS7 iv 3)

obv. 25 maš-da$_3$ nita$_2$
15 maš-da$_3$ munus
u$_4$ 3-kam
ki Ab-ba-sa$_6$-/ga-ta
rev. [Ur]-šu-ga-lam-ma
i$_3$-dab$_5$
iti ki-siki ^{d}Nin-a-zu
mu Hu-uh$_2$-nu-ri/^{ki} ba-hul
left 40

675: SM 1918.01.037 (AS6 iii 12)

obv. 3 udu niga
2 gukkal
2 udu aslum$_x$(A.LUM)
u$_4$ 12-kam
ki Ab-ba-sa$_6$-ga-ta
rev. Na-lu$_5$ i$_3$-dab$_5$
====
iti u$_5$-bi$_2$-gu$_7$
mu Ša-aš-ru^{ki} / ba-hul
left 7

676: SM 1918.01.038 (Š45 x 10)

obv. 1 u$_8$
2 maš$_2$-gal

1 sila$_4$ ga
ba-ug$_7$ u$_4$ 10-kam
ša$_3$ Tum-ma-al/^{ki}
rev. ki En-diĝir-ĝu$_{10}$-ta
Ur-ni$_9$-ĝar
šu ba-ti
iti ezem An-na
mu Ur-bi$_2$-/lum^{ki} ba-hul

677: SM 1918.01.039 (AS4 vii 24)

obv. 1 udu
u$_4$ 24-kam
ki Ab-ba-sa$_6$-/ga-ta
rev. Lu$_2$-diĝir-ra
i$_3$-dab$_5$
iti ezem ^{d}Šul-/gi
mu En-mah-gal-an-/na en ^{d}Nanna / ba-huĝ
left 1

678: SM 1929.01.003 (AS8 viii 20)

obv. 1 maš-da$_3$ munus
2 amar az
ba-ug$_7$ u$_4$ 20-kam
ki Lu$_2$-diĝir-ra-/ta
rev. ^{d}Šul-gi-iri-ĝu$_{10}$
šu ba-ti
====
iti šu-eš$_5$-ša
mu en Eridu^{ki} / ba-huĝ
left 3

679: SM 1929.01.009 (AS1 xii 24)

obv. 1 udu
1 sila$_4$
ba-ug$_7$
u$_4$ 24-kam
rev. ki Na-lu$_5$-ta

Ur-ni$_9$-ĝar
šu ba-ti
iti še-KIN-ku$_5$
mu ^{d}Amar-^{d}EN./ZU lugal

680: SM 1929.01.010 (AS2 v 23)

obv. 2 sila$_4$ ga
3 kir$_{11}$ ga
1 maš$_2$ ga
u$_3$-tu-da
u$_4$ 23-kam
rev. ^{d}Šul-gi-a-a-/ĝu$_{10}$ i$_3$-dab$_5$
iti ezem ^{d}Nin-a-zu
mu ^{d}Amar-^{d}EN.ZU / lugal-e Ur-bi$_2$-/lum^{ki} mu-hul
left 6

681: SM 1951.02.001 (AS6 viii 28)

obv. 1 sila$_4$
e$_2$ uz-ga
mu-DU
Šu-Kab-ta$_2$
Ur-^{d}Ba-ba$_6$ maškim
rev. u$_4$ 28-kam
ki Ab-ba-sa$_6$-/ga-ta ba-zi
iti šu-eš$_5$-ša
mu Ša-aš-ru^{ki} / ba-hul
left 1

682: SM 1951.02.002 (AS8 v 12)

obv. 5 udu
2 sila$_4$
u$_4$ 12-kam
ki Ab-ba-sa$_6$-ga-/ta
Igi-^{d}En-lil$_2$-še$_3$
rev. i$_3$-dab$_5$
====

iti ezem ^{d}Nin-a-zu
mu En-nun-e-^{d}Amar-/^{d}EN.ZU-ra-ki-aĝ$_2$ en / Eridu^{ki} ba-huĝ
left 7

683: SM 1951.02.003 (IS1 v 6)

obv. 10 1/2 ma-na siki / ĝir$_2$-gul
bar udu mu-DU-ra
u$_4$ 6-kam
Lu$_2$-kal-la
šu ba-ti
rev. ĝiri$_3$ Nu-ur$_2$-$^{[d]}$EN.[ZU] / dub-sar
----
iti ki-siki ^{d}Nin-a-zu
mu ^{d}I-bi$_2$-/^{d}EN.ZU lugal
seal i [^{d}I-bi$_2$-^{d}EN.ZU]
lugal kala-ga
lugal Uri$_5$/^{ki}-ma
lugal an ub-/[da limmu$_2$-ba]
ii Nu-[ur$_2$-^{d}EN.ZU]
dub-[sar]
dumu I-[di$_3$-Er$_3$-ra]
arad$_2$-[zu]

684: SM 1995.03.092 (AS2 viii --)

obv. 1 maš$_2$-gal niga
1 gukkal
1 [ ]
3 kir$_{11}$
1 [ ]
ba-[ug$_7$ u$_4$ x]-kam
rev. ki Lu$_2$-diĝir-ra-ta
Ur-ni$_9$-ĝar
šu ba-ti
iti šu-eš-ša
mu ^{d}Amar-^{d}EN.ZU / lugal-e Ur-bi$_2$-/lum^{ki} mu-hul
left 7

685: SM 1995.03.093 (AS2 viii 10)

obv. 2 maš$_2$ ga
1 ^{munus}aš$_2$-gar$_3$ ga
u$_3$-tu-da
u$_4$ 10-kam
rev. ^{d}Šul-gi-a-a-/ĝu$_{10}$ i$_3$-dab$_5$
iti šu-eš$_5$-ša
mu ^{d}Amar-^{d}EN.ZU / lugal-e Ur-bi$_2$-/lum^{ki} mu-hul
left 3

686: SM 1995.03.095 (ŠS2 iii 24)

obv. 4 udu
1 sila$_4$
ba-ug$_7$ u$_4$ 24-kam
ki Na-lu$_5$-ta
rev. ^{d}Šul-gi-[iri-ĝu$_{10}$]
šu ba-[ti]
iti u$_5$-[b]i$_2$-[g]u$_7$
mu ma$_2$-dara$_3$ abzu / ^{d}En-ki-ka ba-ab-/du$_8$
left 5

687: SM 1995.09.004 (ŠS2 i 5)

obv. 1 sila$_4$
saĝ-ba zi-ga
mu en ^{d}Nanna-/ka-še$_3$
u$_4$ 5-kam
rev. ša$_3$ Ga-eš^{ki}
zi-ga
ki Ur-^{d}Ig-alim
iti maš-da$_3$-gu$_7$
mu us$_2$-sa ^{d}/Šu-^{d}EN.ZU lugal

688: SM 1995.09.006 (AS2 viii 28)

obv. 1 sila$_4$ gaba
1 sila$_4$ ga
1 kir$_{11}$ ga
ba-ug$_7$ u$_4$ 28-kam
ša$_3$ Tum-ma-al

rev. ki En-diĝir-ĝu$_{10}$-ta
Ur-ni$_{9}$-ĝar
šu ba-ti
iti šu-eš-ša
[mu ^{d}]Amar-^{d}EN.ZU / [lugal-e Ur]-bi$_{2}$-/[lum^{ki}] ba-hul

689: SM 1997.01.005 (Š38 ix)

obv. 11 udu šu-gid$_{2}$
52 maš$_{2}$ šu-gid$_{2}$
udu Sa-bu-um-ma
ki En-diĝir-ĝu$_{10}$-ta
rev. Lu$_{2}$-^{d}Nin-ĝir$_{2}$-/su kurušda i$_{3}$-dab$_{5}$
iti ezem mah
mu us$_{2}$-sa bad$_{3}$ / ma-da ba-du$_{3}$

Index of Names of Deities and Deified Kings

Index of Personal Names

Index of Geographical Names

Index of Selected Words and Phrases

Printed in the United States
by Baker & Taylor Publisher Services